Queen Emma's
Church In Kealakekua

Crossroads of Culture

Nancee Pace Cline

Copyright © 2010 Nancee Pace Cline
All rights reserved.

ISBN-10: 1456351729
EAN-13: 9781456351724

To all the ordinary saints of Kealakekua

Table of Contents

Foreword	ix
Chapter 1	1
Once upon a time	2
Historical Context	14
The First Vicar	17
Mother Nature	23
Problems	24
Chapter 2	27
Samuel H. Davis, the second Vicar	27
Community Outreach	31
In the Cemetery	33
Neighbors	33
History Detective: The Magic Lantern	35
Victorian Eye-Witness	36
Historical Context	40
Another Visit to Kona Historical Society	41
Return Visit	42
History Detective: Eucharist bread or wafer?	44
Heavenly Wine	44
Historical Context	45
The Painted Panels	47
Photography Project	48
A Trip to the Archives 1	49

Different Voice, Different Pen: Ting Sing	55
The Final Years	56
Commentary: Captain Cook	57
Profile: Charles Lambert	60
Historical Context: the First Lifeguard	62
Follow Up: The Transit of Venus	63
Gifts for the Expedition	66
History Detective: A Trip to the Archives 2	67
Profile: The Last Hawaiian Queen	70

CHAPTER 3 — 73

Different Voice, Different Pen: Liliuokalani Explains the Hanai Custom	73
Commentary: Gift Culture	74
New Names	78
Then and Now: Entertainment (plays)	78
Different Voice, Different Pen: Heidi Edson	80
A New Era	81
Women's' Work: The Christ Church Guild	82
The First World War Years	88
Historical Context: Technology	91
Then and Now: A problem with the local teenagers	93
Goodbye to a Faithful Wife	96
Exiles in Molokai	97
Then and Now: Ecumenical Gatherings	100

CHAPTER 4 — 103

Within Our Memory	103
Kenneth Miller, sixth Vicar Of Christ Church 1937-1944	104
Follow up: Girls' Friendly Society	110
Different Voice, Different Pen: December 7, 1941	111
Interview: Alfreida Kimura Fujita	113
My Little Grass Shack in Kealakekua Hawai`i	116
Follow-up: More About the USO	118
Then and Now: Pidgin	119
Burton Linscott, seventh Vicar Of Christ Church 1945-1950	122

Different Voice, Different Pen: In Memory 126
Commentary: Passing the Peace 128

Chapter 5 131
Morning Prayer in the Celtic Style 132
Interview: Terry Angelo 132
Follow-up: Pumpkin- squash soup 134
Family Tree 134
Interview Terry Angelo #2 135
Henri Pickens eighth Vicar Of Christ Church, 1950 137
Historical Context: Statehood 1959 141
Interview: Billy Paris 144
Different Voice, Different Pen: on Vicar McKinney 148
Change of Status 151
Blessed Are Those Who Mourn 152
Different Voice, Different Pen: The Bells 155
The War Memorial 156
Doctor Theodore Yeh, 15th Vicar of Christ Church 1970-72 157
Different Voice, Different Pen: Cookie Dough 166

Chapter 6 167
The Reverends David and Alice Babin, 1980-1986 167
Different Voice, Different Pen: Sunday school children 171
Reg Rodman, Rector of Christ Church 1987-1996 173
Interview: Pat Taylor 179
Follow up: Hospice 181
Interview: Betty Hodgins 181
Stained Glass Window 183
Interview: Cynnie Sally 184
History Detective: Not the Oldest Trees 188
Different Voice, Different Pen: The Vestry 190
Commentary: Married to the Ministry 194

Chapter 7 199
Interview: Thelma Tyler 200
Different Voice, Different Pen: Labyrinth 203

Interview: Brenda Machado Lee	205
First impression- Linda Melson	208
Interview: Stephanie Ackerman	208
Interview: Stephanie #2	210
Follow-up: Christ Church Cemetery Rules and Regulations	212
Follow-up: Cremation	213
Interview: Mona Ewing Gurrobat	215
Follow-up King Kamehameha butterfly	218
Interview: Edward Ahuna, September 16, 2007	218
Follow-up: Genealogy	219
Different Voice, Different Pen: Lao Tzu	221
Race Relations	222
Different Voice, Different Pen: Joy McElroy	222
Historical Context: Evensong, September 30, 2007	224
Interview: Robert Mist	225
The Photographs	228
History Detective: Sand Dash Finish	231
Interview: Norm and Alter Grandparents	232
CHAPTER 8: CONCLUSIONS	**239**
The Weaving Metaphor	239
What is a Church?	241
A Backward Glance	242
Then and Now: Dancing for Evensong	244
ACKNOWLEDGEMENTS	**247**
PHOTO CREDITS	**249**
BIBLIOGRAPHY	**251**

Foreword

⚜

The English historian Thomas Babington Macaulay wrote that "History falls between Reason and Imagination…History begins in novel and ends in essay." In the Middle Ages history was supposed to reveal the handiwork of God to the faithful. During the Renaissance, history revealed forgotten truths and ancient wisdom. Enlightenment history framed a proper study of mankind to ensure a better future. By the nineteenth century history was written to glorify the past achievements of a race, people, or a nation. In the twentieth century history served both as a form of entertainment, and in the development of critical thinking. Much of history was rewritten: not only the winners told the stories, but the losers were given a legitimate voice as well.

This is a collection of stories, interviews and commentary concerning the history of a little Anglican church in Kealakekua, 143 years old. The denomination first came to the islands with Captain Cook, and returned officially at the urging of Queen Emma and Kamehameha IV. This church was started by a young vicar from England for the British pioneers in the area.

We know a great deal about the American missionaries and the eventual Americanization of these Hawaiian Islands. Americans won the Revolutionary War against England, and in some ways, continued to fight it out here in these spheres of power. Although America won again, the British influence has not been insignificant.

Kealakekua, far from the religious and political battles carried on in Honolulu and the press, offers a simpler, quieter story of life and change and aloha in Hawaii. The little church tells its story through letters, receipts and thank you notes left behind. The first vicar left his initials on the beams he used to build the foundation. The second vicar left photographs and a small monthly publication. There is a receipt for a donation Queen Emma made toward the purchase of the organ. There is a note about King Kalakua's visit at Easter.

Just walking through the cemetery we see history unfold: first we see the old British names on the tombstones, the Hawaiian, then the Chinese and the Portuguese, then the Japanese. We see the same family names, again and again.

The parish hall has served as home and community center in many ways. To list a few: a Red Cross center during WW 1, a USO center in WW ll, Girl's Friendly Society, Scouting Programs, Alcoholics Anonymous, Quilting Club, schools including boarding schools, Waldorf, dyslexia center, and currently, a Hawaiian Immersion School.

We can also trace the technological change in society with the first electric light at the church, the first telephone, the first automobile, the first computer.

"Interdisciplinary humanities" looks at life as multifaceted and interconnected rather than as neatly separate disciplines. History is not treated as a subject by itself, but tangled up with literature, music, philosophy, attitudes, trends, conflicts, opinions. This book is my *interpretation* based on the facts, colored by my own values, the stories and opinions of the people I interviewed, and, the authors I read.

It is not like a *traditional history* in four significant ways. First, I don't try to stay objective and invisible; instead I am very much in the story and I invite the reader into it too. Second, I try to show what happened, but more importantly, I try to give the reader a <u>context for caring</u> about it. Third, I try to build bridges between the past and the present. I try to keep it all grounded; I may ask hypothetical questions, but I bring the reader back to the earth literally, the cemetery, or the actual church building.

If I could interview every gardener that cared for the land at Christ Church for the past 143 years, I would have a very different view of its history than if I interviewed every choir director...or every Sunday School teacher. I like the view from the pew—imagining what it was like for the ordinary person who was baptized, married and buried here.

This project started out as a joint venture. The original desire to write the book came from our previous rector, Carol Arney. She felt a call to preserve the papers moldering away inside the old boxes in storage at CCE. She asked me to help her. As a team we interviewed people who had been born and/or raised here. We flew to Honolulu to work in the archives of the Cathedral, and at the Bishop Museum. While I focused on the view from the pew, Carol represented the view from the pulpit. She holds a broader view that encompasses church politics, church dynamics, and financial issues. She looked for facts, while I concentrated on feelings, opinions and stories. Eventually we realized that our project needed to be two different books. I imagine them as companion pieces; together they celebrate this place where we gather.

CHAPTER 1

Queen Emma. This appears to be Emma dressed in widow's weeds, in London. She visited Queen Victoria there in 1865. (Courtesy Bishop Museum Archives.)

Once upon a time

Once upon a time there was a fragile blue and green planet named Earth. On this planet, in the middle of a vast turquoise liquid, was a volcanic island. On the western slope facing the pink sunset, was a tiny church with a red roof and a pointy steeple. If you stand at the front door to gaze at the sea, you must look through the headstones of a cemetery. Our story begins in the cemetery.

Here, in this place of departures, we celebrate new life. New life? Don't I mean past life? No. It is Easter morning. Lovely, fragrant flower leis are draped over the headstones. Dotted in, and around, and behind the Celtic crosses and the marble markers, are Easter eggs. This one special morning the children—dressed in yellow, pink and lilac, just like the eggs—wander over the graves of their ancestors with delight. Can you imagine the pleasure those ancestors might feel as well? The circle connects for a few moments, a symbolic reuniting of old souls with young innocent life.

Here, in this tiny piece of paradise, is a cloud of witnesses freed from time and space. I shall be a gatherer of their stories, a weaver of memories. I shall sort them out and tease out the tangles.

Like so many old stories, our story has a queen in it: Queen Emma. Like good and beautiful queens in fairy tales, she loved her people and always wanted the best for them. So she had this church built—this tiny church on the slope of the volcano in the middle of the liquid blue. Queen Emma saw in the Anglican tradition a grace and dignity that she found irresistible. On a high arch inside the chapel are the words, "Worship the Lord in the beauty of holiness." These words help us remember.

The church has stood for 143 years. Not everyone who enters in lives happily ever after. In their stories I hear of injustice, of scandal, of hurt feelings, even of murder. But if you stand back, far enough away to see the whole tapestry, you can see threads of grace, silken threads that hold it all together.

Let us turn around now and face the little church. Climb the steps and enter the double doors. It seems too dark at first to see anything because we have just come in from the tropical daylight. After a moment our eyes adjust to the dim light coming in from the stained glass windows, and we begin to see a doll house of a chapel.

There are eleven windows, three on each side lining the rows of wooden pews, two next to the north choir stall, and three up high above the altar. The first one, closest to us by the door, acknowledges the coming of Christianity to Hawaii. Christianity actually arrived right here, in our own Kealakekua Bay. The writer of the *Stained Glass Windows* pamphlet explains:

> First came the Hawaiians in their sailing canoes, using the stars, Hokupa'a, (the North Star) and Hokule'a (Arcturus) for navigation, much like the wise men once followed their star. Many years later, the malihini (newcomers) came to the islands in tall ships and started a new era, their sails resembling the Makahiki Banner. The first Christian service was held on the shore of Kealakekua Bay. It is mysterious irony that the words Ke-ala-ke-kua mean *Pathway of the God.*

Near here is the place of *first contact* between the Hawaiians and the representatives of Western Civilization. Captain James Cook was one of those there that day. We know from journals kept on his voyages through the Pacific how other indigenous islanders reacted to the white sailors. The Aboriginal people of the Great Barrier Reef believed them to be overgrown babies. The New Zealanders thought they were goblins. But the Hawaiians believed that Captain Cook, in his magnificent ship with sails like wings, was a god.

Why is anyone surprised? The Hawaiians lived in a semi Stone Age society. They did have agriculture and had learned to domesticate animals, but there was no copper, no metal on these very young islands. This seriously limited their technological development. Cook brought wisdom from thousands of years of culture: Greek, Roman, Arabic, Hebrew and Christian, the world of mathematics, science and medicine, the Renaissance, the Enlightenment. He also brought all the technology of the Bronze Age, the Iron Age and the beginning of the industrial revolution, literally thousands of years of human invention. On the ship were such things as the nail, wheel, gun, knife, canon, spy glass, mirrors, clocks, things beyond the wildest imaginations of the Hawaiians who greeted them. That *first contact* was a mighty meeting! Good and bad would both surely result, but let us not get ahead of ourselves. Mystery and wonder were certainly present! Full hearts and thanksgiving all around. The Hawaiians gave abundantly of their hospitality, gave without reserve, offered their beautiful gift of aloha.

The first Christian service recorded on Hawaiian soil was at Napo'opo'o, January 28, 1779. It was a funeral for Seaman William Whatman. You can visit the site today; it is only minutes away from the church. The second recorded Christian service was on February 21, 1779, another funeral, this time for Captain Cook. The infamous spot of Cook's death is just across the bay; you can kayak over to it. The funeral service read was from the Anglican Book of Common Prayer. Both services were recorded in the ship's log, but regular Sunday Prayer Services were not written in; they were just routine. In fact, they were required by the Royal Navy. So it is probable that *Morning Prayer* was read on land, in Hawaii, every Sunday the seamen went ashore.

From then until the first service at Christ Church is a very long time. As eager as I am to start raising the rafters here, I need to fill in these 88 years. The history of Christianity in Hawaii does not unfold as one might expect. No, the Anglican Church in Canterbury was a bit too preoccupied with other things to pay attention to the far off needs of the Hawaiian Islanders. Here is a brief and biased summary of what happens next.

George Vancouver was with Captain Cook on his second and third voyages, and was at Cook's side in his final moments. In 1792 Vancouver returned to Hawaii now as the Captain. He came back in 1793, and 1794, bringing oranges, sheep, and cattle. In terms of our story, his most significant act was that he told Kamehameha about the "One true God, the Creator and Ruler of the Universe" (Jarves 88). Vancouver promised to ask King George to send others to teach the Hawaiian people about this Supreme Being.

With the Hawaiian Islands on the map, whalers and trade ships on their way to the Orient found a safe haven for stop-overs. Occasionally a seaman was left ashore, or was held hostage. John Howell, Isaac Davis, and John Young were three who were left on this island. All three were Anglicans, and their influence "was considered good and wise, on the side of humanity and civilization" (Stanley, 1).

Tradition, according to Restarick, says that King Kamehameha asked Howell (a clergyman) for a sacred rite to "tie" Young and Davis "to the soil." He needed them.

Young and Davis became close friends and trusted advisors to Kamehameha.

These white men did not participate in the traditions of kapu. Most of us have read that Hawaiian women could not eat roasted pig, turtle, coconuts or bananas, men and women could not eat together, and that one could not step on the shadow of the ali'i. But there were many other laws about kapu. An early witness described what he witnessed while one kapu was being observed; "A general gloom and silence pervaded the whole district or island. Not a fire or light was to be seen, or canoe launched. None bathed; the mouths of dogs were tied up, and fowls put under calabashes or their heads enveloped in cloth; for no noise of man or animal must be heard" (Jarves 33).

The author described the many ways death might be inflicted on anyone guilty of breaking a kapu. These gruesome details do not really pertain to our story, but you can check the references.

Jarvis's one area of praise was for the sanctuary available—the City of Refuge:

> These sanctuaries are somewhat analogous to the Israelitish cities of refuge and originated, doubtless, from the barbarous and sanguinary customs, common to both nations, which required a safe-guard from the evil passions constantly kept in excitement by the universal prevalence of the law of retaliation, and the bloody character of their warfare (Jarves 34).

With new weapons (the white man's guns) and new knowledge, Kamehameha unified the eight Hawaiian Islands into a kingdom, and established order and law. After his death, with the coming of new leadership, the system of kapu was broken. This remarkable shift in religious tradition was influenced by the example of the white men: they ate with their Hawaiian wives and nothing bad happened! They showed no fear of the Hawaiian gods or the kapus. First the Hawaiians were frightened by the white men's arrogant indifference to the gods. But no punishment ever came. On the contrary, the white men lived well.

Between first contact and the arrival of the American missionaries, a great deal has happened. Howell, Young and Davis have been the accidental emissaries of Western Civilization; by their continued presence they have quietly changed the kapu system. Young and Davis have married ali'i brides in Anglican Prayer Book ceremonies. They have advised the chiefs in new ways to govern, trade, and share power. They have assisted the Hawaiians in using and caring for the new technologies and the new livestock Vancouver has introduced. It is impossible to know all the ways these three men provide transitional assistance for what is to come: the onslaught of whalers, merchantmen, and American missionaries.

In 1820 missionaries arrive...but not from England as Vancouver promised. In fact, when they tried to land, the King refused to allow it. Young however, "gave his decided advice in favor of the missionaries and said to the King and chiefs, "missionaries from America are the same as missionaries from England; they worship the same God and teach the same religion" (Jarves 43).

Well, some would say, *not quite* the same religion.

These other missionaries—the New England Calvinist missionaries—have a mixed reputation. It is true they taught reading and writing to the children of these islands. They brought clothing and medicine, order and discipline. Although they didn't introduce the islanders to Christianity (Captain Cook and the English seamen left behind did) the missionaries brought a systemized program for converting. I don't think it would be ungracious of me to say that not everything done in Christ's name was actually Christ-like.

If you have read James Michener's Hawaii, then you surely remember the excesses he illustrated in his portrayal of the more zealous missionaries. They dressed in wool as they did in New England, and refused to bathe, ever. They believed fiercely that flowers in church were offensive. They refused to believe equality with Hawaiians was possible—even faithful, baptized, Christian Hawaiians.

Michener is of our own age. Let us hear the evidence from others who lived among the missionaries long ago. James Jackson Jarves lived with his aunt and uncle for five years starting in 1837. He wrote, "The gospel taught by the missionaries was one of fear." Christianity became a list of prohibitions; writing about the new converts Jarves explained:

> Their white instructors, in taking away their games, dances and festivals and wars had given them nothing as an outlet for their natural energies. A polka or waltz was proscribed as the dances of the devil. Theatricals were something worse. Horse racing no better than hell's tournaments. Smoking was a capital sin. Native songs and festivals all smacked of eternal damnation. There was nothing left to the poor native for the indulgence of his physical forces. The most rigid principles of the most rigid Protestant sects were made the standard of salvation (Jarves, 158).

One reverend, a Mr. Stewart, wrote that when he asked a native what the chief commandment was, he answered, "Do not smoke tobacco" (Jarves, 54).

A local Christian chief named Boki, pleaded by letter with England "to be allowed to cook and bathe on Sundays," because the missionaries would not allow it.

Keeping the Sabbath became the test of piety for the convert. William Ellis wrote about a Sunday spent at Kailua:

> The Sabbath was spent in a most gratifying manner. No athletic sports were seen on the beach, no noise of playful children, shouting as they gamboled in the surf, was heard throughout the day, no persons were seen carrying burdens nor any canoes passing the calm surface of the bay. It could not but be viewed as the dawn of a bright, sabbatic day for the dark shores of Hawaii.

About 8000 Hawaiians were excommunicated by the missionaries between 1823 and 1863 for various offences such as dancing hula, swimming, smoking (Restarick, 82). Accustomed to keeping kapu, the Hawaiians unfortunately understood the restrictions of the Sabbath. Not exactly *Good News!*

But there was good, much good, and it would be untrue to leave it out. Summed up by Bishop Resterick, the missionaries "reduced a language to written form, translated the Bible and other books, led the way to universal education, originated industrial schools" (73).

This form of religion did not satisfy Kamehameha ll; he still longed for Vancouver's promise. In 1822, Kamehameha ll wrote a letter to England's King George lV declaring, "Our former idolatrous system has been abolished, as we wish the Protestant religion *of your Majesty's dominions* to be practiced here."

In the following year Kamehameha ll and his Queen journeyed to England to meet with King George. There was speculation that they intended to ask the British Crown for protection, as well as for the faith teachers that Vancouver promised. The weather was harsh in London, however, and the Hawaiian King and Queen caught measles. What was a simple childhood disease for the English proved fatal for the king and queen.

So when we ask, "why did Queen Emma choose the Anglican Church?" it is not so hard to imagine the answer. Both her grandfather, Seaman John Young, and her hanai father, Dr. Rooke, were Englishmen, so Emma had Anglican blood in her veins and she was raised in an Anglican home. Also of significance, the Anglican Church in England honored the monarchy, whereas America (including the missionaries) had recently waged a Revolutionary War and done away with kings altogether. But besides the heavy political and national overtones, there were simple reasons: the Anglicans allowed flowers in church, loved ceremony and liturgy. Instead of focusing on sin and degradation, they focused on the splendor, the mystery and majesty of God.

This is a significant difference. A wonderful, ecumenical English teacher/writer of today, Brian McLaren (not even an Anglican) sums up our church in the loveliest way. Since I can't do it half as well, I want to share his words. He highlights three treasures of our tradition: First is the practice of dynamic tension:

> When you choose both/and rather than either/or regarding Catholicism and Protestantism, you learn to live with dynamic tension in other areas as well. You resist the reductionist temptation to always choose only one thing over another, and you learn to hold two or more things together when necessary.
> Second is the practice of compromise: "Compromise is a dirty word for many Christians. It suggests a lowering of standards. But it is a beautiful word if you are trying to live in community with others, with Scripture, reason, tradition, and experience in dynamic tension. In this light, compromise and tolerance suggest keeping a

high standard of unity and a high level of respect for your brothers and sisters who disagree with you.

Third is the practice of beauty: What keeps Anglicans together if they have so much diversity? It is their deep appreciation for the *deep beauty* of liturgy that helps them make room for one another. Even if they disagree on what the liturgy means or requires doctrinally, they are charmed by its mysterious beauty and beautiful mystery, and that is often enough to keep them together long enough to share, evaluate, and integrate varied understandings. In contrast to Christians who argue about the fine points of doctrine but show little taste for the beauty of truth, the Anglican way has been *to begin with beauty, to focus on beauty, and to stay with it, believing that where beauty is, God is.*

Whenever I read the high arch in church now, I bless Queen Emma for her dedication and steadfastness in bringing about her vision.

Right where the arch begins, on the left side by the organ, there is a new gift given to our church. The quilting club has used Wallace Hall for years and they have made us a thank you gift. It is a handmade quilt, a copy of the stained glass window of Queen Emma and Kamehameha IV that hangs in the Cathedral in Honolulu. There is actual braid around the king's jacket; there are real earrings attached to the quilted queen. It is all done in orange, blue and brown. The King and Queen look very much like European monarchs. They look regal yet beneficent. Both the King and Queen are official saints in the Anglican Communion. I have referred to Emma but what about the King? He died before Christ Church was built, but his work and devotion influenced all Anglican work in Hawaii that came after.

The author Kuykendall writes that Alexander had the manners and the bearing of a European gentleman. He was well educated and familiar with the best in English literature. He was a master of the Hawaiian language as well.

As a prince, Alexander visited both America and England. In America he was subject to incidents of racial prejudice, yet in England he was treated with dignity. It is believed that this made a great impression on him, and influenced his political relationships later as king.

Alexander and Emma knew each other as children. They attended the ali'i school together. When Emma and Alexander were married, June 19, 1856, an Anglican wedding ceremony was performed. It was "the grandest affair of the kind that had ever occurred in Hawaii" (Kuykendall, 83).

As king, Alexander, now Kamehameha IV, asked the Church of England–once again—to send missionaries and to establish an Anglican Church in Hawaii.

And finally, *finally*, after so many years, it did. In England both *The Society for the Propagation of the Gospel in Foreign Parts,* and *The Society for Promoting Christian Knowledge* raised funds and pledged support.

Manly Hopkins wrote to educate the British people about Hawaii. He expressed concern that clergy for Hawaii "must be truly earnest in the Christian cause, and be of a liberal habit of mind, so as to endear and not to estrange other workers in the vineyard." There had been enough tension between denominations, and Hopkins hoped for some sensitivity on the way it was to proceed. But England does not select a humble clergyman of liberal habit, it chooses a bishop.

While awaiting the bishop's arrival, King Alexander began translating the *Book of Common Prayer* into the language of his people. He donated land in Honolulu for a church building. The Queen prepared the young prince for baptism.

All this preparation, eagerness and anticipation, was interrupted by tragedy. The beloved little prince died. Nobody was sure of the cause; the four year old was playing happily one day, fell ill, and died. Doctors now speculate that he had appendicitis. The King, however, believed that he himself was to blame for his son's death. Although they had planned a baptism with the new bishop, they could not wait for him. The prince was baptized in his final hours.

Six weeks later, October 11, 1862, the first Bishop of Hawaii, Thomas Nettleton Staley, arrived in Honolulu. We can assume that he arrived ready to celebrate, only to find the King and Queen in mourning. Though they surely would have preferred isolation, they had official duties to perform, and perhaps the preparations were a help in the healing process.

On October 21, Queen Emma was baptized in a private ceremony. Her name, Emma Alexandrina Frances Agnes Louder Byde Rooke Young Kaleleokalani, is the first in the register of St. Andrew's Cathedral.

On November 9, Morning Prayer was celebrated in the Hawaiian language for the very first time. The King corrected the sermon beforehand and had the preacher practice it several times to make sure it was right. The King also wrote an explanation for the Prayer Book. It begins:

> The Church is established here in Hawaii through the breathings of the Holy Spirit and by the agency of the chiefs. Vancouver, years ago, was requested to send us the True God. . . Your king [Kamehameha ll] went to a distant and powerful country to hasten the advent of that which our eyes now see . . . the very Church here planted in Hawaii, but how long we have waited.

On November 28 the King and Queen were confirmed into the Anglican Church, and two days later they took their first communion. *The gifts of God for the people of God.*

On December 21, David Kalakaua, the future king, was confirmed into the Anglican Church.

The King continued with his translations. The church worked to build a firm foundation in Honolulu. But there was still nothing here in Kealakekua. We do have a story of the King visiting Kona in 1863. He was staying at the summer palace on

Ali'i Drive, while the Queen stayed behind in Honolulu. The following story shows the heart of the King, but it also illustrates the difference between the Calvinist and the Anglican presentation of Christianity to the native population. According to biographer George Kanahele:

> The last time King Alexander Liholiho had visited Kona was when the young prince was still alive and when he himself was in better health. While wandering through the house, the memories of that happier time greatly affected his moods. When he chanced upon a box containing the playthings of his son, he could not hold back his grief.
>
> Near his summer residence was a Congregational Church, and when Sunday arrived, feeling sad and alone, he decided to attend church services. The sermon he heard presented such an alarming and terrifying picture of a vengeful Christian God delivering eternal punishment on the Day of Judgment that the king announced that he himself would hold a second service that afternoon and deliver a different kind of sermon.
>
> The church building was crowded with his eager but respectful subjects. Major H, wearing a white surplice, opened the service by reading from the king's translated version of the Prayer Book. Then the king, also wearing a surplice to symbolize the religious office he now assumed, gave his sermon using as his text the passage from the Gospel of John, "Jesus wept." He described a God of sympathy and mercy rather than one of fear and recommended that abounding love and beneficence and long suffering be the reason for holiness and hope. The congregation was held spellbound not only by the power of his words, but by his mana. For here was their ali'i nui, a Kamehameha, suffering from his own deep pain and uttering words of compassion and solace.

November 30, 1863, King Alexander died. Only a few months after preaching in Kona, Kamehameha IV was dead at only 29 years of age. He had not been a perfect king. I have not shared in this short and focused history his weaknesses, nor have I shared what some would consider his greatest gift. But I have shared that which earned him the position of saint in our church.

The queen has lost both her child and her husband. Emma sat with the casket in the throne room for 60 days. Bishop Staley writes:

> The Queen sits almost incessantly by the coffin. She has prayers in the room night and morning, in the Hawaiian language, so that all present may understand, taken from the Book of Common Prayer, and I read to her from the Psalms or other consolatory passages of Holy Scripture every day. It is beautiful to see how she seeks for consolation only in God. . . among all the classes of people there is one common feeling of sympathy with her in this hour of her anguish. For by her works of charity and mercy, she had endeared herself to the hearts of all.

The *Polynesian,* on February 6, 1864 reported that 800 children walked to Honolulu to march in the king's funeral procession, to "testify their love and regret, and their gratitude to the memory of a prince to whose heart their cause was ever nearest."

HISTORICAL CONTEXT

What else has been happening in Hawaii and in the rest of the world in the 88 years between *first contact* and the arrival of the first Vicar Of Christ Church?

In 1779 the Revolutionary War finally ended and the new United States of America ratified an amazing Constitution filled with unheard of personal liberties.

In the year 1783 Ben Franklin invented bifocals, a wonderful invention that many of us use daily with gratitude.

While Kamehameha fights to control the islands, on the other side of the globe, starving French peasants, (inspired by the audacity of the American Revolution,) plunge into their own revolution against an indifferent and opulent French monarchy.

In 1792 the Kona orange, which originated in Southeast Asia, was introduced to Hawaii.

In 1804 Lewis and Clark, with the invaluable help of Sacagawea, set out to map new territory, and explored all the way west until they reached the Pacific Ocean.

In 1805 typhoid fever killed 5,000 Hawaiians and decimated the army of Kamehameha.

In 1808 Beethoven started to compose, and in 1811 Jane Austen began to find success in her writing.

Don Francisco de Paula y Marin, the Spanish advisor to Kamehameha, introduced pineapple and coffee to Hawaii in 1813. This first coffee is Brazilian. The pineapple is named after the pinecone.

In 1823 papayas arrived. William Ellis grew them in Kona; he called them *pawpaw apples*.

Mango came to Hawaii from the Philippines in 1824. It is in the poison ivy family, and many of us are seriously allergic to the sap on the skin. Mangoes are found in the fossil record 25-30 million years ago!

Guava, which is part of the Eucalyptus family, also came some time before the 1830's. It was growing wild by the 1850's.

Charles Dickens' name was on the calendar by 1837, stirring up the middle class and creating a social conscience through his novels.

In 1838 the Cherokee walked their "Trail of Tears," giving the world an unforgettable image of injustice in a country which declared itself "the land of the free and the home of the brave."

Although it had been killing Hawaiians for two decades, influenza became so deadly that it killed nearly every baby born in Hawaii in 1848 (Tayman, 25).

The first Chinese contract workers arrived in Hawaii in 1852.

The 1853 small pox epidemic took the lives of 5,000 Hawaiians.

Charles Darwin wrote his earth-shaking (and faith-shattering for some) *Origin of Species* In 1855.

The cornerstone was laid for the Queen's Hospital, Honolulu, in 1860. This was the first hospital for the Hawaiian people. Because they had no immunity to the germs of simple childhood diseases (measles, mumps, whooping cough, chicken pox), or the adult complicated ones (syphilis, gonorrhea, typhoid, influenza, or small pox,) this met a tremendous need. It was also a tangible sign that the culture was moving away from traditional healers to modern medicine. It was explained to the reluctant ones: the kahunas are good for our own sickness, but we need the white men's medicine for the white men's diseases.

In 1861 the Civil War, the War Between the States, Lincoln's War to free the slaves, to heal the wounds of a nation, began.

In 1865 Queen Emma visited England, Queen Victoria, Alfred Lord Tennyson, and Paris.

In 1865, the myna bird, loud, aggressive, and comical, came from India to visit Hawaii. Like so many of us, it decided to stay.

Beginning in the year 1866, individuals suspected of having leprosy in Hawaii were exiled. Over the next hundred years, over 8,000 individuals were exiled; this was one in thirty residents. No ethnic or economic group was spared; Hawaiian royalty as well as prominent lawyers, judges, and children of doctors were banished to Molokai. The tough decisions and laws enacted began as a sincere attempt to save the Hawaiian race from extinction.

1867 marked two events in Honolulu for the newly formed Anglican Church: the laying of the cornerstone of St. Andrew's Cathedral, and the Dedication of St. Andrew's Priory, a girl's school which was a project dear to the heart of Queen Emma.

In 1867 Alaska natives learned that 2 foreign countries bought and sold their entire territory without consulting them.

The First Vicar

Now we are ready for our fair Englishman, our first vicar, with the energy, strength, and the perennial idealism of youth. Did he grow up with stories of Captain Cook? Did he spend gloomy gray winters reading about brilliantly colored gardens of Eden still flourishing in the Pacific Ocean? I wrote to the president of the Captain Cook Society in England and asked what books might have been available to young Williamson. The president, Cliff Thornton, answered:

> When books about Cook's voyages were first published in the late 1700s they were immediate best sellers. The stories and engravings that they contained about strange unknown lands across the seas made fascinating reading. Initially books came out separately for each voyage, but from the late 1780s his three voyages were published together in one book.
>
> To make the story more accessible to the public, some publishers broke the books down into sections published in cheap weekly editions. Cook's story was so spellbinding that it has been retold and republished time and time again, so there was never a period when a child would not have had access to them.
>
> I am looking at a bibliography of books about Cook, and a new book seems to have been published every few years. Here is the data relevant to the years you are interested in:
> 1846 "Voyages of James Cook" illustrated with maps and engravings. With an appendix giving an account of the present condition of the South Sea Islands, etc. Published in London by W. Smith.
> 1852 "Circumnavigation of the Globe- and progress of discovery in the Pacific Ocean, from the voyage of

Magellan to the death of Captain Cook." Published in London, by Nelson.

1852 "The Voyages of Captain James Cook" illustrated with maps and numerous engravings. Published in London by John Tallis.

1853 "Narrative of Captain James Cook's voyages round the world." Published in Halifax by Milner & Sowerby.

1855 and another/ 1856 and another / 1857 and another / Etc.,etc.

So there was no shortage of books, both new and old.

The Captain Cook Society president suggests another important source of inspiration to a young boy's imagination:

> You are talking of the early years of Queen Victoria's reign; she came to the throne in 1837. Victorian England was seen as a very religious period.
>
> The discovery of the peoples of the Pacific seems to have aroused the Christian fervor for proselyting, and the London Missionary Society was established to take the Gospels to the four corners of the world. Often the missionaries returning to England published details of what they had seen in far off lands. I am thinking of William Ellis in the case of Hawaii, although that was a little before 1842. But the principle was the same for later missionaries. So you may wish to consider if young CGW went to church whether he would have been exposed to such missionary tales at Sunday School.

We don't have access to Charles Williamson's early life or childhood dreams, but we know that at 21 he studied theology, mathematics and Hebrew at St Augustine's Missionary College in Canterbury. More importantly, or at least of more practical importance, he studied carpentry and medicine.

Four years later, Charles crossed the Atlantic Ocean, then the Isthmus of Panama, then the Pacific. He arrived in Honolulu on the ship D.C. Murray. Everyone arrived by ship; there was no other way. It allowed one time to collect oneself. No jet lag, no time zone warps. There was more than enough time to pray and meditate and prepare oneself. To let go of the past and to make plans for a whole new life. Time to practice that new language. An enforced Sabbatical.

In a letter dated May 21, 1867, Charles wrote about his first Sunday upon arriving in Honolulu:

> Oh, how I wish that some of our English friends could have been present at the service of that morning! The example set by the natives, as regards devotion and joining in the service, would shame many a congregation in England. You could hear the responses echoed from all parts of the church while the Canticles and Psalms were chanted in Hawaiian, in good taste and with much feeling.

He was also touched by the ecumenical unity displayed in the second service:

> And so it was at the English service, attended by many formerly Presbyterians, Methodists, and American Episcopalians. Each member of the congregation seemed to pour out his whole soul in worship. Our hymns were heart-stirring and full of devotion, and my thoughts were carried back to dear old England when I recognized familiar chants and tunes.

Finally Williamson arrived on the Big Island, on our island, Hawaii, the land of his dreams! This will be his home. He recorded his first impressions of Kealakekua Bay September 1, 1868:

> It is very nearly the same as it was in Cook's time . . . the huts are built of grass under the shade of cocoa-nuts

which line the beach. The people spend most of their time swimming about in the water, or skimming over the clear blue sea in the feathery canoe.

Charles set out to find land on which to build a house of worship. There were places in Kona town, but alas, no one would sell land to him. The ecumenical unity that stirred him so deeply in the English service in Honolulu was not present here. March 1866 he wrote to the *Society for the Propagation of the Gospel*, "It is a source of great sorrow to me that an unpleasant feeling approaching almost to hatred should exist between the Calvinist missionaries here and our church."

Why would his brothers and sisters in Christ (his American Calvinist brothers and sisters) treat him with such hostility? It was because they were very territorial. They actually believed that they were here first!

By and by, (and, we can assume, by the will of God) land was found in Kealakekua. Janion, Green, & Davies, all three Brits involved in the Hamakua sugar industry, owned land which had been abandoned to weeds and wild guava. As fellow countrymen, they willingly loaned the young vicar a two-acre parcel.

Current church member Robert Mist tells me that he is a direct descendent of Green, and has family stories about the old partners. Janion and Green were part of a successful group of men who enjoyed late nights of gambling and drinking together in Kona. To pacify their wives for their sometimes outrageous behavior, they made frequent, generous donations to local churches and charities. These gifts were often the result of guilt rather than piety. Or maybe they were sincerely both. Robert Mist suspects that the free loan of the property for a new mission came after one of these wild nights. Whether this is fact or fiction, Kealakekua became home for the new Anglican Mission.

What we do have are letters from Charles Williamson to document his progress and his insights:

> Considering that I am the first English clergyman on the Island you will not be surprised when I tell you that the principles of our Church are little known. As regards buildings, the people here can give next to nothing; they have no money. Through the kindness of some friends in England I have some money towards building here . . . being the spot where Capt. Cook died, I may expect some to assist in raising a school building which might justly be called a Memorial to the Great Navigator as none has been attempted at present. (SPG May 21, 1867)

Charles Williamson chose a lovely spot to build on: at the crest of the hill with a view of the ocean. The elevation was just right for comfort; not as hot as the beach, not as cold as higher up mauka. There would be plenty of rain, plenty of sunshine. Finding the materials to use, finding the money to pay for them, and finding some help with the labor were new challenges.

> Not being able to find or obtain any building for school, or church purposes, I at once commenced building, with the aid of two carpenters. I have in three months built a church & house, a room of the latter being arranged for a school. The expense of those buildings is a little over $2,000, the great item being the lumber itself, which in this country is very expensive. I am proud to say that fully one third of the work has been done with my own hands, working beneath a summer tropical sun, with, I thank God, no injury to my constitution ... (SPG 9-31, 1867)

Who were the two helpers? Were they Hawaiians, or foreigners? CW and his two helpers built a foundation of low lava rock walls reinforced with ohia logs. They used 5½" tongue and groove Douglas fir to make the nave. The carpenters used square nails to secure the wood shingle roof. The windows were single hung with a Gothic arch. Inside the church the floors were Douglas fir, and the front entry steps were enclosed. The church was painted gray with a sand-dash finish.

CW did not wait for the completion of the building to have his first service. Twenty-five local natives attended his first Hawaiian language service, and sixty haoles attended the English service; this would have included the local British farmers, graziers and merchants, and perhaps visitors from the ships in Kealakekua:

> Some of the natives have shown their good will by subscribing the expenses of the building and $50 have been raised here. I have far more success as regards numbers attending my services than could have been expected at first. I do not wish to express any opinion respecting making good Christian Churchmen out of them; I labour, but "God giveth the increase (Annual Report, 1868).

According to the first register, CW performed the first wedding at Christ Church for bride and groom Pelielii and Nakepalau on May 19th 1867. The first to be baptized at Christ Church were two small brothers, Ashford, 2 years of age, and Charles Spencer, 3 months, on February 10, 1868. He writes in his Annual Report, September 1867:

> There is, I think, a work to be done, not a work of much show perhaps—a still and unnoticed work, a tedious work, a work for Christ, to be done with the Spirit's guidance, bringing souls out of self into Christ, out of error into truth.

Then and Now: Queen Emma

When Queen Emma stayed in the Hulihe'e Summer Palace, she rode her horse 15 miles to attend services at the Christ Church mission. According to a letter Charles Williamson wrote in 1868, crowds of adoring subjects came to church whenever she did. So many attended that they could not all fit inside the chapel; "many have been obliged to follow out the Hawaiian mode of sitting squatted on the ground."

Now, high above the altar are three tall stained glass windows. The middle one is *'The Good Shepherd'* dressed in white, with a lamb cradled in his left arm. The narrow windows on both sides show stained glass flowers, those said to be Queen Emma's favorite. They are large, pinkish-purple spider lilies. The light pours through the pretty pink glass softening the light in the chapel. There are real *Queen Emma lilies* growing outside the front door, offering fragrance and beauty all year around.

Mother Nature

In the spring of 1868 an earthquake estimated as a 7.9 on the Richter scale hit the Big Island. The epicenter was estimated at Ka'u. *Besides* an earthquake, there were volcanic eruptions from first Mauna Loa, then Kilauea; then there were tsunamis, and then electrical storms. Of course there was no Richter local magnitude scale yet, or Jagger Observatory, or early warning systems.

Now CW became an amateur geologist. He kept meticulous notes and sent his findings over the next three weeks to the *Hawaiian Gazette*. CW recorded 128 earthquakes in four days but apologized for being asleep three hours on Saturday night and missing some. On April 2nd, the big one hit. He described it:

> I reigned in my horse at the commencement of the shock, and sat perfectly astounded. No one who has not experienced a similar shock can form an idea of the impression it made... strong kukui trees were bent backward and forward, like reeds in a storm, not a breath of air blowing at the time. With my own eyes, I saw a house fall, and a large portion of the two palis... the terrible convulsion...seemed to affect the water for a considerable

time, the sea running in and out for several hours, leaving fish dry on the rocks.

Water rose 12 to 15 meters at the Keauhou Landing destroying all homes and buildings. Aftershocks continued and an "immense volume of smoke hung like a pall over the earth for several days."

The volcanic emissions created acid rain which contaminated the water in catchment systems. The sulfur dioxide in air and water damaged human, animal and plant life all over the island. Seventy-seven people lost their lives; many more suffered illness. With earthquakes, volcanic eruptions, tsunamis, mud slides and acid rain all mixed up together, people must have feared it was the end of the world.

While churches up and down the coast were leveled and grass shacks torn to shreds, the little wooden church in Kealakekua stood firm.

The young vicar traveled throughout the region over the thin, new lava by horseback to witness the truth of this amazing event, and to offer comfort and support to his new parishioners. I don't imagine anything in his Missionary College prepared him for this!

Problems

As CW made progress in Kealakekua, the Bishop was under siege in Honolulu. There was tension between High Church and Low Church that went far outside the bounds of this particular denomination; "The Episcopal Mission tried to steer a middle course [between Catholic and missionaries] but it collided with both." (Kuy 98)

Unfortunately, Charles Williamson and the Bishop could not see eye to eye on spiritual matters either. Tension between them grew until it seems that Charles could no longer carry on in good conscience. By June of 1869, Charles had returned to England.

Former member of Christ Church, author Sandol Stoddard has published a book titled *The Eloquence of Silence, A Testimony to the Life and Character of Charles George Williamson*. Stoddard chronicles the ongoing strife of the Anglo-Catholic Church in Hawaii, and how it is reflected in the relationship between this gentle priest and his arrogant superior. (*See her 2007 publication for further details and stories she uncovered in her research.)

A last note on Williamson and the property. When he left Christ Church, Charles needed to deal with the ownership of the land. It had only been on loan, and yet he had built a church on it. Theo Davies, the sole owner by this time, wished to give the land to Charles. Charles asked him to deed it to the church. Davies refused to do so. Why would he refuse?

Let us take a short detour here. Besides a British businessman, who was Theophilus Davies anyway? On the internet, his name is associated with the Big 5, the wealthy movers and shakers of Hawaii. In Bishop Restarick's book, Davies' name is almost always in the lists of people present at important events in the early Anglican Church in Honolulu. Davies was also the guardian of Princess Kaiulani, heiress apparent to the throne, and was in charge of her education in London for 8 years.

After his death, the Diocesan Magazine acknowledges that he used his considerable wealth for the Church Missionary Society clarifying that "his benefactions to that society were munificent." Upon further research I find that there are two windows in St Andrews Cathedral dedicated to the memory of Theo Davies, as was the chapel itself at HPA in Waimea.

Theo Davies deeded the original two acre piece of land to Charles Williamson, but folks here don't even know his name. Rich tycoon that he was, maybe this is a good thing. But the point I want to make here is that he refused to deed the land to the Anglican Church because he was so deeply offended by the Bishop. He refused to be bullied or to bow to protocol; Theo Davies' loyalty was to the humble servant of the Lord, Charles Williamson, first Vicar Of Christ Church.

CHAPTER 2

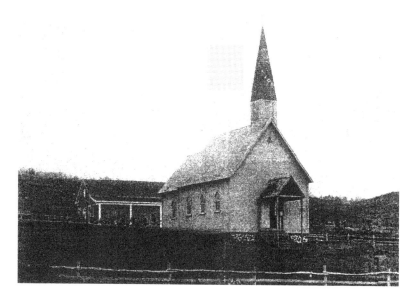

Christ Church 1881. (unattributed, Xerox stapled to The Wanderer.)

Samuel H. Davis, the second Vicar of Christ Church Kealakekua, was born April 7, 1838 in East Combe, Gloucestershire, England. He was actually 4 years older than Charles Williamson; they would have grown up with the same influences in cultural heroes, manners and values. Perhaps they even knew each other at Saint Augustine's Missionary College in Canterbury.

Davis was ordained while serving as a missionary in Zanzibar. We are not sure how he gets from Africa to Hawaii, but Reverend Davis arrives with his wife and a new bishop—the second bishop of Hawaii—in the year 1872. Davis is 34 years of age. He will stay in Hawaii the rest of his life. The Davis years will be peaceful and productive years for Christ Church, but not for Hawaii. While the little Gothic church becomes stable, the monarchy will gradually fall. The Hawaiians and the Americans are the primary players in this struggle, but others–the British, the Catholics, the Chinese, the Portuguese—are all making significant, though quieter, contributions to life in the islands. But first let us arrive with Reverend Davis to this place that apparently has been left to go a little wild.

Three years have passed since CW left. Grass has grown up over the windows of the little mission and the rest of the land has lived in riotous abandon. Davis cleans up the property, and fences off space for a graveyard. He repairs the church, encloses the front steps, has the spire galvanized, adds a new corrugated roof, buys an organ. He builds a hexagonal font from a solid piece of koa. He also builds a schoolhouse. We know a few things from letters Davis wrote. We know a few things from a preservation report that architects made in 1990. We also have access to old issues of the Anglican magazine published in Hawaii. Here we find the statement, "The reverend gentleman – Samuel Davis- has beautified the church and grounds in such a way as to make them a delight to all who visit the neighborhood."

There is also an article about an important visit by the bishop, the consecration of the church, and the naming of it. The *Hawaiian Church Monthly Messenger* reports that on the 3rd Sunday after Easter in 1874, the Bishop of Honolulu, Alfred Willis, comes to South Kona. We have a very long and detailed description. Here is a portion: I have shortened it considerably but kept enough to give a clear picture of the event, as well as the bishop's writing style.

> The Bishop landed at Kealakekua Bay... Thursday evening shortly after sunset, accompanied by Mr. Trembeth and four of the choir boys of the Cathedral at Honolulu. His visit not being expected till a fortnight later, there were no horses in readiness for the party. But

a pack-horse was found to whose back the baggage was speedily transferred...

Our readers will remember that Mr. Davis completed the fencing in of the Churchyard in Nov. last, and they are also familiar with the 'long grass and guava bushes' which choked the ground. On entering the ground by moonlight we found that these historical guava bushes, grass, and every vestige of vegetation had entirely disappeared, and the ground presented the appearance of a garden border ready for planting... Mr. Davis had found his "recreation" during the dry season in clearing the whole ground, and burning the sods, so as to get rid of the Hilo grass, for which he intends to substitute the manie-nie. No one could form any conception of the labour that has been performed unless they had seen the ground in its previous condition.

... On Saturday which was S. Mark's Day... the Church was decorated for the morrow's solemnity. Our decorators in Honolulu would have looked with envious eye upon the flowers produced in the cooler climate of South Kona. The Altar was vested in a rich frontal sent out for the church from friends in England.

It was somewhat vexatious that a bag containing the boys' surplices, Altar Linen, and other things requisite for the Service never reached Kealakekua, so that many of the externals of the Service were unavoidably missing.

The first service on Sunday was of course a Celebration of Holy Communion at 7 a.m. The ceremony of Consecration commenced at 10.30. The Bishop, preceded by the Choir, and the Rev. S.H. Davis bearing the Pastoral Staff, proceeded from the Parsonage to the Church reciting the

24th and 45th Psalms. The Deed of Conveyance was presented to the Bishop at the Altar, and by him laid upon the Holy Table. The prayers always used in the Church at home on these occasions were then offered. The Consecration of the Burial Ground followed. The Bishop followed by the Choir and Congregation made the circuit of the ground in procession reciting Psalms 49, 91, 142. Then kneeling down in the centre of the Cemetery, the Bishop offered the following...

[Here is the first prayer only]
O GOD, Creator of the world, Redeemer of mankind, absolute Ruler of all creatures visible and invisible, we humbly beseech Thee that Thou wouldest vouchsafe to purify, hallow, and bless this cemetery, wherein the bodies of Thy servants and handmaidens are to rest after the brief course of this life, and as Thou hast granted of Thy great mercy remission of all their sins to them that put their trust in Thee, bestow likewise perpetual consolation on their bodies which rest in this cemetery and await the trumpet of the Archangel; through Jesus Christ Our Lord. *Amen.*

After the prayers, the group returns to the church and sings, 'Christ is made the sure Foundation.'

The Bishop preached on "the purchase and consecration of the land on which Abraham built his first altar in the land of Canaan ..." The offertory amounted to $14. The service closed with Hymn 112, 'Christ the Lord is risen again.'

In the afternoon the children were catechized. Bishop left for Waiohino on Wednesday.
Mr. Trembeth and the boys remained over the following Sunday waiting for a Schooner, so that the octave of the consecration was kept with a choral service.

The Bishop from Honolulu named the mission "Church of Christ." Why did he choose this? We have no information about his choice. I asked our bishop, Bob Fitzpatrick, "Who had the authority to name a church? Was it the bishop, or the rector who built it?" He said that churches were usually named by a generous supporter, or in memory of a church in the childhood home of a founding member.

When did "Church of Christ" change to "Christ Church?"

Community Outreach

Education is of critical importance in bringing "civilization" to a new land. The American missionaries have introduced reading and writing, and a rigid morality, but there is still much work to do to bring the Hawaiian people into the modern world. The ali'i have embraced the splendor, the glitter and the glory of the European monarchs. Their palace is full of beautiful European style furniture and décor. Some of the ali'i study English literature and classical music. The Western educated ali'i want the best of what the newcomers have to offer, yet want to keep the best of what they already have: an almost impossible and rather ambiguous dream.

Clock time is an example of a Western concept incompatible with Hawaiian time. Hawaiian time is in harmony with the cycles of nature: sunrise and sunset, the tides, the seasons. In school, however, children are expected to be up at 5:00 (regardless of the sun) to begin their day of prayer, study and work. Schedules are rigidly kept.

Apparently girls are in special need of discipline. Dibble writes, "It seems impossible to restrain them [the girls] from rude and romping behavior, and to confine them to those exercises deemed most proper for females."

Queen Emma dearly wants education for Hawaiian girls, and the Anglican Church takes up her cause. The Reverend and Mrs. Davis open a school at the mission. We have the announcement;

> Family boarding School ...for Hawaiian Girls,
> South Kona, Hawaii
> Conducted by Rev. S. H. Davis and Mrs. Davis.
>
> A large and well-ventilated dormitory has been added to this School and we are now prepared to receive applications for admission of at least twelve more girls as boarders.
>
> The climate of Kona is well known to be the best in the Islands for affectations of the lungs. Mrs. Davis, who is an experienced nurse, would give especial care to children having a tendency to these complaints.
>
> The grounds about the School are large and well kept, giving facilities for healthful recreation.
>
> The School provides a pleasant home, in which girls receive a sound English education, with thorough training in household duties—careful attention being paid to their health and formation of character.
>
> Terms Board and tuition; $100 per annum; washing (unless otherwise provided for), $25; music, $20;–all quarterly in advance. Children under ten years of age are admitted at $50 per annum, as they are entitled to a grant from the Board of Education.

In the records we have a letter from Miss Lillian Willis. She is both the teacher of the mission school and sister of the bishop. She reports that there are ten boarding students, the youngest 4 years old. The boarders do all the housework and most of the cooking. Carry Clerk is the oldest girl, and she does the bread baking. Two Japanese women do the laundry. The days are orderly with Matins at 9am and prayers at 7pm. After the little ones go to bed, the others do needlework and Miss Willis plays the harmonium.

In the Cemetery

There is a grave from this time period that is off in a corner separate from the rest of the cemetery. Esther Waha is buried there, one of the students in the mission school. She dies unexpectedly, right after Christmas, December 1885. The *Anglican Church Chronicle* explains:

> The following week was a very mournful one to us by the sickness and death of one of our pupils, Esther Waha. She had been in the mission schools since infancy at St Cross, Lahaina...where we found her in 1877... Her connections with our schools had not only given her good instruction, but kept her from daily temptations to which she might have otherwise been exposed. She was only 19 years of age. Truly her sun went down while it was yet day.

On the official list of burials it notes that young Esther is buried by the parsonage, not in the graveyard. Many years later Reverend Davis is buried next to her. They are all alone in the corner. The rest of the cemetery is beginning to show the wave of immigrants arriving in Hawaii. Unhappily, there are many infants on the list.

Neighbors

What else is in the neighborhood at this time? There is a general store just down the street and around the corner, belonging to one of the mission parishioners. Built in 1870, the Greenwell store was the first mauka store in the area and served the locals all the way until the 1950s. Now it is part of the Kona Historical Society. I decide to go for a visit to get a feel for life at the time of our second vicar.

We know a great deal about neighbor Greenwell because he kept a daily journal throughout his adult lifetime. Henry

Nicholas Greenwell, pioneer from County Durham, England was an educated man and a hard working rancher. He studied sheep ranching in Australia, and citrus orchards in Pompeii. He listened to opera and visited art museums in Europe. He studied geology, Spanish, French, literature, the prophet Ezekiel, and the Gospel of Matthew during long voyages at sea.

Henry arrives in Hawaii in 1850, just at the time legislation is passed allowing foreigners to purchase property. He buys land on the Big Island; he pours his knowledge and learning into it. He buys land in Kealakekua and plants oranges. He buys land mauka and begins raising cattle.

In 1868, Henry visits Montserrat, in the British West Indies. He finds more than information on the successful lime trade; he also finds a wife. The English born Elizabeth Hall returns with him to Kona. The newlyweds live in Henry's wooden house down the street from the new little Gothic church. In his history book written decades later, Bishop Restarick calls Elizabeth "a true Mother of Israel."

The house is gone now, but the store is standing strong, part of a living history tour. Our docent wears a gray bun and a pink muumuu; she shows a small group of us old photographs of the original Greenwell couple. She sets the stage describing the unique details of the construction of the store.

* The original roof was made of slate.
* Local children dove for the coral that was used in the mortar.
* We can still see the tool marks on the volcanic stone.

We are given a shopping list true to the earlier day, and are led inside. Everything is shiny and clean; basic items once for sale there give us an immediate feeling for time past. The storekeeper is in costume and answers our questions in the character of Mrs. Greenwell. She helps us with our list. There are bags of beans and flour. There are wool shirts and bolts of calico. There is salted cod for the Portuguese. There is strychnine for the wild dogs. In a glass case are spools of thread, a Jew's harp, hat pins. Lanterns and tools hang from the ceiling.

Over on the side is a dining room table and chairs. This, our docent tells us, is where Henry home schools his boys. Brothers and sisters are not taught together; the girls are taught by their mother inside their home next door.

One tourist asks how often people came to shop. Another asks how often the store was open. Our guide answers that the store was open every day but Sunday. She is quick to qualify her answer.... "Not that Henry Greenwell was religious. He was NOT. . . though the rest of the family was."

Now this is a statement that surprises me. I have read his family history and noted his diary entries when he reads his Bible on sea voyages. I noted again when he expresses his pleasure in the Christmas services and church festivities with the Magic Lantern. I have seen the receipts from Henry's donation of 7,673 square feet of land to the church in 1873. Is this just a matter of interpretation? Perhaps the docent means that Henry was not a *Calvinist*. He was known for his temper (Isabella Bird wrote about it.) He was known to drink wine (he left his own written opinion on the quality of what was in his wine cellar.) We even have court records that he went to trial for the murder of a Chinese worker in his employment. He may have been more sinner than saint (and that would be open for interpretation) but the record is clear that yes, he was a religious man.

Henry Greenwell was well known to Hawaiian royalty, worked with at least three Anglican bishops, and two Christ Church priests. Henry died in 1891. He is the first Greenwell to be buried in CC cemetery. His wife and 7 children are there as well as grandchildren, and great grandchildren.

HISTORY DETECTIVE: THE MAGIC LANTERN

When you read the part about the Magic Lantern on Christmas Day, did you wonder what it was? I found references to it three times, twice in Kona (1884, and 1897), and once in Honolulu for a church "Tea -party." I asked several older friends if they knew about it, but no one did, except for my husband. He is the son of a photography buff, however, and his answer was right; I checked on the worldwide web. In the 1890's a traveling group created a Magic Lantern show with projected color images, live music, live drama and/or comedy, and audience participation. A brass and mahogany lantern projected hand painted glass slides on a full size movie screen; it was the fore-runner of the cinema.

There is a *Magic Lantern Society* today that still performs authentic shows. I wrote to tell them about the references here—in the middle of the ocean in the Kingdom of Hawaii during the Victorian Age! Who would have imagined it? I thought they would have been delighted with the historical documentation, but they never answered my letter.

Under 'Christmas program' the Magic Lantern Society reenactment program offers a show with selections including "The Night Before Christmas", "O Holy Night", popular stories like "The Little Match Girl" and a parade of animated toy soldiers. Under 'Bible presentation' it also offers "An authentic 1890's religious show, both fun and inspiring". A dramatized Bible history with "David and Goliath" and "The Passion Play of Oberammergau"; spectacular hymns like "Rock of Ages" and "Amazing Grace."

Henry Greenwell took his ten children to Christ Church to see the Magic Lantern show on Christmas Day and wrote about it in his diary. I wonder how Reverend Davis was able to import such a wonderful gift—not just the technology, but the entire cast—for his tiny parish.

VICTORIAN EYE-WITNESS

Isabella Bird, Victorian extraordinaire, visited the islands in 1873; her letters to her sister were later published as <u>The Hawaiian Archipelago: Six Months among the Palm Groves, Coral Reefs,</u>

and Volcanoes of the Sandwich Islands. These letters offer a view of early Hawaii through the eyes of someone who is quite daring and adventurous for a proper British lady. Because she is writing to her sister, she is unselfconscious, and agenda-free. Clearly well educated, Isabella quotes poetry, and describes the flora and fauna using their Latin names.

Isabella travels the Big Island extensively. She learns to ride astride a horse—like a man—which is a bold and shocking thing (yet, she sees the Hawaiian women and children doing so without harm.) Her descriptions of Waipi'o Valley, a difficult and dangerous trek in good weather, becomes deadly when her little band of travelers gets caught in a flash flood. She visits two volcanoes during their eruptions. She describes the City of Refuge, and the Trade Winds. There are dozens of interesting details about camping on our island; for instance, she describes the plentiful little shrimps in the streams as a common source of food.

She has a keen eye for observing the social life of the foreigners and their relationship with the Hawaiians. Here is one of her remembered conversations:

> I am quite interested with a native lady here, the first I have met with who has been able to express her ideas in English. She is extremely shrewd and intelligent, very satirical and a great mimic. She very clearly burlesques the way white people express their admiration of scenery and, in fact, ridicules admiration of scenery for itself. She evidently thinks us a sour, morose worrying forlorn race.

> "We [the Hawaiians] are always happy; we never grieve long about anything; when anyone dies we break our hearts for some days, and then we are happy again. We are happy all day long, not like white people, happy one moment, gloomy another; we've no cares, the days are too short. What are haoles always unhappy about?"

Isabella writes that this lady expresses the general feelings of her "careless, pleasure-loving, mirth-loving, people." They fulfill the commandment to "Take no thought for the morrow."

We know that Isabella visited Christ Church Mission and spent the night at the rectory. We also know she was a guest of the Greenwells, who provided her with a horse and other travel necessities. Maile Melrose, local historian, tells me that Isabella Bird makes mention of several familiar Christ Church families: Hall, Paris, Greenwell and Davis. Isabella reports that Mrs. Davis was from Saint George's Hospital in London, and that Rev and Mrs. Davis were missionaries in Zanzibar before they came to Kona. I read the whole book waiting for these particular references, but apparently they have been edited out. This is what I did find:

> This is one of the stations of the "Honolulu Mission," and Mr. Davies, the clergyman, has, besides Sunday and daily services, a day school for boys and girls. The Sunday attendance at church, as far as I have seen, of three adults, though the white population within four miles is considerable....among the whites who have sunk into the mire of an indolent and godless, if not an openly immoral life, there is an undoubted field for Evangelistic effort, but it is very doubtful, I think, whether this class can be reached by services which appeal to higher culture and instincts than it possesses.

The old magazine ads from that time say that the mission school was only for girls, but perhaps Isabella is mixing the Greenwell boys into the general population of children at the church. Or maybe Jimmie is included, the hanai son. She has misspelled Davis, but that is easy to do. This is very early in the Davis years, even before the Bishop's consecration, so that is perhaps why attendance is so low. Isabella has a lot more to say about Kealakekua:

> This district [Kona] is famous for oranges, coffee, pineapples and silence. A flaming, palm-rimmed shore with a prolific strip of table land 15,00 feet above it, a dense timber belt eight miles in breadth, and a volcano, smoking somewhere between that and the heavens, and glaring through the trees at night, [these]are the salient points of Kona, if anything about it be salient. ...
>
> Wind indeed is a thing unknown. The scarcely audible whisper of soft airs through the trees morning and evening, rain drops falling gently, and the murmur of drowsy surges far below, alone break the stillness. No ripple ever disturbs the expanse of ocean which gleams through the still, thick trees. Rose in the sweet cool morning, gold in the sweet cool evening, but always dreaming; and the white sails come and go, no larger than a butterfly's wing on the horizon, of ships drifting on ocean's currents, dreaming too! Nothing surely can ever happen here: it is so dumb, and quiet, and people speak in hushed thin voices and move about in lethargy, dreaming too!

Her love for the flowers, the leis and fragrances and the color of Hawaii show up again and again. A few more words about Kona;

> Hot-house flowers grow in rank profusion round every house, and tea-roses, fuchsias, geraniums fifteen feet high, Nile lilies, Chinese lantern plants, begonias, lantanas, hibiscus, passion flowers, Cape jasmine, the hoya, the tuberose, the beautiful but over-powering sweet ginger plant and a hundred others....
>
> Kona looks unutterably beautiful, a languid dream of all fair things. Yet truly my heart warms to nothing so much as to a row of fat English cabbages which grow in the rectory garden...

Isabella realizes that she is homesick, and soon says goodbye to paradise. Once back in the British Isles again, Isabella publishes her letters into a book, and it becomes a bestseller. She also becomes the first female fellow of the Royal Geographic Society. She advises the British astronomy team what gifts they should take as they prepare for the *transit of Venus expedition* to Hawaii.

Historical Context

What did the early church use for the Eucharist?

In an old book there is a reference to bringing flour to Hawaii. Reverend Titus Coan writes of the "weary voyages between islands and the perils of long journeys across ravines, along great precipices, and over dusty, barren stretches of lava or plain."

He explains that "The news of the world and the flour for their daily bread were brought in a four-to-six month voyage around Cape Horn, both arriving in a state of unappetizing staleness. The flour in barrels was often so hard as to require the use of axe and chisel to get it ready for baking." He wrote this in 1881 looking back on the previous years since his arrival in 1835.

In an early cookbook from Kauai, the author explains that she could only make bread when flour was available. She also explains that there was no yeast at all, and so gives directions for how to use potatoes as leavening.

By the time of our Reverend Davis, the Greenwell store provides flour and yeast and all the necessary ingredients for bread making. By this time, it is shipped from San Francisco. Still, bread baking is far too much work for every household. We know that Carry Clerk bakes bread for the church school, but it is the Portuguese women who become the primary bread bakers of this island. The Kona Historical Society honors their labors and shows the public how it was done in their *Living History program*.

Another Visit to Kona Historical Society

Striding across the grass is a man in period costume. Gray vest with watch chain, gray pants, white shirt with long puffy sleeves, a gray bowler hat, a trim beard and mustache, he looks like Dapper Dan. He greets me with a warm smile and a question, "Have you come for bread?" He points the way although with my eyes closed I could find it. The warm sweet yeasty aroma announces itself loud and clear. The loaves are in large brown paper bags with red plaid labels:

> *Portuguese Sweet Bread (Pan Doce)*
> Portuguese from the Azores and Madeira started coming to Kona in the 1870's to help develop and manage dairies, a key phase of the ranching industry in Hawaii. The outdoor stone oven, or forno, was a constant presence wherever the Portuguese settled. Other ethnic groups came to enjoy Portuguese bread and selling bread became an important supplement to Portuguese families' income. This Portuguese bread was baked in the Kona Historical Society's forno, a feature of the Kona Heritage Ranch and Store.

Only 5 ingredients are listed on the Kona Historical Society loaf: flour, eggs, butter, sugar and yeast. The local Portuguese brought butter regularly to trade with at the Greenwell store.
"Do you still use local butter?
"Yes, when we can get it."
"Local eggs?" I ask.
"Yes, when we can get them." When they do get local eggs, the bread turns out a different color because the eggs are so rich.
The stone oven looks like a bee hive, round, about 8 feet in diameter, and as tall as I am. Firewood is stacked nearby and long-handled tools for taking the coals out and putting the bread in. Getting the oven temperature just right for baking bread

is the challenge every bread baker faces. The Historical Society bakes 96 loaves each time they fire up the forno. I will come back on a Thursday morning so that I can see it in action.

Return Visit

The steep path down to the bread oven is green and overgrown this January Thursday morning. Volunteers are waiting for the first loaves of white rolls to come out. The oven is 500 degrees hot. A volunteer comes every Thursday morning at 5:00 AM to start the fire. During the hours it takes to get hot enough–500 degrees for the white bread—the dough is mixed and kneaded, allowed to rise, then punched down, rolled out, shaped, and left to rise again. The temperature and the timing are critical and they are influenced by such things as the humidity of the day, the cloud cover, the condition of the wood.

Once the white bread is done, the oven will have cooled just enough to bake the sweet bread. Two men get the paper bags ready. Two tiny dark women brush egg over sweet bread dough rolled out and waiting its turn. There is always at least one overdone or damaged loaf, and the volunteers take care not to waste it. A new volunteer has brought homemade jaboticaba jam for sampling. There is a little bit of work, a little bit of conversation, but really, the fragrance from the oven dominates everything here. It is a cool day and a pleasant wait.

I am one of the bread bakers at church. Five of us rotate baking the communion bread. It takes most of a day, so I mark my calendar two weeks ahead when it is my turn. I organize my day around it; I prepare myself for a slow motion day. You cannot make bread hurry. No, the bread sets its own pace and you must adapt to it.

I order my own wheat from Canada, hard, red winter wheat. And because whole wheat flour spoils quickly in heat, I buy the whole grain and grind it into flour as I need it. White flour lasts much longer, and so the bread bakers here, 100 years ago, would have used white.

Whenever I bake bread, I start early while it is still cool. I grind eight cups of Canadian hard red wheat and think of the work of the farmer who plants and harvests it. I use local eggs when I can get them. I soften the yeast and think of the small miracle it is.

The parable of the leaven is one we teach in the Sunday School to the three to six year olds. We read the scripture and we make dough—actually two batches of dough. In one we add leaven, and in the other, we leave it out. We cover our two batches with a cloth, put them in the sun, and then go up to church for Eucharist. After church is over, we return to the classroom to see what has happened to the dough.

"What is different?" I ask as I remove the cloth.

"Let's smell them... Let's taste them." The children are delighted to do this.

"Which one do you think has the yeast?" The response is unanimous.

"What a difference there is when the leaven is present!"

"How long did it take? Not very long, but we did have to wait."

"A tiny amount of leaven makes a great transformation."

"Jesus said the *Kingdom of Heaven is like this!*"

In the Mass we act out the wonderful exchange of gifts between heaven and earth. In the kitchen, we bread bakers get in touch with this most basic of symbols. It is an honor to participate in preparing one of the gifts of God for the people of God.

How could the greater church have ever decided to use thin wafers that taste like sawdust for such a magnificent symbol? If this bread represents the bread of heaven, the taste and the texture are important. It should delight in taste and smell and texture; it should be so delicious that you can hardly wait to have more.

History Detective: Eucharist Bread or Wafer?

Rev Carol feels sure that I am wrong about the communion bread. She thinks they would have used wafers in the early days. We both search for any reference but the old books make no mention of it. Stuart Ching, the cathedral archivist doesn't remember any reference, anywhere. It is such a small question, that probably only bread bakers would find it of interest.

According to the Catholic online encyclopedia, the earliest picture of communion bread comes from the catacombs; the bread was round even then. The earliest reference to an 'unleavened' wafer comes from a document from around 1050 AD; the wafer was large, however, and as it was passed, each person broke off a piece.

On our second visit to Father Linscott, we ask him what he used; he confirms that he did indeed use wafers. This would be later in CC history, 1945-50.

After more than a year, Rev Carol finds an answer in the midst of Historic Rubrics. The use of spelling suggests that it is very old:

> *Upon the Sundays and other Holy-days (if there be no Communion) shall be said all that is appointed at the Communion, until the end of the general Prayer* [For the whole state of Christ's Church militant here in earth] *together with one or more of these Collects last before rehearsed, concluding with the Blessing.*
>
> *And to take away all occasion of dissention, and superstition, which any person hath or might have concerning the Bread and Wine, it shall suffice that the Bread be such as is usual to be eaten; but the best and purest Wheat Bread that conveniently may be gotten.*

Heavenly Wine

Well, what about the wine for Eucharist? I have found nothing in the records so far, not even on the shopping lists Davis wrote out in his ledgers. We do, however, know what was in Henry Greenwell's wine cellar just down the street. Let's read his journal entry from December 7, 1890:

> This being Arthur's birthday we had a glass of champagne from Schaefer & Co. I had bought it believing it to be "Veuve Cliquet." It is Eugene Cliquet. I doubt it being champagne at all. It is almost impossible to get good wine here. I have now in the cellar, claret from Love, Tokay form Hamilton Johnson, Champagne from Schaefer and also from Hackfeld, and not one of them do I care to drink; also the sherry I got from Frank is not good. The only good wine I have ever had was that from Holdsworth, Amorosa sherry and Port, both excellent, and no doubt genuine.

Historical Context

What else is going on in Hawaii and around the world at this time? The Hawaiian magazine the *Anglican Church Chronicle* 1887 relates news of the Jubilee Year celebration in England. International Dignitaries travel to London to see Queen Victoria on the fiftieth anniversary of her accession.

There is a notice about the donations given for the starving poor at the East End of London. Sunday School children in Hawaii have collected and sent money so the English children will have something to eat. An ironic turn-around.

In Hawaii, these are the Father Damien years. These are the years that author Robert Louis Stevenson befriends the children on Molokai.

In the commentary section is a letter declaring that "the greatest want of this age is Lei-sure—leisure and the wit and the will to keep it, prize it, and to make the best use of it."

Reading the magazine ads also help us imagine the times:

"New Harness Shop" and "Champion Horse Shoes" reminds us that transportation is still by horse.

"Steam Made Ice Cream Pioneer Steam Candy Factory and Bakery."

"Chinese and Millinery Goods" reminds us of the changing population. After plantation workers complete their years of indentured work, they move on to new ways of earning a living.

In a section on *missions,* news from neighbor islands is reported. In a letter dated April 86, Reverend Davis acknowledges "a parcel arrived by steamship *Alameda* containing a very handsome violet altar frontal and super-portal worked in crewel, a carved oak cross, sets of book markers of the colors." He offers his sincere thanks. How many years would these have been used and treasured at Christ Church? Certainly they would have been in use when the King visited.

> In the April 16, 1888 issue Davis writes,
> Easter day there were two celebrations of the Holy Communion at 7am and again after Morning Prayer. The matins were choral. **His Majesty**, who received his Easter communion {was} present at the 10:30 service. Congregation, (67; communicants at both celebrations 15; offertory for church improvements, $10.75.) Evensong was at 4pm. The exchange of windows in the nave of the church was made in time for Easter and are a great improvement. The church was decorated with stag moss and flowers, with appropriate text. After service **His Majesty** went to the parsonage, where the school children were presented to him by Mrs. Davis. He also looked at the new school, still unfinished, and remarked that it was small.

Later in the same year, an additional shipment arrives for Christ Church–oil paintings. If you have ever once sat in the historic church you have seen them.

The Painted Panels

Above the altar is an oil painting of Jesus as the 'True Vine'. He is in the middle with two evangelists on each side. Each of them has a circle of gold around his head, though the halo of Jesus is different. Part of an angel, an ox and an eagle show at the bottom. The evangelists are dressed in dark red robes and hold books, or tablets. The background is divided in half; the top half is teal, the bottom half gold. Everything is quite dark except for Jesus; he is in white. His arms are extended in a gentle, welcoming way. Vines flow from him, over and around and below, linking him to the apostles.

"I am the true vine and my Father is the gardener....I am the vine; you are the branches." These are the words of John 15, the inspiration for the painting.

The painting looks old. Who painted it? When and where? It is an unsolved mystery until the day at the cathedral archives. In the cathedral newspaper of August 23, 1888, is a letter from Reverend Davis of South Kona, announcing the arrival of "painted panels" of the evangelists: Mareko H, Mataio H, Johane H, Luka H. They have been sent from Miss A. Styan.

A month later, in September 1888, Davis writes, "Our thanks are again due to Miss A. Styan for her kindness in beautifying our church."

Part of the mystery is solved: we know when the art came to Christ Church, who sent it, and who received it. But is Miss Styan the artist or did she commission the work? Was it painted for Christ Church? Or was it already old when it arrived? Was it done in England, or here in Hawaii?

If it was painted in Hawaii, then the vine is one we would all know; our gardens, as well as the church gardens, are full of vines. In the *Gardener's Guide to Tropical Landscape* there are dozens of kinds described. Many have Christian names that point us back to the scriptures: Easter Lilly vine, Bleeding Heart, Passion Fruit, Chain of Love, Morning Glory, Angel Wing Jasmine, Christmas vine.

Many of these are invasive plants that quickly take over our gardens and move rapidly to take over the neighbors' as well. The vines climb the trees, wrap around trunks, venture out on the frailest of branches and then decorate the tree with a flower not its own. As responsible gardeners we are cautious about controlling vines, but I invite you to think about their extravagant activity as a symbol for our life in Christ. Imagine quiet, introverted Episcopalians moving about like lilikoi, or wood rose vines, always in the background, covering fences, arbors, trellises, banks, and borders *with abandon*.

If you stand right up close to the painted panels, you can see that the vines are not lilikoi or wood roses. There are blue clusters of grapes hanging from the vines, as would be accurate from the original story. But the grapes are so dark that in 5 years of sitting in the front pew, I have never seen them. Up close the painting looks very old indeed; the paint is peeling in many places.

Jesus ends his little gardening sermon with the words "You did not choose me, but I chose you to go and bear fruit—fruit that will last." And just what is the fruit of this vine? He tells us it is Love; we are to let his love grow wild in us, over and around and through us, in every direction.

Photography Project

We know that besides running a boarding school, Reverend Davis sells guava jelly. The accounting shows up in all the records: the sugar costs, the tin costs, and the labor. The guava jelly account is the beginning of the endowment fund.

Reverend Davis is also a photographer and he sells his photographs. We have his published ad offering "Six Views of Kealakekua Bay and Ka'awaloa, Hawaii, the place where Captain Cook was killed." Unfortunately, we can find none of the old photographs to view.

At this time in history, photography is still quite new. What kind of a camera did Davis have? And how did he get it? We know from the Magic Lantern that he has an interest in the technology. Here is a time line of camera and film development:

    1884 George Eastman invents flexible, paper-based photographic film.
    1888 Eastman patents Kodak roll-film camera.
    1898 Reverend Hannibal Goodwin patents celluloid photographic film.
    1900 First mass-marketed camera—the Brownie.

While the British admired and respected Captain Cook as a brilliant navigator, the Americans did not. Neither did the fire-and-brimstone Reverend Sheldon Dibble. On the contrary, he is responsible for creating a satanic caricature of Cook which he spread among the American missionaries as truth, blaming Cook personally for everything bad that came to Hawaii. Unfortunately, this anti Anglo propaganda was never really cleared up, and Cook's reputation here is questionable to this day.

For the Anglican vicar and the British immigrants that attended Christ Church—and their relatives back home—cameras were still new, and photography exciting. A photo of the actual place where the legendary Captain Cook died must have seemed an irresistible novelty!

A Trip to the Archives

Finally, after two and a half years of asking, waiting and hoping, I am allowed into the Kona Historical Society archives.

Maile Mitchell Melrose leads me through a small book-filled room to a desk, where there is a small pile of white gloves. I select a pair that turn out to be a bit too tight. I think of OJ Simpson as I struggle to get them on, and then direct my thoughts to the box Maile has brought out. There are two boxes and four volumes in the 'Christ Church collection.' They are full of the original records; the oldest are hand written in ink that has turned brown. There are ledgers, beautiful hard bound volumes, and smaller composition booklets, the kind once used in colleges. Sacramental records for burials begin in 1867; there are lists of confirmations and marriages.

Since these are clearly official records, I ask Maile why the Historic Society has possession of them... Why doesn't the church have them? She explains that when Reverend Rodman was in charge, he got rid of all the old stuff. He threw these beautiful, hand written historical documents in the trash. Someone witnessed this and moved to rescue them. Indeed I find that they are "a gift of Helen Weeks, Feb 5, 1988."

The first document is "Church and Personal Accounts Record Book kept by Rev. Samuel H. Davis." This is a book filled in from both directions—first the normal way, front page to back, but then it was turned over, upside down, and the writing starts again, wherever blank space is available.

Records of Davis' photography sales begin in 1883. (This is one year *before* the list of camera developments on the last page.) He lists the prints available to purchase, such as the Captain Cook Monument, Kealakekua Bay, The Little Grass Shack, and the Actual Place of Captain Cook's death blow. The prints are 10 by 8 inches, and cost 25 cents each. The list of those ordering the prints includes bishops and other clergy in England. Reverend Carol has searched for any remaining photographs through the drawers and boxes and files at the church without luck. But Maile says that she knows who has the glass plates.

In a notation from 1893, we find that the donations for a Captain Cook window amount to $38.24. This seems like nothing to us, but we must consider that a 10 by 8 inch photograph—a novelty in the world at this time—sells for 25 cents. As we continue reading, however, we discover that Davis is ready to give up on the idea of honoring Captain Cook in this way. Why? In January 1893 Liliuokalani ceased to be Queen; the Americans were now in control of Hawaii, and Captain Cook was no hero to them.

Davis reports that he is also giving up on his guava jam sales. He has tried several other jams—like China orange, and poha—but the cost of the packaging is high and the small profit is not worth the effort.

The stamps, however, are successful. We have seen his requests for stamps in the Anglican newsletters at the Cathedral archives; we have seen his general expressions of thanks to all the people who have mailed him their stamps. Rev Carol and I were never sure what these stamps were. Maile has an opinion: She thinks all the canceled stamps—from all over the world—are collected by Davis and sold to stamp collectors in England. Or maybe they are canceled Hawaiian stamps? Do we have any old ones to look at? Davis records that the stamps have brought in $443.

We find reference to the purchase of a printing press and book binding materials. Apparently Davis creates his own magazine. In a later paper he refers to "The Banner of Faith, a monthly Magazine of the Anglican Church in Hawaii." He is, however, disappointed that the number of subscriptions has not come up to his expectations.

There are many shopping lists. Here are a few of the items on the "List of Goods to Arrive per Bismarck" dated March 27, 1884.

2 colored petticoats
6 tooth brushes
16½ yards calico
buttons
boots for Jimmie
Mackintosh (like mine only smaller)
Girls and boys magazines
book binding materials

Things for Mary
1 black dress
2 petticoats same as last
2 colored petticoats
1 dozen stockings
1 dozen handkerchiefs
1 pair stays

Waverly novels by Dickens' work if money enough

[Charles Dickens died in 1870 but his novels are still very popular throughout Davis' lifetime. Dickens' novels shocked his "Christian" nation by illustrating the blatant inequalities that existed. This is most especially true concerning injustice and cruelty to children. In storytelling form with unforgettable characters, Dickens caught the conscience of the English-speaking world.]

Who is Mary? Is she the wife, or the sister of Rev. Davis? We know they were both at the mission, but we don't know if it was at the same time. Perhaps the sister came because the wife left. We know the Mrs. returned to England, but we don't know why or when.

Who is Jimmie that needs boots? . . . One boy in a girl's school? Maile explains that Jimmie was the Davis hanai son. This is a surprise! Carol and I have searched for the information on Esther, whom we imagined to be their hanai daughter. Never have we seen any mention of Jimmie Hooper Davis before. Maile says that when Reverend Davis was old, deaf and blind, he lived with Jimmie.

Here is a reference to Miss A. Styan, the giver of the 5 painted panels, and here is an answer to one of our mysteries: it says she has sent them from Paddington, London. There is another entry of interest. Davis writes that while the three light windows over the altar were being installed, the altar carpet was damaged. This carpet (it notes) was a gift from C.W. Williamson! The first rector has been gone for some years, but has sent a gift to this little church that he built with his own two hands.

The reader probably doesn't realize that the information we find does not come to us in any logical order. Seven months after the day at the archives, I am given an old file found in a dusty closet at church. In it are Xerox copies of Davis accounts, years I have not seen yet. I find answers to questions—solve some mysteries—with this new information. It only took 3 years! Miss A. Styan's name shows up over and over again. Davis thanks her for her gifts to decorate the church, as well as books and pictures for the children. And on December 1887, two subjects combine nicely. Davis explains:

> About 4 years ago I commenced to make Guava Jelly hoping by the profit on the sale to make something for Church and Schools. But as the sale has proved so very slow and uncertain, I do not intend to make any more. I have now on hand about 500 1 lb Tins, which I offer @$3.75 per doz. By the case, and @ $4 per doz. If less than a case is taken. Miss A. Styan 27 Norfolk Crescent, Paddington, London, W. has kindly undertaken to sell some for me. The price in England is 2s 6d. per tin.

There are other names that appear regularly under gifts: Miss AF Westmacott is one. Gifts are being sent from London on every ship, or so it seems. Exotic Stamps, Photographs, Jams & Jellies travel one direction, while traditional high church items come back. Who are these generous gift-givers and guava jelly distributors in London? Perhaps they are aunts or nieces or sisters to Rev. & Mrs. Davis, or perhaps they are members of the churches they grew up in.

Another gift acknowledged: in February 1887, Sister Caroline writes from the *Orphanage of Mercy*, Randolph Gardens, Kilburn, NW to the girls at the Christ Church boarding school. She acknowledges with great pleasure the donation these young Hawaiians have sent for the English orphans.

In December 1888 contributions for **Permanent Improvements to Church and School,** we see some important names:

    His Majesty The King, $50
    HRH The (late) Princess Likelike, $15
    HRM Kaiulani, $10

I'm guessing the HRH stands for Her Royal Highness. There are other names with English and French titles, His Ex., Esq., the Hon'ble, Captain, and Messrs.

Under **Clergy Fund** :
    HN Greenwell Esq. $50 and use of 2 cows.

And here is an answer to the stamp questions in the 12/ 1886 account book:

    "Wanted 4,000,000 Hawaiian Stamps

The Rev. SH Davis, Kealakekua, South Kona, Hawaii is collecting *used* Hawaiian Postage and Fiscal Stamps and Post Cards to sell for his Church and Schools." Details follow on how to protect the stamps and how to send them to Kona. Most of the stamps are 1 and 2 cent cancelled Hawaiian stamps.

Years later, 1892, he reports:

> About twenty persons in the Islands and one in San Francisco are collecting and sending me stamps, to whom I tender my sincere thanks.
>
> I feel sure there are many others who would do the same if they only knew and realized how valuable such contributions, of stamps, would be.
>
> I have sent to my Agent in England, during the past year, 13,822 stamps...

Different Voice, Different Pen: Too Sad for Words
By Maile Melrose

There are only four headstones made of lava in the graveyard of Christ Church, and only one is shaped like a cross. This interesting memorial marks the final resting place of Kahula Ting Sing, the first Hawaiian to be buried here. Her descendents still visit her grave and believe her stone was carved by the Rev. Samuel Davis. Church records reveal Davis as a multi-talented man with an unstoppable drive to improve his fledgling mission. If Mr. Davis mastered stone carving to honor Kahula's memory, his care and effort may have found inspiration in her Christian faith and tragic death.

In 1852, the Hawaiian government hired an English sea captain named Cass to bring two shiploads of Chinese coolies to Hawaii to work as laborers. A steep drop in Hawaii's native population had fueled fears that only imported labor would enable the Kingdom to prosper in producing sugar and other agricultural crops. A few of these first coolies ended up in Kona as employees of Henry N. Greenwell.

Ting Sing was one of these new arrivals and he eventually became Greenwell's cook at Kalukalu. He married Kahula Kaapana from South Kona and Christ Church records show they raised a fine family of Chinese-Hawaiian Anglicans. Their children, all baptized or received into the church by Rev. Davis, were: Katarina, David Kaapana, Keo (also known as Charles Joseph), Ana Lupea, and Edward Kumukahili, sponsored at baptism by Albert Sala and Elizabeth Caroline Greenwell.

On Christmas morning in 1879, Mr. Davis had the pleasure of marrying fifteen year old Katarina Ting Sing to nineteen year old Peter Whitmarsh at 9 a.m. at Christ Church. (Peter had been confirmed by Bishop Willis at Christ Church in 1873.) How delightful to imagine flowers on the altar, bright winter sunlight streaming through the southern windows, and a medley of races and faces filling the pews. After a single year of happiness, sorrows of all sorts fell upon the family of Ting

Sing. On February 24th of 1881, Kahula was delivered of twin boys. Rejoicing soon gave way to grief when Kahula died on March 6 and was buried the next day. On March 19, a smaller hole was dug and one baby boy was buried close to his mother. In a cruel coincidence, daughter Katarina gave birth to twin sons in April of the very same year. On the 25th of April, Rev. Davis noted in his record book that was St. Mark's day and he went to Ting Sing's home to hold a celebration for Katarina. Alas, the young mother died on April 29 at the tender age of seventeen. The ordeal of childbirth took mother and daughter within two months. Katarina's little boys, Brookes and William Peter, died in 1882 and were buried next to their mother. Ting Sing lived to see Mr. Davis bury his eldest son Kaapana at the age of nineteen not ten feet away from his mother.

Ting Sing grew old. He left Kona and was buried in a cemetery in Honolulu. His grave is not forgotten by his family and neither is that of his lovely Hawaiian wife. Although no church record exists to tell the whereabouts of Kahula's other little twin son, the family knows he lies beneath the green grass of the cemetery in his mother's arms. Why Mr. Davis did not record his name on the stone is a mystery. Perhaps, it was just too sad.

THE FINAL YEARS

Gradually the Reverend's hearing begins to fail, and then his eyesight. Christina Greenwell's diary notes that week after week Rev. Davis, with either his sister or Jimmie, comes to call Sunday afternoon. They have cake and lemonade. They often sing. There is one reference to his deafness, and how it is now a problem in the mass. There is also a reference to his skull cap. Indeed, in an old photograph of him, he is wearing a black skull cap.

Rev. Davis writes to the bishop asking to be relieved of his duties. Eventually a new rector is sent, but from the brief news in the Anglican journals, we know that Davis continues to baptize new babies; it seems he is the beloved wise one. His replacement does not last long. Davis lives till the age of 88; he is fully deaf and blind by this time.

We know more about Reverend Davis than any other rector, yet his personal life is a bit of a mystery.... Why did he wear a black skull cap? Why did his wife leave? Were Esther and Jimmie really his hanai children? Why is he buried up in the corner, alone with Esther?

COMMENTARY: CAPTAIN COOK

Was Captain James Cook a great navigator or evil haole? It depends on who you ask. For some, there is an all too common prejudice which generalizes all European explorers as racist, sexist, violent and exploitative. But really, what does the evidence say?

According to the extensive primary sources about him, Captain Cook had a brilliant mind, and lived like a Quaker.

Cook did not come to conquer. He did not come to claim land. Never does he name a new bay or strait or anything after anyone in his family. Why did he come? Tony Horowitz researches the legends and the truth in his book Blue Latitudes;

> In 1768, when Cook embarked on the first, [voyage] roughly a third of the world's map remained blank, or filled with fantasies: sea monsters, Patagonian giants, imaginary continents. Cook sailed into this void in a small wooden ship and returned, three years later, with charts so accurate that some of them stayed in use until the 1990s.

He came to explore the globe in order to create maps of the world. His mathematical, nautical and astronomical skills combined to make him a brilliant surveyor and map maker.

One modern Cook scholar, Cordelia Stamp, believes that Cook exemplified many Quaker traits. In fact, in his late teens and early twenties Cook lived with a Quaker family in Yorkshire. An example of advice to Quakers at this time:

> Keep to that which is modest, decent, plain and useful... be prudent in all manner of behavior, both in public and in private, avoiding all intemperance in eating and drinking...walk wisely and circumspectly towards all men, in a peaceable spirit (Horowitz, 307).

Indeed this kind of behavior is confirmed over and over again in the diaries and journals of his men on the ship. According to them, he was never given to excess drink or riotous living. When the men partied, he withdrew. When the food was scarce, he was content. And, he was faithful to his wife at home.

Was Cook confident, assertive, courageous, dedicated, and demanding? Well yes; these are the characteristics of leaders, whether they are Indian chiefs, generals, CEOs or basketball coaches. There is no question that he was a leader and that he expected to be obeyed. But his years of meticulous journaling show not an egotist, not a conqueror, but a careful, intentional, humble, sober, self-made man. On one page in the ship log Cook discusses "astronomy, geology, meteorology, and animal husbandry. On the next, he offers insight into management, commerce, and diplomacy. Then he veers into lengthy speculation about ocean currents and the formation of islands" (Horowitz, 254).

It is true that his behavior towards the end of his life was questionable: his shipmates questioned it because it was so out-of-character. Historians today believe Cook was suffering from physical illness and emotional exhaustion. They know he suffered rheumatic fever, 'bilious colick', sciatica, and, they suspect intestinal obstruction, roundworm infection and vitamin B deficiency. This last "produces fatigue, constipation, irritability, depression, and loss of interest and initiative—in other words, chronic, personality-changing symptom" (Horowitz, 331).

While exploring new territory Cook had to interact with new people even if he was sick. Did he need fresh water? Did he hope to replenish fresh produce? Certainly, but he tried to protect the natives from exploitation. He did, in fact, threaten the lash to any seaman having sexual relations with the women in Hawaii.

Were there communication problems? Absolutely. Were there significant cultural misunderstandings? Of course. The end was an unfortunate meeting where tempers, pride, and testosterone got the better of a situation. But this happens everyday—before and after Cook—in barroom brawls between people who speak the *same* language.

I was really quite indifferent towards Cook before I studied him. That did not last. The facts and the stories and the adventures all mixed together, and the more I read, the more I grew to admire him. The thing that bothers me the most about common criticism of Captain Cook is that he has been blamed for all the bad that came later.

Just think of the Wright brothers. They pioneered the exploration of the world from the sky. Access to distant and isolated places brought change good and bad. It seriously altered life on the planet. No one blames the Wright brothers for this. . . or for air raids in World War ll. . . or for the Atom bomb.

Think of all the bad that has come from the internet—massive fraud, international espionage, untold suffering from pornographers and predators. But I have never heard anyone condemn those who invented it, for the bad that came in its wake.

With manifest destiny hard-wired into human DNA, if Cook hadn't come to Hawaii, someone else would have. Hawaii could not have maintained her isolation, innocence, independence—or her good health—indefinitely.

I never studied Captain Cook in school. Perhaps he was left out of American history books because he was British and his adventures coincided with the Revolutionary War years. But he was not unknown at the time...in fact, Benjamin Franklin "issued an extraordinary order, in the midst of the revolutionary war, commanding American naval officers to treat Cook and his men as friends rather than foes" (Horowitz, 4).

PROFILE: CHARLES LAMBERT, CHRIST CHURCH CEMETERY, 1874

The grandest grave in the cemetery is that of Charles Lambert, who died November 1874. There is a large Celtic cross on a large triangular base, surrounded by a series of iron posts with a chain, waist high.

What do we know of Charles? We know he was 24 years old when he died. We know he was an Anglican from Chile, a young man on a British man-of-war. We know that he was swimming in Kona when he got into trouble. Mr. Kaai, a local, went out in his canoe to rescue him, and tried, without success, to resuscitate him. Young Charles Lambert was buried by Reverend Davis. A simple wooden cross was erected by Admiral Cator who was Captain of the HMS Scout. Some of this is engraved on the present day stone, but most of it is worn away by 127 years of trade winds and Kona showers. (Is my math wrong? No, keep reading.)

What is interesting about the gravesite is the story of what happens after the burial. The parents of the deceased sail from Chile to England to purchase the granite cross, and then sail to Kona to deliver it. The Lamberts keep a journal of their adventures, and eventually, in 1883, publish it. They document their stops in places such as Cowen, Lisbon, Madeira, Saint Helen, Rio, Elizabeth Island, Fatou Hiva, Peacock Atoll, Tonga. Finally they arrive in Hawaii, where they are greeted by such dignitaries as Queen Emma and Princess Ruth. The Lamberts' descriptions of life in Hawaii at this time are wonderful and detailed. Finally, (*finally!*) on page 223 of their published journal, they sail into Kealakekua Bay:

...we steamed out of Honolulu harbour and shaped our course for Cook's Bay, in the island of Hawaii, not, however, without having first received a pretty present from Queen Emma of flowers, honey, and prawns...We had a fine passage, and a nice clear night, and at 7:30 AM we passed close to Kailua Bay, the scene of our sad loss. At ten we anchored in Cook's Bay, and as soon as the men had finished their dinners, the stones we had brought so far with us were placed in the boats and landed, ready to go up to Kona in the ox-waggons ...in the afternoon we landed, and spent some little time in a house belonging to Princess Likiliki, which she had kindly placed at our disposal; nearly opposite to us was the obelisk, erected to the memory of Captain Cook, almost on the spot where he stood, before receiving his death blow. The cliff rises from the shore perpendicularly, to a height of nearly 600 feet, its face honeycombed with caves, the burial-places of former chiefs. The people must have been lowered from above with the bodies, to place them in these very secure resting-places.

At 8 AM we landed, with thirteen of the crew to help in loading the wagons, and to accompany them on foot, and help them up the steep climb over cinders and broken bits of lava, and through the most desolate country, with nothing to be seen but slag and scoria. After wearily ascending this road for some three miles, we came to some stunted vegetation, grass and scrub, which improved as we got further on, until we reached a pretty flowery lane, shaded by paradise and blue gum-trees, which brought us to the little church with its quiet graveyard. It is very beautifully kept...

I must record our gratitude to the incumbent Mr. Davis and his wife, for the care and attention shown to our dear son's grave. We were told by the neighbors that for years fresh flowers had been constantly placed upon the grave and hung on the plain oak cross. Having seen the stones taken out of the cart, we retraced our way to the ship, passing a quiet day on the Sunday.

From Monday to Wednesday we were busy finishing the work which we had come for, and on the latter day had the satisfaction of seeing everything completed, and bade farewell with full and grateful hearts to Mr. and Mrs. Davis and the quiet resting-place in Kona churchyard.

Charles died in 1874; the stones were delivered 1881. The sailing part of the trip takes two years. What an ordeal! From sailing halfway around the world, to the hike up the cliffs of Kealakekua, it was a physically demanding task. From just a few words we recognize the pain of losing a loved one in a far-away land. Their pilgrimage is a simple (though not easy) act of love. And they find that the locals...the members of Christ Church... have cared for the grave of their son with tenderness and affection until they arrive. I have always thought of Charles Lambert (with his big, showy gravesite,) as a tourist, but I have changed my mind. Now he represents all the sons who die far away, and my heart (more than a hundred years later) goes out to his parents.

HISTORICAL CONTEXT: GEORGE FREETH, FIRST LIFEGUARD

There really was no such thing as "lifeguards" in the 1880s when young Charles Lambert drowned. There was no such thing as a lifeguard in Hawaii—or on the mainland – either. It would not be until 1907 that a hapa-haole named George Freeth, the best surfer in Waikiki, was hired to be a "body guard" for tourist Jack London when he tried surfing. London describes Freeth on a wave "standing upright with his board, carelessly poised, a young god bronzed with sunburn.."

With the prose of this famous writer, surfing became of international interest. When London returned to Hawaii eight years later, he was amazed to find that there were hundreds surfing now, "a new brood" riding at "astonishing slants." He writes, "Judges of the Supreme court in Hawaii with their wives and daughters, ex-governors and their families, and the greater proportion of the prominent businessmen are now surfboard enthusiasts...masters of the art that was for so long believed to be possible of attainment only by the native born Hawaiian."

George Freeth and other good surfers became the natural lifeguards on the beaches, official or not. My husband was a California beach lifeguard long ago, but I know he is always aware of potential trouble for the tourists now. It is a responsibility hard to turn off. On the pier of the California town where we grew up is a statue of George Freeth. He became the first official lifeguard in the United States. He saved countless lives with his bravery, and was awarded the Congressional Medal of Honor, the Carnegie Medal for Bravery and the U.S. Life Saving Corps Gold Medal.

I wonder how many Christ Church members over the years have been rescued by lifeguards... How many have been lifeguards... Keeping our beaches safe is an important job in Hawaii, and many dedicated swimmers and surfers have been unsung heroes.

Follow Up: The Transit of Venus

I have read the story of the Lambert grave from a number of sources, but only now (3 1/2 years into this project) have I discovered WHY Charles Lambert was here in Kona. To understand the answer, you need to know about the transit of Venus. According to the NASA eclipse page:

> A transit is the passage of a planet across the Sun's bright disk. At this time, the planet can be seen as a small black

disk slowly moving in front of the Sun. The orbits of Mercury and Venus lie inside Earth's orbit, so they are the only planets which can pass between Earth and Sun to produce a transit. Transits are very rare astronomical events. In the case of Venus, there are on average two transits every one and a quarter centuries. A transit of Venus occurs only if the planet is in inferior conjunction with the Sun (between Earth and Sun) and is also crossing through the Earth's orbital plane (the Ecliptic). During the present period in Earth's history, Venus's orbit crosses Earth's orbital plane in early June and early December each year. If Venus is passing between the Earth and Sun at that time, a transit will be seen.

Let us back up a little. Captain Cook's mission to Tahiti in 1769 had been *for this very purpose;* at Matavai Bay, Cook observed the transit of Venus for a full six hours using clocks, quadrants and telescopes. According to Michael Chauvin, "The purpose of such observations {is} to better determine the value of the astrological unit (AU)—the Sun-Earth distance—and thereby the absolute scale of the solar system."

In 1778 Cook placed Hawaii on the map by determining its location astronomically. For the next transit of Venus, 1874, Hawaii was the right place to be to observe it. All scientifically sophisticated countries were in competition to do so.

The chase after this celestial yardstick was intense and had serious implications for the future of astronomy, navigation, and surveying. The HMS Scout—the ship Charles Lambert was on—brought seven British astronomers and all their technical paraphernalia to Hawaii for this rare event. King Kalakaua received them graciously and assisted them in every way he could.

George Forbes, the most important of the British scientists, set up a telescope on a brick pier in Kona. Michael Chauvin's book <u>Hokuloa</u> documents the story with the scientific and mathematical details. It also offers personal details from the scientist's letters. Here is where we find out about Charles Lambert, young sailor and friend to the scientist:

> Nov. 20. Friday. Mr. Lambert & I went to bathe this morning before breakfast, as usual. The sea was very rough. We anticipated no danger as we were both fair swimmers; & the Hon: Simon Kaai, the only other person of the beach foresaw no danger. A very strong under-current from the shore had set in. The wind suddenly got up & the sea with it. . . Mr. Lambert appears to have been immediately overwhelmed by the size of the waves. He was much exhausted when I reached him, swallowing water with every wave until I turned his face to the shore. I seized him under the left armpit by my right hand, & struck out for the shore. By watching the rocks on my left, I perceived that instead of making way I was being drifted out. A crowd of natives who were collected on the shore saw our danger, but did nothing for some time. There was a channel among the rocks on my left; if they had pointed this out to me I could have taken Mr. Lambert there. As it was, my only duty was to keep Mr. Lambert's head out of the water with the back of it to the waves. I did not give up swimming towards the shore, though I made no way. Two natives came out for about five minutes & then left us. Eventually a canoe was launched with great risk. At the same time a native called Kaea relieved me of Mr. Lambert's body (he had been dead for some minutes.) The bottom of the boat was stove in, but we got to the shore in it. All means of resuscitation were attempted in vain. We had been in the water ¾ of an hour.

Really, we have spent a lot of time on one grave, but the story is so interesting in terms of historical connections. Besides Charles Lambert and his parents, we have Rev. Davis, astronomer George Forbes, King Kalakaua, the Hon. Kaai, and even Isabella Bird who advised the scientists what gifts to bring the Hawaiians.

Besides the transit of Venus, the HMS Scout had a second job to do on this expedition: it delivered construction materials to Kealakekua Bay. On November 14, a new Captain Cook Memorial was unveiled. "One hundred years of British presence in Hawaii became glorified in concrete. Kealakekua Bay now sheltered and sanctified a monument to the man whose astronomically attuned ability had, one century earlier, pulled the Sandwich Islands into the orbit of the British Empire." Charles Lambert had been a part of this too.

So this story points backwards, but it points forward too: this expedition lays the groundwork for the observatories now on Hawaii, Kauai and Oahu.

(And just in case you are curious, the next transit of Venus is 2012.)

Gifts for the Expedition

A week before the British Expedition sailed from Liverpool, astronomer Forbes received a letter from Isabella Bird, who was once again home in Edinburgh. The Victorian world traveler offered the scientist a list of gift items that she believed would be welcomed in the Islands. Isabella writes:

> My dear Sir
> It is always pleasant to leave some trifling gift as a remembrance with strangers, and in some quarters on the islands, where white people are very poor but insist on giving one accommodation without remuneration, it is really essential. I suppose your gifts must be neither heavy or expensive so I will just suggest any of the following articles, some of which may appear a little queer to your ideas, but would be very acceptable to anyone out of the Capitol.
> For any lady ½ a dozen of those "Windsor Scarfs" which are 4/s a dozen in blue pink and mauve.
> Mounted photographs of the best Madonnas, Ecce Homos and Holy Families.

Any of Scotts Poems bound in tartan. . .

Any of the innumerable stands or easels. . .

For a gentleman a good knife or better still one of those picnic knives in case which when separated makes a knife and fork.

Portable metal drinking cups which draw out. I only saw 2 on the islands.

Plain strong English riding whips...

Bottles of eau de cologne are much valued.

Those pretty ornamental . . . stationery would make nice presents, as paper and envelopes are enormously dear on the island, and these two would delight the natives, as well as bright ribbons (2 yards) and bright bandana handkerchiefs. White pocket handkerchiefs please the natives very much too (both sizes) and scizzors.

Hoping some of these suggestions may be useful.

Believe me

Very Sincerely Yours
Isabella L. Bird

I wonder what George Forbes decided on. It's hard to imagine him shopping for poetry bound in tartan, or eau de cologne in the last few hectic days before departure.

I wonder, too, what "trifling gift" Isabella left as a remembrance for the Rev and Mrs. Davis.

[George Forbes Papers, Incoming Correspondence, 1874, no. 14, University Library, St Andrews, Scotland.]

HISTORY DETECTIVE: A TRIP TO THE ARCHIVES

To use the archives at the Bishop Museum, I must go through a security check, wear a name badge, and leave my backpack in a locker. Ink pens are not allowed, and only one book at a time may be on a desk. One must write down exactly what is hoped for, and a gloved official will bring it.

From my research over the last year, I have a list of dates that refer to times that Queen Emma visited Kona: the third Sunday of 1869, March 1869, mid November 1873, January 1874, February 1880, May 23, 1883. We have access to a letter Emma wrote Charles Williamson in 1869, and the receipt for Emma's contribution for a new Christ Church organ, dated 1881. I would like to read her diaries around all these dates to see if there are direct references to attending services in Kealakekua.

The museum has a diary for four different years; only one, 1881, is on my list. The archivist brings out a copy of it. This copy is not the original, nor is it a Xeroxed copy. Rather, it has been written out in long hand by a Bishop Museum employee. The words are Emma's, but unfortunately, it is not the real diary.

January 1881 begins with details of church life in Honolulu. David Kalakua leaves for his world tour.

In February there is a smallpox outbreak and Emma's home is put under quarantine. The next six months she writes the small details of a strictly limited life. Most of it is about the illness: who dies from it, who has or hasn't been vaccinated. Emma has been vaccinated, and she is safe, but many die. (There were 789 reported cases in Honolulu, 289 fatal.)

My favorite entry is from February 17, in which she refers to John Young, (the Anglican seaman who became advisor to Kamehameha I,) and her baby (who is already in heaven.)

> I have been all day rearranging my jewelry . . . and put them away all in one great tin box and sat it within my mirror wardrobe, / my own and my own dear little Prince of Hawaii's navel were found amongst them together with grandfather's two last teeth, which dear mother always had kept with such affection.

With Emma's jewelry is also the ring of Kamehameha IV "with my name, Emma, composed of <u>E</u>merald, <u>M</u>alachite, <u>M</u>alachite, Ruby, making the name."

Emma's loveliest words are written praising the beauty of her garden, the flowers and the bees. In her February 15 entry she writes:

> How very lovely the early mornings & moonlight nights have been of late & this morning is no exception. It is so calm & delightful, the golden sunlight of the early day bathing the different foliage of Tamarind, the great feathery arms of Cocoa nut leaf, the gorgeous bloom of the purple Bougainvillea which makes my Mother's cottage Polihale one gay mass, the fine delicate foliage of the Poinciana, & the still more delicate Algaroba, all in its golden sheen. How very lovely all nature is to be sure.

But there is no mention of Christ Church or Kona at all during these months of confinement; indeed she could not have visited. The diary stops in June when the quarantine ends.

I ask the archivist if I can see the *real* diary. . . not touch it, just see it. I have to convince him that seeing Emma's own handwriting, the size of the book, the kind of paper…all matter. After some time away, he returns and places it before me. I have to ask him to turn the pages.

The most interesting thing is that the handwriting is tiny. Emma squeezes two lines of writing within each lined space. She ignores the margins, writes all the way to the edge of the paper. Yet she only writes on the top half of the page. Page after page, the top is cramped with tiny writing, and the bottom is blank. What could this mean? By 1881 Emma is 45 years old. Perhaps her eyesight is changing, but wouldn't it be changing in the other direction? Perhaps she is a very private person and does not want her servants reading over her shoulder. Or perhaps, like Davis, she intends to flip the book over and write in it the other direction. Still, my question is why?

The archivist takes away Emma's diary and brings me Liliuokalani's Bible. It is embossed with a crown over her name. This means it was a gift to her when she was a princess. The Bible is a Hawaiian translation, third edition, 1869. I see a few places with tiny pencil checks by scriptures.

Last of all, the archivist brings out Liliuokalani's *Book of Common Prayer,* published 1883, at Charring Cross. Is this the one the Bishop gave her while she was under arrest? The archivist doesn't know.

The ink is brown—all the ink—on every old document. Did everyone use brown ink at this time in history? Or is it black ink changed with age? The archivist doesn't know the answer to this either. In fact, he has never even noticed it before.

Profile: The Last Hawaiian Queen

After the Eucharist we sing a song written by Liliuokalani, the last Queen of Hawaii. In the lyrics both sadness and hope are expressed. Sadness that the Hawaiian people have lost their monarchy; hope that God's grace will sustain them.

The story behind the fall of the monarchy, as told by Liliuokalani, is the epitome of injustice. In her autobiography, Hawaii's Story by Hawaii's Queen, she meticulously details each step of the conspiracy to overthrow her kingdom. She is careful in documenting every accusation, recording dates, signatures, and participants in each event. She approaches her subject with dignity and restraint; she is clearly a well-educated and knowledgeable woman. It is a very sorry story for those of us brought up believing in justice and liberty for all.

When Liliuokalani is arrested, even her long-time pastor at KawaiaHa'o Church deserts her. Imprisoned in 'Io-lani Palace, she is left with only her music for personal solace. And so she writes songs, pours out her heart into haunting melodies. Hawaiian slack key guitarist, Keola Beamer, says of her, "She made music of soulful heart and tenderness held in the arms of her own personal melancholy. After all these years, one can still feel her sadness singing in the quiet spaces between the notes." (CD liner notes)

Eventually the captive queen is allowed the use of her autoharp and guitar. Eventually she is allowed to receive flower bouquets from her friends, and letters, after they have been censored. Her jailers give her permission to care for her potted ferns, to do handwork, and to take pleasure in the company of her canaries. After a time, some books are permitted, but no newspapers of any kind. The Anglican Bishop sends her a *Book of Common Prayer.*

Bishop Willis has been outspoken for her cause. In an article in the Diocesan Magazine, he maintains that Queen Liliuokalani is still the rightful sovereign of the Islands, and that it is "a fundamental principle of Christianity. That those who are sent to preach the Gospel should be loyal to the government of the countries in which they live . . . [and] the church is bound to be loyal until it is changed by the will of the nation."

But nothing changes. Six months later, in another article, the Bishop writes, "The liberties of Hawaii are still trampled upon in the name of liberty . . . it is impossible that the American people will allow the pages of its annals to be sullied with the record of a crime which has no parallel in ancient or modern history."

And later, "It is not a mere question of polities. It is a question of right. What wrong have the Hawaiian people done to America that after a half century of well ordered government she should use her forces to put them under the heel of a handful of men whose fathers came here to preach the Gospel?"

Bishop Willis continues to attack the Republic and expects to be arrested for it.

Upon annexation, the Bishop makes the official changes in the Prayer Book: "God save the Queen" is replaced with "God save the State." Where the people of Hawaii once prayed for the royal family, now they are to pray for a president.

Liliuokalani joins the Anglican Church. She writes that the Bishop has been a great comfort to her, and that he has made the

Christian faith more real to her than it has ever been before. She is not actually allowed to attend church services for some time, but eventually she does gain freedom of movement again.

But the monarchy is over; it is the end of an era. It is the end of the Anglican Church in Hawaii as well. Now that Hawaii is American, the church authority will pass over to the American Episcopal Church. This is a change that will directly affect our little Christ Church in distant, quiet Kealakekua. We don't know how closely it paid attention to all the political drama that unfolded on Oahu; we don't know how long it is before they change the wording in the prayer book. But we do know that with the changing of the guard, so to speak, Reverend Samuel Davis, from the Anglican Church of England, will have to be replaced by an American priest.

Now, more than a hundred years later, we sing *The Queen's Prayer* in Hawaiian, every Sunday morning. As we walk back from receiving the bread and the wine, we remember our heritage, here, in this land. Her song connects us to our roots—to the Queens and the monarchy, to the true language of these islands, to the hope that God will heal the injustices that shape our world. It is a beautiful, haunting, humbling song. Here is a translation:

> Your love is in heaven,
> And your truth so perfect.
> Behold not with malevolence
> The sins of man,
> But forgive and cleanse.
> And so, Oh Lord
> Beneath your wings,
> Be our peace
> Forever more.

CHAPTER 3

Charles Lambert and HN Greenwell graves, @ 1892. Photograph by Rev. SH Davis. (Courtesy Kona Historical Society.)

DIFFERENT VOICE, DIFFERENT PEN: LILIUOKALANI EXPLAINS THE HANAI CUSTOM

Immediately after my birth I was wrapped in the finest soft tapa cloth and taken to the house of another chief by whom I was adopted. Konia, my foster-mother, was a granddaughter of Kamehameha I, and was married to Paki, also a high chief; their only daughter Bernice...was my foster-sister. In speaking of our relationship, I have adopted the term customarily used in the

English language, but there was no such modification recognized in my native land. I knew no other father and mother than my foster parents, no other sister than Bernice.

I used to climb up on the knees of Paki, put my arms around his neck, kiss him, and he caressed me as a father would his child; while on the contrary, when I met my own parents, it was with perhaps more of interest, yet always with the demeanor I would have shown to any strangers who noticed me.

My own father and mother had other children, ten in all, the most of them being adopted into other chiefs' families. Although I knew these were my own brothers and sisters, yet we met throughout my younger life as though we had not known our common parentage. This was, and indeed is, in accordance with Hawaiian customs.

It is not easy to explain its origin to those alien to our national life, but it seems perfectly natural to us. As intelligible a reason as can be given is that this alliance by adoption cemented the ties of friendship between the chiefs. It spread to the common people, and it has doubtless fostered a community of interest and harmony.

COMMENTARY: GIFT CULTURE

Chinese, Portuguese and Japanese workers have been coming to Hawai'i for some time now. They have been here long enough to finish their labor contracts and move on to better jobs, or to their own small coffee farms in Kona. The children born here are now American citizens, and with this new and amazing status, change is inevitable. With a voice and new possibilities, the next generation will not necessarily stay in the fields.

The sugar plantations are still growing, so additional cheap laborers are needed. The new century brings a wave of new ethnic groups. Several hundred American Negroes come, then Puerto Ricans, Koreans, and finally Filipinos. Each brings different customs, language, foods, and beliefs. The implications are complex and far-reaching.

According to anthropologist Lewis Hyde, you can tell a lot about a culture by looking at the way it gives gifts. A gift economy demonstrates "a total social phenomenon, one whose transactions are at once economic, juridical, moral, aesthetic, religious, and mythological" (Mauss, xv).

In a gift economy there are three related obligations: to give, to accept, and to reciprocate. In the example of one Caribbean tribe Hyde studies, gifts move in a circle around a group or around an island, and eventually, come back. (A offers a gift to B; B to C; C to D, until Z offers a gift to A.) The gift increases as it moves, and the status of the gift-giver does too. Hyde explains that in many places a person "came into his social being through the dispersal of his gifts, the big man being that one through whom the most gifts flowed."

In most tribes, food is always given as a gift and the transaction "is governed by the ethics of gift exchange, not those of barter or cash purchase" (Hyde, Xiv). We see this at a potluck or at a party; food is a gift freely given without reservation or repayment. Food bartered is quite a different matter.

The sharing of food with the hungry, the unfortunate, and the stranger is a theme that shows up in the folk tales of most cultures. The gift given this way never gets used up, rather it increases. The lost child who shares her meager bread crusts with the birds is magically rewarded for her unselfishness. The fish thrown back to sea grants wishes to the poor fisherman. The king, or an angel, or a god pretends to be in need, and rewards the peasant who responds unselfishly.

In Hawai'i there is a legend about Madame Pele concerning this theme; on a fateful night in 1960, she disguises herself as an old woman and begs for food in the town of Ka-poho. She is turned away again and again. Nobody responds to her pleas until she arrives at the Cape Kumu-kahi Lighthouse. The lighthouse keepers care for the old woman. Very soon Pele responds severely;

the town is destroyed by lava, but it stops within a few feet of the lighthouse. The flow splits into two paths and goes around it. You can visit it today and see just what happened! It is a cautionary tale to remind us that caring for the hungry is important, and generosity is rewarded.

To give a daughter in marriage is another example of a culturally based gift exchange. A dowry, a daughter and her fertility (the children she will have) are given. The entire tribe/community is witness to the event; there is a feast; there are more gifts given, both practical and symbolic.

In ancient Hawai'i the custom of giving away children—hanai babies—was common. Both Queen Emma and Queen Liliuokalani were hanai daughters.

The gift exchange has three parts and so does the gift cycle. First is giving back to nature. Second is sharing with the tribe. Third is an offering to God. "The inclusion of the Lord in the circle changes the ego in which the gift moves in a way unlike any other addition. It is enlarged beyond the tribal ego and beyond nature....the gift leaves all boundary and circles into mystery" (Hyde, 20).

In our own Christian tradition, we have many examples of a gift economy: the first fruits of every harvest are to be offered to God. Jesus challenges the practical minded and models generosity in giving—he feeds the five thousand, he praises the extravagant act of the woman with the alabaster jar, he claims that the widow's mite is more valuable than the great offerings of the wealthy.

A paradox of the gift exchange is that when the gift is used, it is not used up. Hyde writes that the passage into mystery *always refreshes*.

The European /American capitalist does not hold to these spiritual truths. On the contrary, "modern capitalist societies, however richly endowed, dedicate themselves to the proposition of scarcity" (Hyde, 22).

Let's look at some of our most common English proverbs: *A penny saved is a penny earned. A stitch in time saves nine. Better to be safe than sorry. A bird in the hand is worth two in the bush.* These are meaningless to the hungry child who feeds the birds, the generous lighthouse keeper, and the widow with her insignificant coin. But in the market society, getting rather than giving is the mark of a wealthy person.

Gifts given in a patronizing way are something altogether different. In some societies it is the duty of the rich and powerful to be benefactors to the poor and weak. (The French called it "noblese oblige.") The poor are expected to have a proper sense of obligation to the patrons. This is not the same as giving and receiving; it is not acknowledging interdependence. It is rather a way to assert superiority over others and to maintain it. The plantation system in earlier Hawai'i is a local example of this. (Even if one was treated as an indentured slave under terrible conditions, one was supposed to be grateful for it. The 'superiority' of the plantation owner was not questioned.)

One man's gift must not become another man's capital…it must remain a gift. When it does not, there will be cultural conflict. European capitalism clashes with the native Hawaiian gift economy. As the twentieth century unfolds in Hawai'i, we have not only the conflicts between the native Hawaiians and Western Civilization, but we add the "gift economies" of Eastern Civilization–the Chinese, Japanese, Korean, and Filipino— as well.

These touch our little congregation in ways both tangible and intangible. The church, although modeled on communal sharing and generosity, has to survive in a capitalist society. Our priests can teach God's abundance, but must keep careful accounts of every dollar spent. Add new worshippers with a Buddhist background. Add a few rich, and a few poor. There are ample opportunities to grow in holiness, but there are also plenty of opportunities for misunderstanding.

The lei is a beautiful example of the coming together of cultures in Hawai'i. Let's look at the flowers used for lei today, and acknowledge where they came from: the Polynesians brought ginger, the missionaries brought bare-root roses, the Chinese brought orchids and pikake. Plumeria flowers came from Tahiti, bougainvillea came from Mexico, bird of paradise from Africa, and jade vine arrived with the Filipinos.

In the lei we have the most fragile gift; delicate visual beauty combines with exotic perfume. The investment in time (for nature and the lei-maker) is great, and yet the value quickly fades. Every wedding, graduation, funeral, awards ceremony, the greeting of every dignitary, every winning athlete, and the welcoming of many, many island guests—all are honored with flower leis—transient beauty in the spirit of aloha.

New Names

When Hawai'i becomes a US territory, an American Bishop is needed to replace the English one. There is a lot of political conflict in the changeover, but eventually, Henry Bond Restarick, Dean of Southern California, is chosen.

The church gets a new name as well. Under Bishop Staley it was The Reformed Catholic Church. Under Bishop Willis it was the Anglican Church in Hawai'i. Now, at the beginning of a new century, it is to be called The Protestant Episcopal Church in the Hawaiian Islands.

Then and Now: Entertainment

The Anglican Church Chronicle 1904

News from the Missions
Christ Church, South Kona
On December 20th [1903] an entertainment was given in the hall, kindly lent by the Kona Sugar Co. The first part of the

programe consisted of vocal and instrumental solos and duets, a humorous recitation and a most amusing dialogue in character.

During the interval which followed, ice cream and cake were sold.

The second half was a representation of the screaming farce, "Poor Pillicoddy" which was well received and much enjoyed by a crowded and enthusiastic audience.

Thanks to the kind friends who gave or loaned all the materials necessary for the stage, scenery, etc. and to the gentlemen who were clever enough to construct the same, the expenses were nil and the net result including one or two donations was a clear $142 handed over to the committee.

Our friends at Holualoa kindly got up a subscription dance, which took place on January 8th, and after a most enjoyable evening, handed over to the committee the sum of fifty-five dollars to be added to the organ fund

August 17, 2007

Original Play Festival

The Aloha Performing Arts Company is renting the Queen Emma Community Center for its Original Play Festival. The room is full. Overflowing actually.

The playwright for tonight–day five of the festival—is Diane Aoki who happens to be a church member as well. She warned us in advance her play has adult language and adult themes. She doesn't want those of us from church to be offended. She is lovely in a dressy black and green muumuu with a black and green lei. Her mother made the lei for her. They are both Hawaiian born of Japanese ancestry.

The play is about the tension between a slick land developer and a local Hawaiian protester. The latter is writing her dissertation on local sites of cultural significance and is not open to compromise. The two facing each other on this hot topic were once young lovers, so the personal and the public get all tangled up.

The love of the land is held up as the highest value. I think of the land this church building sits on. Do we love the land enough? The old tension between progress and preservation is lived out over and over all around us.

The play is tough and confrontive and poignant, the issue left unresolved. The audience is attentive and worked up as well. Social criticism, social commentary delivered from our own church hall. Serving our community in a unique way. But the message is for us too!

Different voice, Different Pen: Hear the Prophet Speak Today
By Heidi Edson

Seminary Assignment: Heidi was supposed to imagine what one of the Old Testament prophets would say if he were here today.

Hear this word from God, you Americans who travel to
Hawai'i to remain:
You who come to Hawai'i in droves
And occupy our islands; hear the word of the Lord.
Your palaces are built where the Hawaiian's shacks stood.
For this intrusion, I will cause the salt of the ocean to rust
your glass dwellings.
The tsunamis shall arise to drown your marble-ladened
dwellings.

You shut out the *Aloha* with your locked gates.
Yet you cannot shut out my judgment against you.

Behind closed doors, you say smugly to yourself, 'What need
have I of *Aloha*?
My wealth will sustain me."
For this arrogance, your wealth will slowly dwindle in rising
rates of interest.
The *Aloha* so freely given to all will escape your realms of
existence.

My eyes burn with anger because of your blindness towards
the keiki.
Your concern for their welfare is paltry.
You, who could give such ones the gift of health and
education,
Choose instead to lavish goods upon your own offspring,
sending them to spacious schools while the keiki are crowded in
their halls of learning.
For this evil, I will cause your children to be dulled through
their Nintendos and stereos
while the keikis of this land dance the *Aloha* full of life and
love.

I have had enough of your abuse, says the Lord.
Your greed is a noxious odor in my nostrils.
Your opulent living has made you fat.
When will you turn from your isolation and indolence?
For this wickedness, I will cause destruction to fall upon
your houses of bricks.
No more will you hear the call of *Aloha*
from the goodwill of the Hawaiians.

A New Era

According to the memoirs of Bishop Resterick;
"The story of Christ church at Kona from 1905 is that
of Mr. Wallace and his excellent wife. None could have

come who would have made themselves a part of the community as thoroughly as they.

Mr. Wallace's charge extends from Christ church to Pu'u-wa'awa'a, the residence of Robert Hind, 32 miles in one direction, and to Wai-'ohinu, about 43 miles in the other. At first Mr. Wallace had a horse and conveyance, but when automobiles became common, the District Branch of the Woman's Auxiliary assisted him in the matter of acquiring a car when he needed it, this being more economical than owning one.

The Bishop writes that DD Wallace came from the diocese of Sacramento, California. According to the Greenwell family lore, however, DD Wallace came from Salt Lake City where he ministered to the Indians. His old congregation was sorry to see him go and missed their beloved priest. Two of his parishners, came all the way from Australia to visit him in Hawai'i. A Scottish lassie named Maud was one of them. She fell in love in Kona; she married William Henry Greenwell, and became the second matriarch of the large extended family.

Canon Douglas D. Wallace was the 4th Vicar of Christ Church and served from the years 1906-1933. There were tremendous changes in the world during this time; one of them was the changing role of women in society. We are going to shift our attention to the women now: Mrs. Wallace, "the excellent wife," and Mrs. Wood, the faithful secretary. In this new era the women become significant in making "church" happen, and we have the stories to prove it.

Women's Work

To imagine the realities of daily life in the first decades of the twentieth century, I think back on stories about my grandmother. She never came to Hawai'i, but her experiences run parallel to those of her English-speaking Christian sisters here. She was feisty and strong willed and although she was supposed to be submissive, she had a way of getting what she wanted. Let's look at three examples.

My grandmother, Sister Pace, had a problem with spittoons in church. She believed their presence was disgraceful and she spoke loudly and often about it. The men politely ignored her—the preacher's wife. She continued to complain and they continued to remain deaf, so to gain some attention, she bobbed her hair. Now cutting her hair was an act of rebellion and an affront to femininity. In fear that the church sisters would follow my grandmother's lead, the spittoons quickly disappeared.

Sister Pace was a hard worker; she had tons of energy and will-power to match. She worked hard for everybody else, but I guess she considered her little bit of free time as her own. I don't remember ever seeing her read anything but the Bible, but my grandfather found her reading a novel one day, and told her he would not allow such a thing. She told him that she was a grown woman and she would read whatever she wanted; then she threw the book at him.

My third story is about a vacuum cleaner. My grandmother was the first in her town to have one. The church women in alarm gathered together and came to her house to exhort her: the vacuum cleaner was "of the devil!"

The themes of these stories would have run through Kona too: Freedom to choose things the men might not like, such as wives cutting their hair or reading romance novels; the age old desire for women to clean up the men folk and improve their manners; the ongoing experience of new technology as threatening.

Women did not have the vote (at least not during the early Wallace years.) Women did not have birth control—in fact it was *against the law* for hospitals to even discuss the subject. Divorce was rare and generally unacceptable. Higher education was also rare. Gathering together for friendship and support in some kind of woman's group was an important part of a woman's identity. In groups they had some power, as well as companionship. It was an acceptable place in the community to effect change. It was a place to share and shape their opinions, to develop their own voices.

The Guild at Christ Church was the first woman's organization in Kona. The year it began was 1905. Its motto, "Yes, thank you." Meetings were held every first and third Tuesday afternoon at various homes. The group included women from other church denominations; it was an inclusive group and all the lady teachers at Konaweena School were invited. Initiation dues for joining the Guild were 25 cents, then 10 cents dues for each meeting. This fee was reduced for those members with large families.

The names of the pioneer women and their (now) grown daughters dominate the Guild notes. Among the names are a few connected to the larger history of the island, like Mrs. Jagger, wife of the vulcanologist.

Mrs. R.V. Wood is most often listed as the secretary of the Guild, and what we know of it comes from her pen. Unfortunately, she is most proper in her note-taking; she sticks to the facts. How I wish for a little gossip, an opinion, a joke somewhere in the many, many details. But no, we must imagine the gatherings: women sipping fresh lemonade, and balancing dainty plates of ginger cake, or guava whips on their laps. Some of the hostesses would have brought china with them from England or Scotland or Ireland. Perhaps there would be Kona coffee. They would have used cloth napkins. Certainly the women would be wearing their best dresses, full length Mother Hubbard style, and often they would have done the dressmaking themselves.

After refreshments, the sewing basket would come out, and projects resumed. Can the oldest member still thread a needle? Do a few use magnifying glasses so they can see the tiny stitches? Here are direct references to their sewing projects taken from the notes:

> Orders for dressmaking as well as embroidery kept the Guild members busy earning money for the Church as well as a reputation for beautiful handwork.

The members devoted one afternoon to sew on Miss Mary Ackerman's house linen as she was about to become Mrs. Thos. O'Brien.

White silk Frontals for the Lectern and Credence Table and white bookmarks were made and donated for Easter.

A purple Pall for use at funerals was provided in 1914.

An epidemic of Influenza caused the ten members present on March 18 to set aside all other work to answer an emergency call, and one dozen pillowcases, one dozen Japanese towels, two kimonos and one child's ditto were the result of the afternoon's work. (Another outbreak of Influenza in March 1920 kept members too busy as amateur nurses to hold any meetings that month.)

Besides sewing, the Guild raised funds to replace Bibles and Prayer books, and to cover the cost of building repairs. Here is another list of specific Guild contributions:

> The brass cross for the Altar, costing $33.00, was purchased by the Guild as an Easter gift to the Church in 1906.
>
> The year of the earthquake and fire in San Francisco, the Guild sent a donation of $10 to the fund for destitute Episcopal Clergy of that city.
>
> Mite boxes were distributed and subscriptions for the Hawaiian Church Chronicle collected.
>
> Embroidery on a new White Altar Cloth was started and finished in time as an Easter present to the Church in 1909, the work principally of Mrs. D. Douglas Wallace,

Mrs. Robert Wallace, Mrs. E. E. Conant and Miss Amy Greenwell.

Last year the silk foundation having worn out, the embroidery was cleverly lifted onto a white brocade by Sister Katherine Helen of the Priory and the Honolulu Altar Guild.

In 1909 the brass Altar Lectern was presented by the Guild on Trinity Sunday.

The Transparencies for the East window were provided.

A gift of $15 for the purchase of music made to Chester Blacow as an appreciation of his playing the organ on Sundays and choir practice on Thursdays.

In 1910 the Guild opened an account as one of the first depositors in the Kona Branch of the First Bank of Hilo, now the Bank of Hawai'i.

The Guild assumed responsibility for the Insurance of the Church Property, $45.

1917 the Guild had a telephone installed in the Parsonage when it became the Red Cross Center under Mrs. D. Douglas Wallace.

In 1923 Meetings changed from Tuesday to Wednesday on account of altered Steamer Schedule.

1929 the Guild gave new Prayer and Hymn Books to the Church.

An additional fundraiser referred to in the file concerned plans for an ice cream booth at the parsonage fair. The ladies all plan to wear white dresses with pink aprons. Mrs. Paris and Mrs. Ackerman have volunteered to donate the ice cream, white, strawberry, and vanilla.

Education begins to show up on the agenda. Indeed by 1934 the Guild has an Educational Committee. The Guild during Lent in 1933 made a study of "Living Issues in China" and in 1934 the Educational Committee gave interesting papers on "Christ in the Modern World" and "The Never-Failing Light."

We have a very special celebration on record in the Guild notes file:

> When the Christ Church Guild met at the residence of Mrs. E. C. Greenwell on May 2, 1934, as Mrs. Greenwell entered in her wheeled chair the members all rose to congratulate her on the 93rd anniversary of her birthday and Mrs. Robert Wallace presented a lei from the Guild. Miss Marguerite Bryant brought the birthday cake with many lighted candles to her grandmother who smilingly blew them out in time-honored fashion.

Most of these items were taken from a history that Mrs. R.V. Woods compiled to read for the birthday party. It is quite lengthy, with lists of those who served as officers from 1905 until 1934. All the women are called by their husbands' names, so it is easy to get confused as to who they really are.

To back up just a little, references to a Woman's Auxiliary begin to show up, mixed in with Guild reports. Perhaps you wonder what exactly is the difference between the Guild and the Woman's Auxiliary? The Woman's Auxiliary is a branch of the Board of Missions, so their sewing and fundraising would be for missionary work—for outreach. According to Bishop Restarick, the two groups were combined in the smaller parishes, as there were not enough women for two separate groups. The Guild met year round, but the Auxiliary sometimes met only during Lent. According to the notes, the Christ Church Guild was organized by the Reverend D. Douglas Wallace on April 11, 1905.

A Branch of the Woman's Auxiliary was started in February 1908 with Mrs. D. Douglas Wallace as President. Each group kept their own officers.

Mrs. R.V. Woods served as secretary for both, and sometimes treasurer too. What do we know of her? Her first name is Alice. She is from England, and is married to a sea captain who has retired in Kona. She generally writes about herself in third person. She is also the faithful correspondent to the *Hawaiian Church Chronicle* year after year. Most of what we know about the Wallace years comes from her careful reports.

THE FIRST WORLD WAR YEARS

After leaving Kealakekua, Charles Williamson served in Honolulu where he published St Andrews Magazine. Described in Stoddard's book, this 25 page illustrated magazine "contained news from the Church in America and England, matters of interest & information to both of the Honolulu congregations; papers on the origin and history of the Bible, a 'children's corner,' a short sermon each month, and selections of religious prose and poetry" (Stoddard 65).

Over the years new names were given to the Diocesan paper: *Honolulu Magazine and Church Chronicle, Hawaiian Church Monthly Messenger, Honolulu Diocesan Magazine*. Because of Hawaii's isolation, the importance of print material cannot be overstated. These publications were a reliable and respectable source of news, as well as culture and religion. They were critical in creating dialogue and shaping opinion.

In 1913 the magazine's name is *The Hawaiian Church Chronicle* and has added "Speaking the Truth in Love!" to its title page. Here are some of the ads and articles:

> September 1913 friends at sea will appreciate a Wireless Message! The rate from Honolulu and from all the Outer Island points to ship at sea 20 cents a word. Address and

signature counted. A telegraph line runs from the station on Hawai'i to Hilo

ads:

The Auto Piano the best Player Piano Victor talking machines and records

Silent Barbershop hot baths, 25cents/four bootblacks in attendance! /Arlington Hotel

Essay: "The Church and the Negro"

Story and photos: Father Damien

The headlines for November announces **President Wilson's First Thanksgiving Proclamation,** *peace throughout the world is a blessing.*

January edition 1914 offers Burial Insurance and
Fountain Pens of All Kinds NON-LEAKABLE caps!

Ackerman obituary

August 13, 1914 The American Ambulance of Paris/ Urgent Appeal to Every American at Home

September 1914 headlines; **President Wilson- Call to Prayer- National Day.**

October 4 is chosen as a day of prayer and supplication "to serve the cause of peace."

November 1914 headlines: **Pastoral Letter of the House of Bishops** encourages neutrality, self sacrifice for charity, prayers for peace

In his retrospective book, Bishop Restarick writes that while many pulpits were preaching pacifism, he made a clear stand for just wars:

> While we should do everything in private and in public that would make for peace as individuals and as a nation, yet we should be prepared to resist wrong, injustice and cruelty by force, if necessary, that is, if other means failed. ...that when Christ said that he did not come to bring peace but a sword, he spoke to the duty to struggle for the right and to overcome the powers of darkness.

Restarick summarizes the actions of the church in Hawai'i:

> Our people in Hawai'i did their full share, taking a leading part from the beginning and continued to do so when the Hawaiian chapter of the Red Cross was formed. By the end of 1917, the Hawaiian Red Cross had 16,650 members and a higher portion of life members than any State in the Union. Red Cross Units were formed in every Island, in all of which our people had their full share.

Some specifics:

* The Guild started a fund for children in the war countries; presents to the value of $1600 were sent on the "Christmas Ship."

* The Guild raised money to pay the passage of four Red Cross nurses from Honolulu to London.

* It provided 232 god-mothers for Belgium soldiers.

* Church schools gave money for barrels of flour to be sent to Belgium.

* Children in Sunday school forgo their own Christmas gifts to send candy to children in Europe.

Christ Church mission participated in the National Day of Prayer and made a special collection for the Paris Hospital. When the war starts, CC becomes a Red Cross center. From the Guild notes we know that the women cut and rolled bandages and gauze, made hospital shirts, garments and comfort bags. They made donations for the hungry children of war. Unfortunately we have no old sermons to read, but we can assume that DD Wallace lead the congregation week after week in prayers for the boys, for victory, for peace.

The bishop's wife, May Restarick, provided a service flag for the Cathedral with a star for each son of Hawai'i in the service. There were red stars for those who entered the British service, and blue stars for the Americans. Gold stars were for those "who gave all for God, for County, and for Humanity."

Queen Liliuokalani made a flag too, a Red Cross flag to hang over Iolani Palace. Volunteers worked in the palace throughout the war.

I once asked my grandmother about her many years of ministering as a preacher's wife. She said the hardest thing was to bury young men that she had once given baby showers for.

One of the 7 known dead listed at the Cathedral is Henry Bryant, only son of Carrie Greenwell and Gerald Bryant, and first grandson of HN and ECH Greenwell. A pilot with the British, Bryant was shot down over Italy. There is no mention if Christ Church had a flag with the gold star.

HISTORICAL CONTEXT: TECHNOLOGY

The first telephone at Christ Church was installed in the parsonage in 1917 while it was being used as a Red Cross Center.

Today telephones are such a normal part of life that we can hardly imagine life without them. Although they heralded a significant change in communications, it was a change not everyone felt good about.

What were some of the problems? Mychilo Cline, in his book <u>Power, Madness, and Immortality,</u> explores the impact of new technologies on society.

First of all, talking on the telephone was like speaking to someone in the dark. One could not see the traditional cues, the non verbal cues, the facial expression, body language, gestures. All of these are tremendously important in communication. Furthermore, one could not tell the age of the speaker, the race, the economic level, or the marital status. We accept this now without question, but at the time, the telephone raised many serious concerns.

With the telephone, society had to renegotiate social norms. What exactly was acceptable behavior on the telephone? What about privacy?

In a post Victorian world, issues of modesty were of great concern; what might be the ethical implications of a telephone conversation while not properly dressed? Another problem was that married men talking to the telephone operator (always female) was a constant source of jealousy among wives. How could one maintain boundaries?

The French were very much against the adoption of telephone communication because it promoted dialogue—two way communications—and this disrupted the established hierarchy. Servants were expected to live in submissive silence, and dialogue suggested equality.

> Courtship patterns changed forever.
> Society had to adjust to the rapid spread of information.
> People had to learn how to avoid deception, theft and fraud.

Christina Greenwell makes numerous references to the telephone in her 1896 diary. There does not appear to be one in her home, but phone messages are delivered to her family. The German immigrant Luther Aungst is the one who is responsible for telephone service in Kona. He and his wife, Emma, are buried in our cemetery.

How would all this affect the work of the vicar? It would influence the speed and organization of information in conducting daily business. Certainly it would be beneficial for responding to emergencies in the lives of his flock. It would also be a constant interruption.

Here are some of the dates on the telephone timeline:

>   1876 Bell patents telephone   (Davis years)
>   1878 telephone introduced in Hawai'i
>   1889 patent for first coin-operated telephone
>   1898 first telephone message from a submerged submarine
>
>   1917 the telephone company runs its first ad for army operators and receives 7,000 applications (Wallace years)
>   1917 the first phone is installed at Christ Church
>   1929 the first phone is installed in the White House.

Does this seem strange? Wallace Hall had a telephone before the White House?

THEN AND NOW: A PROBLEM WITH THE LOCAL TEENAGERS

One

The first few moments before church starts are lovely to me; it is the time to kneel and pray, to let go of the past and the future, to intentionally surrender to the present. This morning, when I open my eyes, the first thing I see is a little paper airplane. It is underneath the organ bench just inches from where I kneel.

There is a story going around that a few of the teenagers from the high school up the street came by, took all the little welcome/visitor cards in the pews and made paper airplanes.

When the church secretary came in, they were running around throwing both paper and pencils and being silly. Just kid stuff really, but disrespectful. Of course they were chased away and now the church is locked during the day.

It is my intention to retrieve the paper airplane as soon as the service ends, but I change my mind. I decide to wait and see how long it remains there in secret. I decide to use it as a weekly reminder to pray for the unhappy teenagers who literally keep showing up on our doorstep.

Two

Stephanie Ackerman, cemetery director, stops me in the market to tell me that some of the local teens got into a big brawl on the labyrinth before school. The police were called and broke it up, but the fight resumed later in the cemetery. There was some damage done to the gravesites. Insurance should cover it, but we have a far bigger problem here.

With the high school up the street, the church is an easy drop-off and pick up place. Teens sit on the rock wall, fool around in the parking lot, have sex under the coffee trees, smoke where no one can see them. They want to use the phone and the bathrooms, but have been so messy and disrespectful that it is no longer allowed. The worst thing of all is that a few of the kids aim excessively foul language at Reverend Carol whenever she speaks to them.

We need youth at our church and these youth could stand a little hope and inspiration, but how do we reach them? As a church we have talked about the problem, and although some ideas have come forth, no committed follow-through has.

Three

The first historical reference to local high school students is in the 1920s. According to the World Wide Web, Kona established its first 9th grade class in 1921. The high school continued to establish 10th, 11th, and 12th grade classes as each group was ready to move up. The first graduating class of Konawaena High School was 1925.

For 40 years Konawaena operated on what is known as the "coffee schedule." Summer vacation was shifted to the harvest season, September through November. Children helped with harvesting coffee cherries. This coffee-picking schedule made it impossible for Kona to have a football team because the kids were all needed for the harvest. Eventually, child labor laws eliminated the coffee schedule.

Four

In our little Christ Church parking lot there is a sign, a necessary sign perhaps, but a sad sign nonetheless. It says:

> Private Parking
> No trespassing
> No alcohol or drugs
> No skateboarders
> No rollerblades
> No scooters
> No loiterers or littering
> Violators will be prosecuted

Every Sunday morning I see the sign as a reminder of a need unfulfilled. What if we changed the wording?

> **God's Property**
> Welcome to all who don't yet belong here
> Alcoholics and drug addicts are invited to sample
>   Heavenly Wine
> Skateboarders, rollerbladers, scooter enthusiasts, come meet the One who
>   designed speed, gravity and centrifugal force!
> Those who have nowhere to go, please come inside,
>   unburden your heart, receive a blessing.
>
> ***Violators will be prayed for.***

Goodbye to a Faithful Wife

Editor, the Hawaiian Church Chronicle,
 Having known Mrs. D. Douglas Wallace since her arrival in Kona, it has been my privilege to write the enclosed tribute of appreciation of her life amongst us....
 Mr. Wallace is carrying his load of sorrow most bravely but we all know the ache of loneliness will be dreadful for him.

By MRS. R.V. WOODS.

In Memoriam
 MRS. D. DOUGLAS Wallace passed away on St. Andrew's Day, Saturday, November 30, [1929] at 11:30 p.m., after a few days' illness. She was laid to rest in the burial ground of Christ Church, Kona, on Advent Sunday, the service being read by Rev. James Walker of Kohala. The funeral was largely attended by representatives of all nationalities from North and South Kona and friends from Ka'u and Kohala, who came to pay the last tribute of affection and respect.

Canon and Mrs. D. Douglas Wallace came to Kona in 1905. During those almost 25 years Mrs. Wallace had endeared herself to the Kona people by her loving whole-hearted service. Her training as a nurse in Ireland and subsequent experience as Superintendent of nurses at St Luke's Hospital in Denver enabled her to give invaluable help when an epidemic of typhoid visited Kona and a temporary hospital had to be improvised of which she took charge. Years later when Kona possessed a hospital but both doctor and nurse were among the first sufferers of a terrible visitation of influenza; Mrs. Wallace took charge and directed the energies of a band of willing, but inexperienced helpers until two trained nurses could be secured.

She directed the women's Red Cross activities during the war, supervising the various units of all nationalities throughout the district. These were among her public activities but her private deeds of kindness were innumerable. Was anyone sick or sorry? She was the first to offer help and comfort.

When advancing years and poorer health were a handicap, in some ways she still continued her many kindnesses. Her first thought was always, "What can I do to help?" Mrs. Wallace was the first and only [president?] of the Woman's Auxiliary, which together with the Christ Church Guild, Canon Wallace and she organized soon after their arrival.

Her wonderful skill with the needle gave many pieces of lovely embroidery to the church and her work was always much sought after at the Guild Sales of Work.

The whole district extends heartfelt sympathy to Canon Wallace in the loss of his devoted wife and helpmate.

Call her not dead! She has but swiftly passed
Within the veil that screens the outer hall,
The vestibule of silence she must cross
To reach the presence chamber of her Lord.

EXILES IN MOLOKAI

No history of Hawai'i is complete without an understanding of the history of disease here. In the two decades after Captain Cook arrived, ten thousand people died of syphilis and gonorrhea in Oahu alone. Traders, missionaries and whalers brought 'simple' childhood diseases: measles, mumps, whooping cough and chicken pox as well. Because the Hawaiians had no immunity to these germs, the diseases were too often fatal. When typhoid broke out, it killed over 5,000. Next, between 10,000 to 15,000 died from smallpox. When leprosy arrived, the tough decisions and laws enacted began as a sincere attempt to save the Hawaiian race from extinction. Although heartbreakingly cruel, exile was deemed the best possible measure to stop the spread of infection.

Although leprosy is found all over the world, no other place received the attention that Molokai did. Here was *Paradise for the Lost*, a place of unbelievable suffering set against the backdrop of the majestic green pali and the raging blue surf.

Between the years of 1866 and 1969, over 8,000 individuals were exiled. This was one in thirty residents of Hawai'i. No ethnic or economic group was spared: Hawaiian royalty, as well as prominent lawyers, judges, and children of doctors were banished.

Researcher John Tayman has recorded in careful detail the experiences of about a dozen victims in <u>The Colony, the Harrowing True Story of the Exiles of Molokai</u>. He studies the medical files, personal letters, newspapers, Father Damien's journals, and finally, conducts personal interviews. He also documents the medical research throughout the world, the detours, failures, and eventually the discoveries that lead to treatment.

The story of the creation and the management of the settlement on Molokai is a volatile, contentious melodrama. Those responsible for it are a collection of quacks, criminals, politicians, frauds and even a slave trader. There are also dedicated doctors, a few just legislators, and (thank heavens!) a few saints. Countless unnamed kokuas and nuns join with Father Damien, Mother Marianne, and Civil War vet Joseph Dutton, to give their lives in compassionate service. Other characters in the overall story include Robert Louis Stevenson, Jack London, Mark Twain, Isabella Bird, Queen Emma, and Kings Kamehameha I, III, IV, and V.

This is a ghastly chapter in history, but it is not without beautiful stories of courage, integrity, creativity, compassion, love, devotion, respect, redemption and grace. My favorite story is of Robert Louis Stevenson. While suffering from tuberculosis, he traveled to Hawai'i to take advantage of the weather. Initially his requests to visit Molokai were refused by the board of health, but King David Kalakaua granted permission. Stevenson first went to Ho'okena where he documented the scene as victims where loaded into whaleboats as their families wept in mourning. At the colony, Stevenson taught the girls in the orphanage how to play croquet. It is a tender story full of joy and gratitude. On the steamer leaving Molokai, Stevenson wrote in his journal, "I have seen sights that cannot be told, and heard stories that cannot be repeated: yet I never admired my poor race so much, nor (strange as it may seem) loved life more than in this settlement."

Father Damien felt the same way. He refused to take precautions against infection, sharing pipes and poi with the dying patients under his care. He refused to leave Molokai, even when his replacement arrived. In October of 1888, Father Damien wrote to his brother in Belgium, "I know that my days are numbered. My illness progresses quickly. Both my face and my hands are beginning to decompose....I think I am the happiest missionary in the world."

When I encouraged my husband to read Tayman's book, he looked doubtful and said, "I don't imagine that it has a happy ending." On the contrary! The cause and cure of leprosy have both been discovered. The most dreadful disease in the history of mankind is no longer considered a curse by God, a crime against humanity, or a death sentence.

In the year 2004, Canadian scientists found a *genetic quirk* in victims of leprosy (by this time renamed *Hansen's disease.*) The gene PARK2 is necessary for a person to be vulnerable to the germ. An additional gene, PACRG, is required for an infected person to actually get sick from it. (Like tuberculosis, one can be a carrier, and yet never become ill.) According to the researchers, this genetic quirk occurs in about 5% of the population and follows ethnic bloodlines. For some reason, the Hawaiian and the French populations have the highest rates. Father Damien, from Belgium, had the proper DNA to contract the disease, but he worked many years before he showed any signs. Numerous kokuas, and many babies born on Molokai, were immune.

Because doctors now realize that leprosy is only contagious among 5%, it is treated–and cured—on an out-patient basis. The disease still exists, but it is unlikely that any one of us will ever have reason to know our own genetic status.

Neither will we ever know how many from Christ Church went to Kalaupapa. Reading the tombstones in our cemetery we may be able to recognize when the Spanish flu came to Kona, but those who were sent to Molokai are buried there. I find no reference in the Guild reports of any donations or outreach to Kalaupapa, but surely if any member, or neighbor, or relative went, contributions would have followed. Perhaps Rev. Davis met Father Damien. Maybe Mrs. DD Wallace, a skilled and compassionate nurse, wrote to Mother Marianne

What implication does this story have on our world today? It seems to me that the lessons learned about leprosy have been applied to the treatment of, and legal protection for those with AIDS. In one brief poignant encounter in Tayman's book, a victim of leprosy meets a victim of AIDS. They admit—with shame—that they are afraid of each other.

Caution around a contagious fatal disease is a natural and necessary thing, but even so, as Christians we are called to comfort the sick and dying, and to treat each one with dignity. Jesus is our first role model for caring for the leper. He inspired Saint Francis, who inspired Father Damien. In our own lifetime, we can look to Mother Teresa as a beautiful example of love in action. These three followers of Christ were motivated by infinite compassion, but not overwhelmed by it. This, I believe, is a distinction worthy of our continued meditation.

Then and Now: Ecumenical Gatherings

from

Hawaiian Church Chronicle December 1933
ARMISTICE COMMEMORATION Services in KONA CHURCHES

It seems that all these years after World War One, people still take the day very seriously. In fact, they take the whole weekend seriously:
        Friday night – Armistice Service
        Saturday – Private Devotions in chapel
        Sunday – a Special Commemoration Service

At least three churches gather to participate. Rev Masao Yamada from Kona Central Union Church, Rev. Oyakawa from Holualoa Church, DD Wallace (Rector Emeritus of Christ Church) and Bishop S. Harrington Littell shared the sermons, prayers and benedictions. A choir of young people offered a special rendering of "O God of Love, O King of Peace."

November 2002 – Thanksgiving Eve
Commitment to Living Together in Peace

During the years immediately following 9-11, Kona held an Interfaith Thanksgiving Eve Service. Reverend Carol Arney always took a major role in making it happen. The two largest church buildings in Kona—St. Michael's Catholic, and the Hongwanji Mission—took turns hosting it, though even at these sites there was an overflow of people at every door and at every open window. The service was planned by representatives from the Buddhist, Jewish, Protestant, Catholic, Baha'i and New Thought communities. Everyone brought offerings for the food bank.

We sang hymns and *God Bless America,* and *Hawai'i Aloha.* The Tongans from the Methodist church stunned us all with their haunting songs: the men in their white starched shirts and lacy apron skirts, great big strong men with babies on their shoulders. Their booming voices held us in awe, as they sang in a lilting African/ Victorian style. And then, the *Traveling Jewish Wedding Band* just about brought the house down! Literally hundreds of people were on their feet, clapping passionately, with tears running down their cheeks.

Here we were, a totally mixed crowd singing and praying and holding hope together. It seemed a beautiful, amazing moment of shared commitment and grace; we would respect each other's uniqueness; we would live in peace.

Chapter 4

"The Little Grass Shack" at Christ Church, William Gaa, civil defense and grounds keeper, and M. Talbot, USO director. 1945. (Courtesy Charlotte Miller Melrose.)

Within Our Memory

This page marks a transition in our storytelling because there are those among us who actually lived through these times. In this section we therefore move away from history books and crumbling letters, to the spoken word.

It was a pleasure and an honor to interview Thelma Tyler and Uncle Billy Paris who were born here in Kona in the 1920s. Charlotte Miller Melrose and Robert Pickens lived in the vicarage as children of past Christ Church priests. Norman Wessel is the grandson of one. Dear Father Linscott was interviewed twice before he died at 96 years of age. Others who shared their stories are descendents of native Hawaiians, Chinese, Japanese, Portuguese, Filipino, and European families. Most interviews cover several decades and so they overlap.

The interviews are edited. If you listen to one of the tape recordings, you will hear our conversations head off in many different directions, take detours, get lost, retrace covered ground. You will hear interruptions, and incomplete sentences. Usually the day after an interview I know what parts I want to use... the stories that caught my imagination. Then I go over my notes looking for the themes I want to develop. In each case I have choices to make: what to use, what to leave out. I have to make a judgment call on what is most valuable, what will hold your interest, and what story best captures the essence of the person.

If you have ever been to a large family reunion you will have heard siblings and cousins tell the same story but with a different interpretation as to what it meant or why it happened; it is kind of amazing as a social phenomenon. You may not agree with the opinions expressed in the following interviews. If you lived through these times, you will have seen things at least a little differently. But that is the beauty of our diversity.

Author Barbara Kingsolver wrote, "Memory is a complicated thing, a relative to truth but not its twin." Of course each member of the family—or a church—would remember the past differently.

KENNETH MILLER, SIXTH VICAR OF CHRIST CHURCH 1937-1944

Reverend Kenneth Miller wrote to Bishop Littell, April 1937:

> I want you to know that I am not a world beater, but simply an ordinary parish priest who knows something of the responsibilities required in the Gospel of our Lord

of His servants. I have never aspired to be a "successful priest" in a "big parish" and probably never will be successful in the way that many of the clergy seek to be. I am most happy, and my wife with me, when we can do a good work but be, at the same time, free from undue financial worry. In short, we would LOVE to accept your call, and our Charlotte Anne would love to go also.

Please do not expect too much of me, but be prepared for us to give all that we can to the work of the mission in Kona, should we go.

We have more correspondence and some good photographs of Reverend Miller, but more importantly we have little Charlotte Anne all grown up. After a life in Episcopal work around the world, she has returned to Christ Church; she says she has come full circle. Seventy years later, Charlotte Miller Melrose, looks back to share what she remembers of the great adventure of coming to Kealakekua.

"What," I ask Charlotte, "did your father bring with him to Kona?"

Her eyes light up and she is clearly proud to answer:

A fine education; he was a Yale graduate.
A beautiful voice; he had been in the Yale Glee Club, and had experience as a well-paid soloist.
A heart for other cultures and experience ministering to the Spanish Puerto Ricans and the North Jersey Dutch for 10 years.
A love for books, ideas, and his library.
A knack with tools.
A photographic eye.
An interest in science; he kept a seismograph in their home and shared his data with his friend, the volcanologist, Thomas Jagger.

"What about your mother, Gertrude? What was she like?"

Charlotte thinks for a moment and then describes her mother as beautiful, open, social, and gracious.

> Sunday dinners were always open to visitors, and she was a lovely and generous hostess... My mother loved things like having tea with Aunt Ellen or Maud Greenwell. Her education was a source of discomfort to her though, because she only had an eighth grade education... My mother was reluctant to venture opinions, but focused on pleasing others instead.

The Miller's home was where the community center is now. It had 2 stories with a servant's room upstairs. Vestry meetings were held in the house. Reverend Miller passed out cigars at the vestry meetings and the smoke floated down the hallway. Charlotte remembers crawling out of bed and down the long hall staying underneath the layer of smoke.

In his early letters we read about the beautiful garden the Millers left behind in Connecticut. It was the first real garden the family had, and they loved it. But they came to paradise, and the opportunities to create beauty were all around them.

Last summer Rev. Carol and I interviewed Father Linscott (seventh Vicar of Christ Church) and one thing he asked about was Father Miller's cherry trees. So I ask Charlotte, "Do you remember cherry trees?"

> Yes, I was in love with the cherry tree. I was an only child remember – I spent a lot of time sitting in the cherry tree . . . I was going to buy that little plot under the cherry tree. It was a very big tree and it was very climbable and you could sit in it and eat cherries; it was my refuge. [Those are the kind of things that stick in my mind.] The cherry tree was very special to me and the cherries were wonderful, sweet and dark.

"It was a rare and delicious cherry?"

"Yeah – it really was. It was right next to the porch of the church, and at the time of the year when cherries were in season, I mean, there would just be purple all over the ground."

"Father Linscott also asked if *the carnival horses* were still around. He thought they were still on the property – some kind of burlap carnival horses."

> On the back porch of the old rectory, my father had a major workshop. He loved woodworking . . . and he made a lot of crosses and candlesticks and sold them. He loved turning things on his lathe; it is what he would do in the late afternoon. I spent a long time out there with him. But carnival horses specifically? He loved making things and he could very well have made that kind of thing. He had a very playful side – he loved fun ways of learning and fun ways of doing things.

While in Connecticut, still quite young, Charlotte had learned to ride a race horse. She laughs as she describes riding the local Greenwell ranch horses with her friends. Posting was not something Hawaiian cowboys had ever seen before.

Charlotte attended the little private school at Mrs. Cushingham's home, which is now the public library. There were 2 girls and 3 boys.

Her father loved to invite people to spend time with him in his library. He loved books, he loved ideas. At parties he often sat with Charlotte and played games with her. He took her with him when he visited the mission, Waiohinu, in Kau. He also took her with him when he went to Volcano to visit his friend, Thomas Jagger. She remembers that Jagger had a little pet monkey that spit.

Gertrude started a *Girls' Friendly Society* for the locals. This was the one place where the local children and the haoles played together.

It was just like Girl Scouts – we did all kinds of craft projects; we worshiped together; we sang together. . . It was an organization of the Episcopal Church that I don't think exists anymore. I think it was a missionary outreach idea and my mother loved it, I know that. She really loved that aspect of it.

Charlotte says that she had a hanai sister for a short time: Annie Lanakila, a little Hawaiian girl from Milolii. Annie had a congenital heart defect and lived too far away for medical care. So while Charlotte was at school at Punahou, the Millers brought Annie to live with them at the vicarage.

"How would you describe her?" I ask.

"I remember her as being a very happy little girl, round cheeks and smiling. I remembered she could be very active."

She only lived to be 10 years old.

The family raised rabbits in the yard, and a pig which eventually paid Charlotte's tuition to Punahou. That is where Charlotte was boarding when World War ll came to Hawai'i. She didn't know a lot of what went on in CCE those years, but she does remember that Wallace Hall became a USO center. And she remembers that her father was directed to train locals for civil defense in the event that the Japanese invaded. Sure that invasion was imminent, many families left the Big Island and church membership dwindled.

During the war years, Charlotte came home during the summers. She worked as a waitress at the Kona Inn. She was the first haole waitress they ever had. There were plenty of servicemen there, she adds with a laugh.

According to Charlotte, Christ Church was definitely a haole church. She remembers that their faithful Filipino yardman was once told that he had to sit in the back of the church. Charlotte is tentative and a little sad as she explains that this was a disappointment for her father. He had loved his earlier multicultural ministry.

He had always had a black congregation as well as a white congregation and generally had a mixture at least in his white congregation. It had been a very mixed church in Puerto Rico. He had a full black congregation in New Jersey and a mixed one in Connecticut.

Miller had come to Hawai'i with the hope and expectation that he would serve in that way again. Outside of church Miller attended every hukilau around. Charlotte's mother started the girls club to reach out to the locals. They adopted a Hawaiian hanai child. Looking back, Charlotte concludes that nevertheless, her parents were happy in Kealakekua. They couldn't really leave because of the war, but in their own way, they found fulfillment in their life in ministry here.

But it ended way too soon, and tragically. While burning trash out in the lava tube, Reverend Miller caught on fire. Although he survived, the stress on his heart was too much; he did not recover. His bed was moved to a little place in Napo'opo'o where he could hear the waves breaking. He died of heart failure while Charlotte was away at school.

"Did your mother call you?" I ask.

"No." Although there were telephones by this time, Charlotte has no memory of ever receiving a call.

"Did your mother send a telegram?"

"No." Communications were slow and she was not told about the fire or the heart condition until later. This saddens her even now, 62 years later. She had been close to her father, and she did not get to say goodbye.

As she tells her stories, she adds the disclaimer that she was only a child. As if the view of a child isn't valuable or quite trustworthy. But I disagree: children are wise—sensitive and insightful—in many ways. Even Jesus says so.

Follow up: Girls' Friendly Society

The *Girls' Friendly Society* is an international organization affiliated with the Anglican Church.
When did it start?
The GFS was founded in 1875 by Mary Elizabeth Townsend, the first organization for women in the Church of England. It was a rector's daughter, Elizabeth Mason, who organized the first American GFS branch in 1877.

> Its purpose was to provide a place for girls who were not married and who had been sent to the city by their families to work in textile mills, to experience friendship and recreation in a fellowship of Christian love and service. As this new organization was a place for finding comfort and friendship, the name Girls' Friendly Society was decided upon.

What is the focus of the group?

> On providing a support system aimed at developing the whole person through a program of worship, service to others, study, and recreation, designed to empower girls and to help them grow mentally, emotionally, physically, and spiritually.

When I looked up the *Girls' Friendly Society* on the internet, I found a website in England that explained their current outreach to third world countries. The society has groups in 23 countries, and is open to girls of every race, religion, and nationality between the ages of 5 and 21.

According to another site, fundraising for GFS groups in the past has been through Christmas card sales. Issues of the official magazine of GFS are full of reminders to order plenty of cards early.

I wrote to a dear friend, Elaine Friedricks, 94 years of age, and a cradle Episcopalian. Did she know anything about the *Girls' Friendly Society?* Yes, Elaine did know about it. Not as a child, but as the rector's wife she helped organize a chapter for her daughters to be involved in. She remembers making capes for the girls to wear, with badges on them, symbols for things the girls earned. Elaine once taught sacred dance at their creative arts camp. She once stayed in a GFS House in London while traveling. But she didn't happen to have an old Christmas card. "The Christmas cards came later. The fundraising during my era was selling U.N. Cookbooks. As treasurer I had them all stacked under my bed."

As a member of the GFS, I promise...

To share God's love for all people,

To worship and serve faithfully,

To make my words true, and my actions right,

To grow strong in mind, body, and spirit,

To make the world a better place to live.

In the cathedral archives I found a reference to *Girls' Friendly* in Honolulu in 1907. We know that Gertrude Miller started GFS at Christ Church before WW ll, but we don't know how long it lasted.

Different Voice, Different Pen: Blood Donors of December 7, 1941
By Blake Clark
(From his book *Remember Pearl Harbor*)

This English teacher from Tennessee, eyewitness to the attack on Pearl Harbor, writes about the quiet helpers of the day, those outside the military. "In a hundred humble ways, they merely did what they could, said little, hoped, and waited." One of the ways locals contributed was to give blood. Clark documents the story of those who lined up to give blood at Queen's Hospital; 500 were in line half an hour after the radio station announced the need.

This waiting line was an amazing thing. Here were Honolulu's masses, a unique amalgam in the history of the world—a people who did not communicate with each other except on the level of pidgin English, but a people emotionally united. Honolulu society women stood in line or sat on benches by the wall beside the city's great good-humored lower classes. A well-known woman painter, a wife of a corporation president, and a waterfront washwoman waited together and talked about "what a treacherous thing it was." Japanese by the hundreds were there, many of them members of the Oahu Citizens for Home Defense Committee. Some older, alien Japanese were there too, dressed in black, which they traditionally wear on occasions where respect is due. They stood in attitudes of infinite patience, waiting to register a silent protest with their blood. A Portuguese blind boy of nineteen and his blind sister three years younger were there, brought in by their mother. They had heard the call over the radio and insisted that she bring them down.

…A bunch of huge Hawaiians came lumbering in from the Honolulu Iron Works. Dirty and oily, when they leaned against the wall, they left big smudges. They were all taken into the same room for their lettings. They laughed and joked, teasing a Puerto Rican among them who was scared. "Wait till you get that shot of brandy at the end of the line, boy. You feel numba one swell!" The average extraction was about 400 cc, or something less than a pint. Several of these Hawaiians gave 750 cc. and went back to their job at the Iron Works.

…A Dutch ship was in port for only a few hours. The entire crew came up to give their blood.

…Whole families came at once. The preferable age limits were from eighteen to fifty, but young boys lied and old men asserted their rights in order to be included in the line…

Did the Episcopalians and the Anglicans give blood? Surely they were in that line, or another one. A thousand unsung heroes participated in the daily sacrifices that were called for. ...A hundred humble ways.

INTERVIEW: ALFREIDA KIMURA FUJITA

When the Second World War started, many haole families sent their daughters to the Mainland for safety. Lorraine May (Sohm) was sent to LA. Some of the local girls were already there attending college: Dorothy Mitchell was at Vassar; Grace Bubie (Ackerman) was at Syracuse. But not every young girl had the freedom to leave: unless they were interred, the Japanese had to stay. In fact, their movement was limited; a line was drawn between South and North Kona, (near where the hospital is today) and the Japanese were not allowed to cross it without police permission.

Alfreida Kimura Fujita was here during that time, and she graciously agreed to share her memories. She has just finished a Kona Coffee Festival planning meeting, and there is paperwork all over her lanai table. "Coffee is the backbone of life here," she affirms. She has worked for the Kona Coffee Festival for a very long time: "It is my life now."

Does she have any memories of the 'Coffee Blossom Festival,' Kona's version of the 'Cherry Blossom Festival? Yes, she remembers it from when she was very little. The families all gathered together in the field; the adults drank sake, and they all clapped and sang songs. She sings part of one ... "if you get a bride, get one from Kona...she will be hard working..."

Alfreida was born in 1926 in Holualoa in her grandparents' store. She attended grammar school in Holualoa, and after school and Saturdays, attended the Japanese Language School. She learned a lot more than language, for instance sewing, exercise, and discipline. Saturday afternoons, once classes were over, the children had to clean the school, top to bottom, windows and outhouse included. "If we didn't work then we got a good licken."

December 7, 1941 Alfreida went with her friends to the beach. Mr. Nakamura, the local candy salesman, took the kids in his candy wagon. The kids were playing in the surf when they were abruptly told they had to leave. At home she found her Grandfather listening to the short wave radio in disbelief. He said "Can't be. No...Can't be," over and over again.

Alfreida said she was not afraid; it was all "just words to me." She didn't really understand what was going on. But life changed quickly.

Martial Law was declared for the first time in America since the Civil War. Black outs were mandatory throughout the islands. Short wave radios were confiscated, and those who had them were questioned.

The Japanese temples and the Language Schools were shut down immediately. The priests and the teachers were taken to the military camp at Volcano, and 40 of them were sent on to the mainland detention camps. The families of those considered potentially dangerous could go or stay. Mr. Nakamura, the candy man, had to go, and his family chose to leave with him. Alfreida watched them go, a very sad sight. Of course no one knew what would happen.

Alfreida attended high school at Konawaena, and the school bus was allowed to cross the North/South boundary. Everyone had an identification card. (As we talk Alfreida looks through all her wallets to find hers to show us.) The card has her height and weight, her blood type, and fingerprints. Everyone had them, not just the Japanese. And everyone was issued a gas mask too. The students had to have them at all times, on the bus, in the classroom. She says that even for high school graduation they wore their gowns and carried their masks. During school drills, the children had to run and hide in the coffee land. Then she was afraid.

During the war years Alfreida attended the Congregational Church in Holualoa. This is where the young gathered. She went to Bible study, and Girl Scouts; they put on plays and went on camping trips. The church really appreciated everybody's culture, she explains. She remembers her Buddhist grandparents sitting in the front row for a church play; they were proud of her, and she—looking back—is proud of them; "I really marvel my grandparents enjoyed it."

She explains a little of their story. Grandfather came to Hawai'i to build a bridge in Hilo. When he finished his job and was free, he sent for his wife. Where would they live? The wife had an uncle in Kona, so they decided to come here; they walked all the way from Hilo. As they traveled, there were always kind Hawaiians who shared their food. Alfreida remembers that her grandparents always took in the homeless Japanese, built a little house in the coffee land for them to use while in transition. These homeless were those who left the plantations, some free, some runaways. She refers to her grandfather often in her stories, remembers his wisdom, and quotes him.

During the war the Kimuras pasted newspapers over the windows, and spent their evenings downstairs underneath the store. They had kerosene lamps, but if any light got out, the block wardens yelled at them and threw rocks at the roof. Who were the block wardens? Local Portuguese or Hawaiians; they could not be Japanese.

Everything was rationed; not just rice, sugar, and gas, but everything. Alfreida remembers Gertrude Miller, from Christ Church, coming to the store often. Maybe it was because Alfreida's mother was a seamstress. With Gertrude was her tall, skinny daughter. Charlotte—that was our Charlotte. Alfreida knows Charlotte Melrose, but did not know she was the same person as the tall skinny girl from long ago.

One of Alfreida's favorite memories is of a church youth group trip. They went to sing for an encampment of soldiers. It was a Sunday; the hymns were all in English. Most of the church group was Japanese. It was a happy time and she was proud.

Later, after the war, after Alfreida was grown, she became a Girl Scout leader. This is when she came to Christ Church. Leadership meetings were either at the vicarage or at Jean Greenwell's home. Mrs. Downey was wife of the rector then, and she was very involved with Girl Scouts. Mrs. Downey became a friend and role model for Alfreida. In fact they are friends to this day, sharing birthday cards and visits over 60 years. "We got along so well...we laughed... She was a kick in the back."

My Little Grass Shack in Kealakekua Hawai`i
By Bill Cogswell, Tommy Harrison & Johnny Noble

I want to go back to my little grass shack
In Kealakekua, Hawai`i
I want to be with all the kanes and wahines
That I used to know long ago

I can hear the old guitars playing
On the beach at Hônaunau
I can hear the old Hawaiians saying
Komo mai no kâua i ka hale welakahao

It won't be long till my ship will be sailing
Back to Kona
A grand old place
That's always fair to see, you're telling me

I'm just a little Hawaiian
A homesick island boy
I want to go back to my fish and poi

I want to go back to my little grass shack
In Kealakekua, Hawai`i
Where the humuhumunukunukuâpua`a
Go swimming by

This song was first introduced in Kona, Hawai`i at the 1933 Fourth of July canoe races. It became popular everywhere. Every once in a while now, the kamaaina at church will spontaneously break into song; Meg Greenwell is the most enthusiastic. Just imagine her showing how the humuhumunukunukuâpua`a swim by.

The Little Grass Shack was made into a song in 1933, but Rev. Davis referred to it in his photography project in 1883: a 10 by 8" photograph of The Little Grass Shack sold for 25 cents. Obviously Hawai'i was full of little grass shacks, but this one must have been exceptional to get special attention by Davis, and made into a song 40 years later.

Reverend Miller built a "Little Grass Shack" for the USO which operated out of Wallace Hall at Christ Church during the Second World War. Servicemen would stand underneath the sign and have their photographs taken to send home to their loved ones. Of course soldiers were not allowed to tell their families just where they were, but since everybody knew the song, the worried families would know their boys were in Hawai'i.

Old photos of Thanksgiving Day show long tables set up on the grass outside of the historic church where a traditional dinner was served to the soldiers. They waited for their turn to stand in the "Little Grass Shack" to get their photos made.

Charlotte Miller (Melrose) came home from school in Punahou during Christmas and summer vacations, so she was a part of the activities. She remembers all those young men in uniform! But she was still young, just barely a teenager at this point. Alfreida Kimura (Fujita) was too young to attend the USO dances, but she knew older girls who did. She recalls name after name, but they are all gone now.

Question for Alfreida: Did their (Japanese) mothers feel OK about their daughters participating?

Yes, Alfreida answers. It was at a church, and the events were always in the day time ... no one could drive at night because of the blackout.

How did the girls get there? Gas was rationed, and coming from Holualoa they would have to cross the South Kona border...

Oh, the soldiers would drive around and pick up the girls [young women] in the jeeps.

FOLLOW-UP: MORE ABOUT THE USO

The United Service Organizations (USO) have provided a bridge between the American people and the U.S. military during all the wars since the Second World War. It has tried to create a place for R&R, a home away from home. The website at *missionbf.tripod.com*/USO.*htm* gives a brief history:

> Six decades ago, President Franklin Roosevelt conceived an organization--the USO--for the singular, but enduring purpose of reaching out directly from the American people to those in military uniforms who serve them. Non-governmental, but civilian and voluntary in makeup, the organization would serve as **a link of compassion and reassurance from the ordinary citizen, that America cares, remembers, and supports the service and sacrifice of those who defend her. It would deliver morale enhancing programs and services around the world. Put simply, through its unique and selfless personality and character, the USO would deliver "America"** to those far from home.
>
> Throughout World War II, USO was the channel for community participation in the war effort. In over 3,000 communities, USO centers were established to become the G.I.'s **"Home Away From Home"**. Between 1940 and 1944, U.S. troops grew from 50,000 to 12 million and their need for a variety of services grew accordingly. USO facilities were quickly opened in such unlikely places as churches, log cabins, museums, castles, barns, beach and yacht clubs, railroad sleeping cars, old mansions and storefronts.

USO programs were as varied as the places that housed them. While most aimed to provide off-duty recreation for the mostly male and fairly young service personnel, some were designed for women in uniform, while others provided child care for military wives. USO's could be many things to many people: a lively place to dance and meet people; a place to see movies or find religious counsel; a quiet place to talk or write letters; or, of course, the place to go for free coffee and doughnuts.

The USO truly made history when it came to entertaining the troops. From 1941 to 1947, USO Camp Shows presented an amazing 428,521 performances. There were sometimes 700 or more performances each day, all over the world. Over 7,000 entertainers, "brave soldiers in greasepaint" traveled overseas, from the biggest movie stars to unknown vaudevillians. Some never returned, having fallen beside the fighting men or perished en route in plane crashes. By the end of the Second World War, the USO could claim that more than 1.5 million volunteers had worked on its behalf.

Then and Now: Pidgin

By the 1930s the Japanese had become the majority of the population in Kona. They now had their own coffee farms as well as their own Buddhist temples and Shinto shrines. By this time the Japanese pioneer physician, Dr. Harvey Hayashi, had published a newspaper, "The Kona Echo" for the local Japanese. Besides his medical practice and editorial work, he also helped create an orphanage, a Japanese hospital, and several charitable organizations. Perhaps most important of all, he assisted in the creation of Japanese Language Schools for children. By keeping their language alive, they could keep the old ways alive.

On December 7, 1941, everything changed. Japanese Language Schools were immediately closed, the teachers interred. In a sincere effort to show loyalty to America, typical displays of Japanese customs disappeared, or were done only at home, quietly. No longer did the Japanese speak Japanese in public; language shifted to the local pidgin.

Da Jesus Book
2000

Because I am a recent arrival to Hawai'i, it is fair to ask, what do I know about pidgin? I know what my Hawai'i Community College students have taught me: first, they are extremely ambivalent about speaking pidgin; second, they are sure it has no rules; third, they believe that it is unique to Hawai'i. As an English instructor I know something about the history of the English language. For instance, pidgins are spoken not only in Hawai'i, but also in such far-flung places as West Africa, the Caribbean, the West Indies, and Melanesia.

Pidgins – bridge languages – began with maritime expansion in the 16th century. Sailors from various Old World nations had to find a way to communicate quickly and efficiently. In the same way, Africans from many tribes had to learn to communicate with both their captors and each other aboard slave ships. *Auxiliary languages* are created by groups of people with no common tongue. So when the Chinese, Japanese, Portuguese, Hawaiian and English needed to communicate to work a sugar plantation or a cattle ranch, a pidgin evolved. It is not broken English but a full language system. Once children learn it as their *mother tongue,* however, it becomes a Creole. Technically speaking then, none of my students speaks pidgin.

Technically speaking then, *Da Jesus Book*, published in the year 2000, is not a translation into pidgin, but Creole. Regardless of this distinction, it is an authentic Wycliff translation of the

New Testament. It offers pidgin/Creole speakers the chance to read the scriptures in a vocabulary and a language system that is truly their own

A team of 26 speakers of local Hawaiian pidgin translated the New Testament from the *original Greek*. It took them *12 years*. Reverend Franklin Chun was one of three clergymen among the translators of Da Jesus Book. He visited Christ Church several times, and used pidgin translations in his sermons. It was so beautiful to hear the Good News in a different way; we felt glad and we laughed in pleasure.

My students are generally dismayed by how many rules Standard English has. They are operating under the misconception that pidgin/Creole has no rules. Anyone who tries to fake pidgin, however, is quickly found out by any true speaker. Because case, tense, mood, and voice are generally absent from pidgins, non-native speakers are easily lost. It seems this would be particularly hard for translators, as would be imagery and symbolism, which are based on culture. Idioms (cliché, slang and proverbial expressions) carry meaning only in an original language, so are difficult for all translators in every language.

Word choice and phrasing are also challenges. See how John 3:16 has been translated: "God wen get so plenny love an aloha fo da peopo inside da world, dat he wen send me, his one an ony Boy." If you know the English verse by heart, then you can easily recognize the poetic translation: God *so loved* is now "plenny love and aloha." *Whoever believes in Him may have eternal life*" becomes "life dat stay to da max foeva." It sounds very sing-songy. According to an editor, "The truth is here – authoritative, authentic and accurate but in a new garb." In this case, an Aloha shirt.

Christ Church, of course, spoke the "Queen's English." The Hawaiian girls who attended the boarding school under Reverends Williamson and Davis were taught proper English.

But even by the 1930s, haoles made up only 2% of the local population. The members of Christ Church spoke English to each other, but most likely pidgin to their employees—cooks, gardeners, and ranch hands. I wonder how many of the members invited their workers to attend church with them. I know that the family of the Greenwell's Chinese servant, Tin Sing, is in our graveyard.

BURTON LINSCOTT, SEVENTH VICAR OF CHRIST CHURCH 1945-1950

Father Linscott is a study in blue and white. White hair and bushy white beard, bright blue eyes. Long sleeved blue silk Hawaiian shirt and white slacks. Blue socks and white shoes. He is small, spry, and absolutely charming at 95. After our greetings and introductions he asks in earnest, "Are the cherry trees still there?" He explains that they were a special kind with a split seed. Every single cherry seed split. He praises his predecessor, Father Miller, for his great gardening gift.

Father Linscott's granddaughter serves us tea. After thanking her with affection and appreciation, he backs up to the beginning of his story. Born in Maine, he wanted to avoid the cold so got an inside job. He took business courses in high school, and then worked in a bank. After ten years he looked into the future and felt uncomfortable. No one in his family had ever been to college before, but he secretly started taking classes before work, and during the noon hour, he prepared for college.

The one thing he never ever wanted to be was clergy, but once in college he loved his studies in Latin and Greek. Although raised a Baptist, eventually he became an Episcopalian. It was the beauty of the service that attracted him, especially the language of the Prayer Book. He went to General Seminary and only then could he imagine himself as a priest. He considered the possibility of becoming a monk. He believed he could stand the poverty; he believed he could stand the chastity; it was the obedience he could not commit to. After seminary his superiors decided to send him to the Virgin Islands. When they discovered he intended to take a wife, they said no, that wouldn't work. So instead they would send him to Alaska. Then they discovered he had asthma, and said no, that wouldn't work either. So they sent him to Kealakekua.

He and his bride, Jeannie, crossed the Pacific in a sailing hospital ship in 1945. Surrounded by doctors and nurses, she was seasick the whole time. She was still seasick after they landed. Finally they realized that she was pregnant. Linscott became both the father of a church and the father of two children in Kealakekua. He beams as he talks of those early wonderful years.

The vicarage at Christ Church mission had just been torn down. So the Linscotts moved into the Cushinghams' house next door to the present library. He walked to the church each day, for Morning Prayer and for Evening Prayer. He rang the bells and sometimes people came, sometimes not, but he still held the services. It rained all the time, he recalls, and because he walked back and forth several times a day, he was always wet. He was finally given a bike, and that helped some, but not in keeping him dry.

When the USO moved out of the parish hall, the Linscott family moved in. The hall continued to be used for other things though, and with two children, they needed their own space. There was money for a new vicarage. In the new plan, the roof was designed to collect water and that would dominate all other considerations.

> All the water came from the roof. That was the best water we ever had. Even to this day I remembered the excitement it always was when you had to watch your water tank. But, of course, we had so many because we had church buildings and we also had an underground cistern – that was for an emergency by the Rectory.

Father Linscott was free to design everything else for the new vicarage, and it was a joy to plan exactly what they wanted...every cupboard, window seat, book case. The materials were not first rate, but they used what they could get.

"What about ethnic interactions? Was Christ Church principally white?"

"I was aware of difficulties when I arrived," he explained. The war was over but the USO was still in the parish hall, and had an encampment on the adjoining property. The head of the military spoke to him about the soldiers suffering from shell shock. These soldiers had trouble distinguishing the local Japanese from the Japanese they fought, so Japanese were not allowed on the property. It was for their own safety, it was explained. It was an awkward problem for our congregation, he admits, but it was only for a short time.

When the USO left, they gave him their car. Now he could visit his parishioners and reach out to the greater community.

One special friend was Mr. Seichi Nakamura. He was the local grocer, and he supplied the Linscott household with all their needs. During the shortages, he saved the best for them. When Father Linscott heard that Nakamura was ill, he came regularly to visit. Mr. Nakamura was a Buddhist, but over the visits, he asked many questions about Christianity. Early morning became the most difficult time for the patient, and so Father began to visit him every morning at 4:00, to pray with him until he could take his medicine. Mrs. Nakamura would make Father Linscott rice soup for breakfast.

Mr. Nakamura asked to be baptized on his birthday, Christmas Eve, before he died. Mrs. Nakamura and her six children asked to be baptized with him. Without Linscott's knowledge, Mr. Nakamura had been teaching his family everything he had learned about the faith. On Christmas Eve, they were all baptized at Christ Church. He says, "I had to chase around and get godparents for them all." Each child insisted on answering the baptismal questions individually – not as a group. They were so proud!

When Mr. Nakamura died a few weeks later, he was buried in CCE cemetery. The Buddhist community gave a funeral feast and insisted that Linscott attend. They welcomed him as one of them. They also insisted that he eat the very special raw fish served. Linscott admits he was quite skittish about eating raw fish, but he could see no way gracefully out of it. He laughs now and confesses that he really enjoyed his first taste of sushi.

The Nakamura children became acolytes and sang in the choir. Father says there was complete acceptance of the Japanese community. The difficulties were not racial, but differences in customs.

There was also a Japanese Boy Scout troop at the church:

> They were always there every weekend. There was no place for them except outside but they did all of their drilling and all the rest. Originally we had the baker – who was local and Japanese. His grandfather was getting quite old and he said 'I just can't leave my grandfather to do all the work so he had to give it up. I took it over for a little while then the youngest of the Greenwell sons – he became Scout Master – he was very good. He took us down to Ka-awa-loa for an outing overnight – but he rode his horse and all of the rest of us walked. He offered me a horse—but I only rode on a horse once and I couldn't walk for days afterwards—so I said 'I'll walk with the boys.'
>
> That was an interesting thing. You know, if it hadn't have been for that I would not have gotten to the actual spot where Captain Cook was killed. That is the private property of the Greenwell Ranch. You can see the Monument through the water.

In 1950 the Bishop called Father Linscott to Epiphany Church, Oahu, and so the family left lovely Kealakekua. The goodbye party was held at Teshima's and the restaurant was full. During the meal, the eruptions of Mauna Loa began, and the parishioners joked that these "fireworks" were part of their goodbye.

Father asks us if we would like to see a picture of a beautiful lady. We say yes, and he opens his wallet to show us a photograph of Jeannie. She lived until 90, he tells us with pride.

Throughout this interview he has used the phrases "she was a delight to me..." "He/she/it was a joy to me." These words were sprinkled all through his reminiscing. They seem to reveal a heart full of praise and thanksgiving.

As we say our goodbyes at the door, Father Linscott asks one last question of us: "What about the carnival horses? Are they still there?"

Different Voice, Different Pen: In Memory
By Joan Coupe

The Rev. Burton L. Linscott, 96, of Kaimukí, died Jan. 13, 2010. Born in Bar Harbor, Maine. Arrived in Hawai'i in 1945 as a missionary; retired after 28 years as the minister and principal of Epiphany Church and School. Survived by son, John; daughter, Betty Taylor Hardaway; four grandchildren; four great-grandchildren; caregiver and niece, Pat Saunders. Service 11 a.m. Saturday at Epiphany Episcopal Church. No flowers. Donations to the Father Burton Linscott Memorial Fund, Epiphany Church, 1041 10th Ave., Honolulu, HI 96816.

Father Linscott was a person of unending energy. He taught school, held two services every Sunday, was in charge of the youth choir, and got the entire church out to help with projects. He organized the planting of all the grass below Wallace Hall. I can still see him out there with a shovel digging away. He was very white skinned, but he had shorts on and his shirt and clerical collar. Sweat was pouring down but he didn't stop. He gave us children the job of separating the grass clumps and delivering them to the adults to plant. By the end of the day the place had been completely done and was beautiful.

He was an excellent teacher. He taught grades three to eight all in one room in Wallace Hall. The room was divided by blackboards, so another teacher taught the younger ones there. He not only taught all the different school subjects but religion and PE too.

I will never forget the day I cheated with my cousin on a spelling test. He did not say a word until after school. He asked us to come to him and he said he knew that we had cheated. The punishment was to write 100 times "I will never cheat again." He, of course, called our parents so they would not worry. He also told them not to punish us anymore, as he had taken care of it. To this day I have never cheated again and I cannot tolerate it when I see someone else cheat.

Father Linscott's art classes were absolutely unbelievable. We did things like soap carvings, potato prints, and art for Palm Sunday and Christmas. These art classes were usually held in the sacristy. Once he organized a circus type performance; we made costumes, paper Mache animals, and balance beams. Konawaena High School was so impressed they invited us to perform at their May Day program.

Father Linscott's spirituality was his most outstanding attribute. He taught us to love God, respect the church and love others. He taught our children's choir. We even sang some of the songs in Latin; he explained all the words to us.

He was strict! In these days we did not wear shoes to school; however, he insisted that we wear them in church. I can still remember the excitement of lining up outside and following the acolytes with the cross and Father Linscott into the church. We were taught never to turn around in church, never laugh or talk. If we dropped a prayer book, to bring it to him to be blessed. The church was usually filled for family worship, so we were always in the choir stalls. It was a very special feeling for a fourth grader!

To this day I feel that Father Linscott has influenced me more than anyone else besides my parents. Father Linscott: A working Minister—A caring Teacher and A Teacher of the Episcopal Faith.

Commentary: Passing the Peace

It is hot, dark, and dusty in the storage room. How long has it been since anyone came in here? The fireproof file cabinet bought by the McKinney vestry is in the corner. We find the old record books. Book of baptisms, marriages, confirmations, death. Names we know jump out: Machado, Roy, Ackerman, Wallace, Greenwell. Some have a check by the name, some have x's.

Kealoha Roy is in the kitchen nearby. She is the head of the Hawaiian Immersion Pre-school here in Wallace Hall. Reverend Carol calls out, "Here are some Roys....." and starts listing first names.

"That's my uncle…that's my other uncle…I'm in there too." Kealoha was baptized here, by Father Linscott. She attended here as a child. Not now though, and not for a long time. Why did she (and her whole family) leave? Have they gone to another church? Or dropped out all together?

Rev. Carol says that most have married into other families, or moved away. Sometimes it is medical problems that take people to the mainland, or job transfers. Recently it is the vog.

We feel like celebrating when we find the entry concerning the Nakamura family: six Nakamuras baptized on Christmas Eve 1947! And then, the burial in January.

Most memories I have collected are good and positive memories, but I have also heard bitterness expressed. I have heard complaints based on what appear to be rumors. I think there is a "Book of Grudges" here too, and a long ragged list of old hurts never healed, too often never revealed. Resentments and prejudices and injustices, misconceptions decades old, *nurtured carefully*. How can this go on in a faith community built on the ideal of forgiveness?

"Passing the peace" was originally designed for the forgiveness of our neighbors. One was not supposed to receive Eucharist until one made sure one's own heart was clean. To be at peace with neighbors in church was to release them from whatever you held against them. At the altar, you shared in the Great Thanksgiving receiving heavenly food and wine together. It is the symbolic food for the journey in this land where forgiveness reigns; it is a beautiful ritual. I fear its meaning is forgotten and passing the peace is just a social break.

The Book of Grudges should have a little cross marked by each name.

CHAPTER 5

Christmas Choir @1940. (Courtesy Kona Historical Society.)

A few of my favorite things about living on our island: pink shower trees, saffron finches, roadside lei stands, afternoon tropical rain, balmy nights, turquoise water. And the fragrances! Angel trumpets after dark, so sweet that they make me swoon. In the mornings, the rich heavy smell of roasting coffee beans spreading out for a mile or so in every direction.

A poet named Sarah wrote a poem about coffee that reminds me to be thankful for simple pleasures. It also reminds me to value the people who make those pleasures possible.

Morning Prayer in the Celtic Style
By Sarah Blackmun

> Bless the one who brews the coffee
> Bless the one who brings the coffee
> Bless the growers and the reapers
> Bless the roasters and the grinders
> Bless the machines that grind and roast
> Bless to me the strong smell
> Bless to me the first sip
> Bless to me the last gulp

INTERVIEW: TERRY ANGELEO

If the land could speak for itself, what stories it could tell. The soil, the trees, the flowers and the earthworms could tell of their work, their struggle, and their glory days. They could tell of newcomers and transplants, of extinction. Perhaps they would tell stories of the children who played in and around them. Or the gardeners who cared for them. If I could interview all of the groundsmen that served as stewards of this sacred ground, I would have a very different history of Christ Church.

I meet Terry Angeleo, current groundsman, down by the coffee plants. He is carrying two pumpkin squash and lays them in the bed of the truck. He explains that he planted them in between the coffee rows to cut down on the weeds. Now the vines are climbing the coffee trees and the weight (of the pumpkins) is becoming a problem. He offers them to me, one or both. We sit on the tailgate of his truck in the shade.

Terry is from the Philippines, and from *small kid time* he learned a lot from the Anglican Church there. He was baptized at three. He remembers that in all the excitement, he tore the baptismal certificate in half. In fact, he still has half of it.

As a child Terry attended the missionary school. Eventually he worked for the Cathedral compound, which includes St.

Andrew's Seminary, Trinity University, and St. Mary's. He served as landscaper, groundsman and sacristan.

Now, here at Christ Church, Terry tends all of the property including the cemetery and the coffee land. He does some landscaping, some improvement, lots of weeding and pruning. If there was more time and more money, he says, he would keep it like a park. There is a beautiful Gold Tree that he would like to plant.

Which are the oldest trees on the property? The row of Cyprus standing at attention along the walkway. Or maybe these big coconut palms in the front corner. Since trees in Hawai'i don't have seasonal rings to count for years, how can we know how old they are? Only from some old written record by the person planting them.

Perhaps, he adds, the oldest thing on the property is the cement slab between the mango tree and the rock wall that separates the cemetery from Wallace Hall. Sherwood and Norman Greenwell showed it to him and explained it was from the old sugar mill.

Terry points out the things he planted. The medicinal red ginger by the entrance. The Queen Emma Lilies, a gift from Brenda Machado. The poinsettias from the first Christmas celebrated in the new community center. The newest plants on the property are the ones around the labyrinth. Terry built the labyrinth too, although he didn't really know what a labyrinth was. He followed a pattern, placing steppingstones into a circular pathway into its own center. He'd like to work on it more now, but there really isn't enough time.

The messy and invasive African Tulip Tree needs to be cleaned up or removed. The roots of the trees by the cemetery are pushing up the nearest graves. Plants that block the view from the highway need to be pruned, but other trees were planted precisely to block the storage areas. Everywhere there are jobs to be done. Terry sees the details, whereas I see the big picture, lovely and lush. One of his sons helps him when he can. Terry has six children. I remember when his twin sons came home from serving in Iraq. There was a big, bold sign on the rock wall: "Welcome home Peter and Paul!"

I tell Terry that I have twin sons too. On special occasions I send them the coffee he harvests here, on Christ Church land.

FOLLOW-UP: PUMPKIN SQUASH SOUP

Bake Japanese Kabocha or African kobota pumpkin squash in oven until soft. Cut open and remove seeds. Put pumpkin in soup pan with water or broth and simmer. Sautee onion, garlic and ginger. Add to pumpkin. When ready to serve, put chunky mixture in blender and blend until smooth. Serve with sour cream /or fromage blanc and, cinnamon /or nutmeg. Tastes even better after a day or two. OK to freeze.

FAMILY TREE

There are numerous references in the Hawaiian Church Chronicle about the beauty and peacefulness of our church grounds, "God's half acre." One writer states it was "enlarged and brought up to its present comely appearance by the Rev. S.H. Davis and kept in order by the loving care of the present rector, it stands in its sweet surroundings, an inspiration towards every thing that is good and true."

Notice that the vicar gets all the credit? Of course, most likely, a gardener did the lion's share of the actual work.

Before service this morning, (8-15-10) Natsuko Aoki handed me a wrinkled Xerox paper that came from a family reunion. It concerns the Aoki family, their arrival in Hawai'i and their work in Kealakekua. According to this, Bunzo Aoki and his wife Tano, (whose name he took by yo-shi marriage custom) worked at Christ Episcopal Rectory. Beginning in 1891, "they lived in a cottage on the church grounds while Bunzo worked as a yardman and Tano helped with the household chores for the pastor's family." They had 2 children there. Eventually they moved to a coffee farm and had four more children.

What else do we know about this couple from Kumamoto, Japan?

> In addition to the farm work, Bunzo established a reputation as a master stonewall builder. He was also known for his culinary skills, particularly vegetable carving and was often asked to chef for parties held by his friends and relatives. In the meantime, Tano was involved helping others with home births of babies. With the encouragement and assistance of the local physician, Dr. Dickson, Tano became licensed as a midwife in 1926. This enabled her to deliver many of her grandchildren.

One of these grandsons grew up to marry Natsuko. Their daughter is Diane Aoki, church member and playwright. Diane is the great grandchild of the yardman and housecleaner/midwife for Christ Church at the turn of the century. Perhaps Bunzo is the one who planted the oldest trees on the property.

INTERVIEW: TERRY ANGELEO #2

Terry calls to say that he has thought of more things to tell me about the plant life of CCE. He asks me to meet him in the morning. When I drive into the parking lot, I don't see Terry, but I see his wife, Julia, weeding. She is a silent volunteer involved in a secret tithe of labor.

There is a new purple jacaranda that Terry has just planted. Planting a new tree on church property is important, and he is sure that I will want to document it in the history book. Today, March 29, 2008, a jacaranda is planted to shade the newly restored east wall of the historic church. The expert who worked on the wall talked to Terry about it; the hot tropical sun is hard on the church, and this new wall needs some protection. Terry has provided it and he is proud.

Turning around to face the other direction, we admire the giant magnolia tree. It is probably as old as the church. Could Reverend Williamson have planted it? There is no way to know. There are a few stories about it. One is the wedding of Maude Wodehouse; when it was time for the ceremony to begin, the bride had no bouquet. Someone ran out and picked giant, gorgeous magnolias from this tree for her to carry.

We move up close so that Terry can show me something peculiar. The vicarage was once near by, and there was a chain from it to the tree. Terry says it was to keep the high school kids out. The vicarage is long gone, the chain was forgotten and the tree grew around it. Now the padlock sticks out like a little sore thumb, a permanent part of the tree. You can still spin the dial.

Terry has set orchids around the trunk about shoulder high. The roots have taken hold and the plant has encircled much of it, made itself at home. Until last week. The newest generation of high school malcontents was back, ripping the orchids off, stomping on the purple flowers underneath, bored and restless in their misdirected angst.

We wander around and Terry points out the puakenikeni planted at Barry Machaedo's funeral, the camellias that are good for green tea, and the shower tree that blooms in both pink and yellow. Then Terry mentions the cherry trees down by the preschool. . . the cherry trees that both Charlotte Miller and Father Linscott spoke of so fondly? We go down to see, but these are not old at all; they are not big enough for a child to climb. They may, however, be the grandchildren of those old beloved trees. There are no cherries at this time to see if they have the famous split seeds.

Our last stop is to check on the calabash gourds growing behind Wallace Hall. Terry stomps around, picks out two and gives them to me: one to make into an ipo [traditional gourd drum,] the other to carve. He points out that the second will make a perfect turtle.

Different Voice, Different Pen: Henri Pickens, Eighth Vicar of Christ Church, 1950

One day, out of the blue, a man walked into the office and identified himself as the son of Reverend Pickens. He said that he had lived here briefly, as a child. He offered us part of his father's memoirs. The son also wrote his own memories for us to use in this project. The two follow below, unedited.

Christ Church, Kealakekua May 1, 2008
Attached is an excerpt from my father's unpublished autobiography covering his brief stay in Kealakekua. It is rather personal, however he passed away several years ago and I suspect most of the Greenwell's of the time have also gone elsewhere.

My memories of Kona in those days are very fond. I was born in China in 1940, and came to Kona in 1950 as a 10-year old youngster when my parents and younger sister moved there from Ke-kaha, Kaua'i. As it happened, they flew via Honolulu, however I had a pet dog so rode the inter-island ferry from Kaua'i overnight, and was carried ashore on a small boat along with my dog and other passengers bound for the Big Island, an interesting experience in itself.

The rectory at that time had a main floor where my parents and younger sister (then 4-5) lived, and small room downstairs which was my bedroom. I didn't much care for the arrangement as there was then a banana plantation next door, and the banana spiders would occasionally try to share the room with me.

I enjoyed the school and the playground, and followed the Japanese gardener around watching him graft various bushes and flowers together. I particularly enjoyed the occasional dynamite explosion when it was necessary to free up some space for another few graves in the graveyard (often for one of the Greenwells).

Trips were also exciting…we went down to Kailua-Kona maybe a couple of times per month, and swam in the pool at the Kona Inn. Occasionally we made the long trek to Hilo, stopping at times at the volcano and several times at Kala-pana Black Sand beach, a wonderful spot before Pele covered it up a few years ago.

And I fondly remember the last great cattle roundup and loading onto the boats offshore, which was hugely exciting.

I never wanted to leave the islands, so when I finally retired from the US Air Force after 25 years active duty I came back, and have lived here ever since.

Richard H. ("Dick") Pickens

KEALAKEKUA, HAWAI'I by Henri Pickens, Vicar

After about eighteen months on Kaua'i a job fell open on the Big Island, and Bishop Kennedy thought I might be able to handle it. I liked the idea, and suggested that Kekaha be dropped to a lower status under the care of the vicar at 'Ele'ele, only twelve miles away. This was done, and a visit in 1986 showed that the church remained in this limbo, just as I had suggested almost forty years before.

We arrived in lovely Kealakekua not long after the eruption of 1950, when lava across the main highway was still very warm and thick. Living mauka (up the mountain) at the 1,500 foot level was pleasant, and the ocean could be seen just down there over the bulging slope of Mauna Loa.

The USO had used the church lawn for "The Little Grass Shack in Kealakekua", but after the war (WWII) the shack was moved makai (to the sea) to Kailua as a tourist attraction among many others along the Kona coast of the "Big Island".

At the church was a school named Waipu'ilani. This explains why I was sent there, and why I departed. My predecessor had built up the school with the aid of the local gentry, who did not wish their kids to attend Konawaena public school, with so many nisei [children of Japanese immigrants] children. Waipu'ilani offered a way out, just as did the Hawaiian Episcopal Academy. The latter prep school had just been founded in Waimea, close by the huge Parker Ranch. It has now dropped the Episcopal connection, and become privately secular, while old Waipu'ilani no longer lives.

My jobs at Waipu'ilani were many. I was headmaster of this small private elementary school. Yoshie Kawasaki was most adorable as the teacher for the nursery. Her children belonged to the numerous varieties best seen in Hawai'i: Haole and Hapahaoli, Japanese, full Hawaiian and mixtures. A teacher was hired for grades one to three, and I was the one to teach the rest of the children. My class comprised the grades from four through eight, all in one room (an open porch). All appropriate school subjects were taught, so to speak, and I ran the athletic program as well. I forget whether we saluted, prayed, or did the other stuff recently proclaimed as essential to national survival. In fact, if any of my teaching went right, it should rank as a miracle. I was also treasurer, which was right on the penny, I might add. The combination of Parish and school life at Christ Church, Kealakekua, enabled us to find and keep a cadre of friends over many subsequent years. The work load, however, was far too heavy for such a lovely locale. As it was in Ke-kaha, so it was not in Kealakekua. I never found the right balance.

Taking the services and visiting the well, as well as the sick, I thought a good beginning of my tour of duty at the small parish. The building and some furnishings had come around the Horn, like the tall cedars at the cemetery, mostly to serve the churchy or religious needs of the land-owning ranchers, with their strong links to England.

The family of Greenwells, like others of pioneer lineage, built and paid for these family chapels, of which Christ Church was one. [Commonly believed, but not accurate.] The small colorful and attractive church building, and its adjacent cemetery, stood close to elderly Maude Greenwell's heart, as well as her property values. Any parish dinner would include (free) delightful and tender filet mignon, thanks to generous Ma Greenwell.

Pie shaped land grants ran from the peak of Mauna Loa to the sea, many thousands of feet below. At the 5000 foot level, old ranch houses were full of Greenwell history and, as with the other divisions of the property among the sons, each was hard to get to, but delightful once there. Water was a bit of a problem in Kona, on the dry side of the Big Island. Old bathtubs were often used to serve the thirsty cattle, much as huge wooden tanks were used for family houses far down the mountain. These wooden tanks were at hazard during earthquakes, and occasionally a season's supply of water was lost as the result of a big quake.

Things have changed at Christ Church since then, as they have for Kona, generally, now that the jet age has come to stay. The parade of Vicars and Rectors continues, with no clear hope or expectation of clerical stability along Hawai'i's loveliest coast. In fact, Kealakekua is actually a tourist spot now, and Christ Church has status as a genuine historic monument which, it is said, is no longer safe for public worship, especially with Rite Two.

Buddhism among the local Japanese nisei came with the coffee business of the Kona coast. At the temples they often sang a familiar hymn, "Onward Buddhist Soldiers", much as Christians used to do. Kealakekua was then an area with wealth in cows and Kona coffee, which has somewhat changed lately out of a need to welcome tourism and orchids. There is still room for Buddhist temples and businesses, and a strong incentive to make changes from the old ways, building a more modern Kealakekua. One of the exciting "old ways" was shut down just before we left to start a new life on the mainland. I refer to the periodic cattle loading in Kailua Bay.

One of Kona's last cattle loading events took place at Kailua in 1950. The herd and attending cowboys moved from the ranches through town, and with much prodding and mooing the cows went into the water one by one. Afloat, each cow was guided to an awaiting long boat and tied on. These small boats with their full quotas of beef then rowed out to the larger ships where the wet cattle were hoisted aboard. Once loaded, these ships sailed off to the Honolulu market.

Spectators, enjoying the sights, cheered when any single cow broke loose and swam about in momentary freedom until cowboys could catch them, which they did with much noisy whooping and tossing of ropes at horns on errant bovines. This colorful activity is now another lost memory of Kona's earlier days.

Kona owes much to this progress, some of it to a talented family, once resident makai, close to the blue unpolluted Pacific, with two darling twin daughters. Curt Crellin had much to do with the over development of Kona, and left a fat fortune for his children and Lou. They often visited us in our home, not least among which was the one in Dhahran in 1967. Unfortunately, Curt died in 1980. Lou remarried some years later.

Diane was a cute little girl who was companion for Janet, as her parents, Kay and Andy Dorsey, were for us. Andy, Master Sgt. USA, did not like the soft way recruits were pampered in the new army during the Korean War, so he retired to the ROTC program. Kay was an army nurse with much musical talent. We have been friends a long, long time. Hawaiian glue often really made relationships stick once they were formed in that year at Kealakekua.

For some cause not known to me, one of the numerous Greenwell sons chose to threaten my children, so I flew off to see the Bishop, since I was none too sure Jack had not actually lost all of his buttons this time. I forget how it came out, but most of the Greenwell tribe was embarrassed. The Diocese decided to close the school. I was asked to move to Honolulu and take on a chaplaincy job at 'Io-lani School for boys, but declined.

This time I felt it wiser to call it quits, after so many years trying to be a disoriented worker in evangelism. I thought it best to take my children home for a real American education. In those days that made sense, I think.

Historical Context: Statehood

I find an old LIFE magazine, dusty and fragile, in my parents' garage. It is dated January 26, 1959. The cover shows a saber-toothed tiger preying on a guanaco. The headlines: *Black Africa in Tumult/Darwin's Discovery – A Fossil World of Extraordinary Animals.*

The most interesting story I find inside is about Alaska. The photographs show children waiting for a school bus in the dark, a mother taking frozen pajamas off a clothes line, a mailman with a flashlight at 3:30 in the afternoon. The story begins,

> Last week the Artic sun was casting its frosty sparkle over Fairbanks less than five hours a day, just as it had been doing in Alaska at this time of the year since modern man has measured time. But this 30 below scene, this month, interested more Americans than had ever been the case since Secretary Seward and the Russian minister closed a 4:00 a.m. deal for Alaska in 1867. Next week the first legislature of the 49th state convenes, even though the new 49-star flag does not become official until July 4th.

The fate of Hawai'i is linked to that of Alaska, at least in the halls of Congress. As candidates for admission, the two territories are tied together; *both*, or *neither*, will be granted this status. There is no mention, no hint of this in the essay celebrating Alaska. Nonetheless, LIFE magazine offers a wonderful glimpse into the life of Americana that the two will join.

It is of note that LIFE's lead articles have black and white photography while the ads are in color. The ads are a history lesson by themselves. Let me describe two.

Inside the front cover: "**Go Rambler for '59** – the Compact Car/Get the Best of Both – Big Car Room—Small Car Economy." A clumsy looking brown sedan is parked on snow, with a smiling family holding ski equipment nearby. The suggested price for the car—delivered—is $1835.

The back cover shows a pretty housewife stretched out on a chair with her feet up. She is laughing on the phone. There is a vacuum cleaner at her feet, a small bottle at her elbow. The caption reads "**Only Coca-Cola** gives you the cheerful lift that's bright and lively . . . the cold crisp taste that so deeply satisfies!

No wonder it's the real refreshment. . . anytime. . . anywhere! **Pause . . . for Coke!**"

In terms of world significance, 1959 was the year the first computer microchip was produced. It was the year that Fidel Castro led a successful revolution in Cuba. And it was the year of the "Kitchen Debate" between Nikita Khrushchev and Richard Nixon in Moscow.

What happened in 1959 closer to home? James Michener published Hawai'i. In Oahu, Martin Luther King spoke at Punahou. On the Big Island, Ki-lau-ea Iki erupted. At Christ Church Reverend William Smyth served his last year as priest.

There is not a lot of information about statehood day on the World Wide Web, only a few facts and a general statement that "the neutrality of the information is in question". (Apparently the political activists fighting against statehood contest all the details.)

One uncontested fact is that on March 12, 1959, the members of the United States House of Representatives voted for statehood for Hawai'i. Gavin Daws describes it:

> The news reached the islands within minutes. It was a pleasant spring morning in Honolulu, and no one felt like working. Offices and stores emptied out, the streets filled up, the bells of all the churches rang, civil defense sirens wailed (a take cover signal, oddly enough), a lot of beer was drunk.

I remember the day; it was announced in my California primary school during social studies. I felt joy at the news. Of course, I was only a child and knew absolutely nothing about the politics or the issues. I was just proud that this amazing exotic paradise was now part of us, as if it were a marriage, and the goodness of the new in-laws would spill out over me.

But one thing did bother me. My grandmother had a beautiful handmade quilt of all the state flowers. She and her church friends had embroidered the flowers—poppy, Indian paintbrush, magnolia—onto a peach colored background, long before I was born. I knew that there were 48 squares/states and flowers on the quilt, and I worried—with sincere childish regret, because the quilt would now be forever wrong! And, of course, the American flag too. But the president thought of that, so he passed another bill that allowed the addition of two new stars to the field of blue on the American flag.

Formal statehood for Hawai'i took place on August 21. Of everything I have read about statehood, the one beautiful statement I found was from "The Statehood Sermon," given by Abraham K. Akaka on Radio Station KAIM. It has nothing political or patriotic in it, rather Akaka calls on Hawai'i to remember a far greater reality.

> One of the first sentences I learned from my mother in my childhood was this from Holy Scriptures, "Aloha Ke Akua."
> In other words, "Aloha is God." [Aloha is Love].
> Aloha is the power of God seeking to unite what is separated in the world—the power which unites heart with heart,
> soul with soul,
> life with life,
> culture with culture,
> race with race,
> nation with nation.
> It is the power that reunites a man with himself when he has become separated from the God within.

The 50th state became the "Aloha State." Akaka defines *aloha* as "united with affection in our common life." What a gift to offer to the country. . . to the world.

INTERVIEW: BILLY PARIS

The first time I saw Uncle Billy Paris was at a memorial service. Reverend Carol had pneumonia, and she asked Uncle

Billy to be her substitute. When he spoke, it was clear that he knew a whole lot of local history. It was also clear that he was loved by the listening crowd. I remember that he prayed in Hawaiian, and that he reminded us "sorrow is not for the deceased."

For our interview, we are in Reverend Carol's office. She asks, "What are some of the details of your childhood?"

Uncle Billy explains that the original Paris cottage is the oldest standing house in Kona today. Built in 1854, it is located on the road to Na-po'opo'o; his sister lives in it. Billy was born in the cottage next door in 1922. It had a stone kitchen, which he loved. It was damaged in the 1929 earthquake, ruined in the next one. He remembers watching his mother pack lunches every day for the cowboys. She wrapped meat and rice inside a ti leaf, and then that was wrapped up in newspaper.

When Billy was little he enjoyed being around the cowboys. When he was big enough, he enjoyed working with them.

"It was wonderful to be in that community," he says wistfully. Billy learned to speak Hawaiian from those cowboys, and from hearing it in church.

He remembers that his family raised angora goats for a while. They shipped the pelts to the Middle East for rug making. This was eventually stopped, as the goats were too hard on the land. He talks about cattle, water, roads and transportation problems back in the old days.

Everybody within three miles of school walked every day. There was a bus for kids who lived farther than that. Any child could ride it, but kids who lived in the three mile limit had to pay. Since there was a depression going on, the kids walked. There was a little store where *The Grass Shack* is now, and it is best remembered as a place to buy ice cream on the way home.

The main road was paved, but that was all. Ali'i Drive, even Palani, were just gravel paths. There was a hospital above where the bank sits now, and two doctors for the entire Kona area. They made house calls and the ambulance was their car. There was no fire department, but fear of fire was significant, and so at his home, there was a hose at each corner.

He talks about how hard the Japanese kids had to work, and how sometimes their fathers suffered injustice.

Reverend Carol shows Uncle Billy the list of all the reverends in the 140 years of CCE. Billy looks over the list and then tells us that DD Wallace baptized him in 1923. Although Billy is the descendent of the New England missionaries, his mother was an Episcopalian, so for 12 years he attended CCE. When his family moved to Kainaliu, he joined Lanakila, his great grandfather's church, and has stayed until now, except for all the times he visited other churches. He lists several, including the small Episcopal mission Carol and I discovered in some old papers. He remembers it as "a cute little church" located near Hina Lani.

Billy has an ecumenical heart. "I've been exposed to English ministers; I've been exposed to Hawaiian ministers." Even while dodging bullets in Europe, he says, he didn't care what denomination a church was, he just wanted to worship God. This is one way Hawai'i has changed; "I see the harmony of churches a lot better today."

Reverend Miller was his Boy Scout master. "He was interested in the youth, especially boys. He kept a lot of us out of trouble."

Linscott? Oh yes, he brought a lot of high church. Lots of catholic stuff in the service. As a teenager, Billy was so interested that he attended Father Linscott's early Sunday service, and made it back to Lanakela Church for the later service.

What about Norman Alter? Billy shifts in his seat, leans back and smiles.

"I loved him. Great guy. His ministry was in Hilo before he retired to Kona. My aunt used to go to his church in Hilo. He had a wonderful personality; he was always jolly. He would come to parties and talk to me. Everything was always a pleasure. I knew him in Hilo especially while courting my wife Bertha... He joined us even when we were kicking up our heels.

"I'd say he was an *all around person*. Whether it be social or at the church. He gave a wonderful sermon, preached God's word, yet it wasn't over anybody's head. He was a wonderful deliverer, that I remember."

His eyes scan the list. Did you know Dr. Yeh? Billy laughs, "He was a jolly guy. Kind of punchy." He laughs again. "He had a big boat. Towed it with a jeep. The road was steep going up to his house." He laughs again picturing it. "He didn't have enough horse power."

What else do you remember about him?

"He had smart kids."

Did you know Reg Rodman?

"I liked him. He had an outrigger canoe. He was very active in the canoe club."

Were you aware of the conflict in those days?

"Yeah, there were firecrackers over tearing down the church."

Billy is nostalgic for the Sundays of yesteryear, "church was more a part of people. You would stay several hours, go to meet friends, the pace of life was different. You didn't have all the outside activities. You didn't have transportation."

Reverend Carol points out, "You spent most of your life as a rancher and a farmer, but everybody respects you as a kahu, invites you to give blessings."

"If you love God, it is not too hard. Know your scriptures, read the Bible, that's not too hard to do," he answers. Then he adds, "Every generation gets further and further from Hawaiian."

Billy's memories return to Alter again.

"He was a great person and I loved his funeral services... he always said,

'Sorrow not for the deceased...he is at peace...he is no longer suffering, and from now on, he is in the care of God. You sorrow for yourself when you have lost someone you love.'

Between the memorial service last summer and this interview, Uncle Billy lost one of his daughters. The words are an affirmation, not an abstraction.

Different Voice, Different Pen: Vicar Irwin McKinney
By Maile Melrose

Father Bob Brown and his glamorous wife left Christ Church in 1967. His enthusiasm for creating youth groups and inviting hippies into church shook up a lot of people. Deep sighs of relief, from both pulpit and pew, may have been heard after his departure. Father Tom Kunichika of Waimea, always a favorite visiting priest, filled in the gap until Bishop Harry Kennedy sent a veteran to steer Christ Church safely into a new decade.

The arrival of Vicar Irwin McKinney and his wife at Christ Church can best be compared to the dawning of a sunny day after a period of clouds and rain. His years of experience, his friendly wife who somehow looked like a clergyman's wife (she did not smoke mini-cigars), and his kindly voice instilled peace and happiness in the congregation. Like a favorite grandfather, warm and wise, cheerful and hard working, easy going and polite, Irwin McKinney fit right in. His stay in Kona could not be permanent, but it was a welcome change. One lasting contribution to Christ Church completed under Rev. Irwin McKinney's watchful care deserves special recognition.

Kona Historical Society archives hold a record of Mr. McKinney's correspondence with the A.J. Bayer Company, art metal fabricators, of Torrance, California. In February of 1968, he wrote: "Perhaps you can help us to solve a problem? In this 100 plus-year-old churchyard there are about sixty unmarked graves, some of which we can associate with names, but many are, as we say, 'unknown to man, known only to God.' It is our plan to begin a program of marking these graves. Would you be interested in quoting us a quantity price or an estimate?" In this way, his search for the best designed, most affordable, and most lasting metal markers for these unidentified graves began. Fortunately, A.J. Bayer believed in Bronze ~ The Ageless Metal of Eternity ~ and they welcomed the opportunity to assist.

After several letters to and fro – how quaint the postal system seems today in this era of instant communication – Mr. McKinney sent off the church's first order on April 6, 1968.

"Please accept our order for 36 bronze memorials in your #601 Puritan design in the 16" x 8" size which you have quoted to us at $29.00 each delivered. This order is a start on our program to mark the hitherto unmarked graves in our cemetery. As funds permit, we will place further orders with you, in at least dozen lots.

Yours faithfully, Irwin McKinney"

More letters flew back and forth, clarifying the best method of affixing plaques to concrete blocks (epoxy or screws), and double checking spelling and dates of the dearly departed. During this process, members of the congregation died. With confidence, Mr. McKinney carefully ordered plaques in the Tranquility or Destiny style. On July 30, 1968, Mr. McKinney wrote, "It is a pleasure to do business with you folks." In another letter, he said, "Thank goodness for your catalogue!! With it I can match up with a former order for an adjacent grave."

After the plaques arrived, the daunting task of installing them fell to the Cemetery Committee: Chairman, Mr. Henry A. Greenwell; Junior Warden, Mr. John Weeks; organist, Mr. William (Bill) Buttles; and amateur mason, Mr. Fred von Guenthner.

On October 12, 1968, Henry Greenwell wrote to John Weeks, most fortunately a professional surveyor by trade, to set a date to have "you assist in the proper physical location of these markers, and in fact all other unmarked graves so that we can place these markers exactly in the correct location." He went on, "I know that everyone is busy with politicts (sic) these days but if we are to complete this project by Christmas it will have to be started soon." Let the record show, the Christmas deadline was not met and a year went by. Perhaps there were difficulties.

On April 17, 1970, Mr. McKinney once more addressed A.J. Bayer Co.

"Dear Sirs:
We feel we are in a position to complete the program of placing bronze memorials on the rest of the unmarked graves in Christ Church Cemetery.

Our previous order in April 1968 was for 36 markers, #601 Puritan design in the 16" X 8" size, price delivered $29.00 each.

If the price and design are the same, please proceed to fill this order for 48 more, as per attached lists. If the price has changed, please advise me before you accept this as a firm order, and I will consult with the Cemetery Committee, who have authorized the expenditure.

It has taken a long time to prepare to complete our program, but it is very gratifying to know that, after these last 48 are in place, every grave in the little Churchyard will be marked to the best of our ability, and according to the old records of the church.

Thank you for your interest and moreso, for your very fine workmanship.

Yours very truly,
(signed) Irwin McKinney

In 1970, the Cemetery Committee took the bull by the horns (Henry Greenwell was a rancher, after all) or, perhaps it should be said, the shovel by the handle. By May 20, the first thirty-six plaques were in place. By year's end, the task was complete. In all, eighty-four unmarked graves were permanently and suitably identified. At last, the location of Mr. William Glenney's grave, the first person Rev. Charles Williamson ever buried at Christ Church, was no longer a mystery. Now names of 19th century babies – Hawaiian, Portuguese, Chinese, English, American – took their rightful place in the historic record of the church. Thankfully, relatives could now easily discover their loved one's final resting place.

How pleased the congregation must have felt when this three year project was complete! Thanks were due to many people, but a special *mahalo* must go to Rev. Irwin McKinney. His courteous manner and quiet attention to detail ensured this important task was organized and completed with care. His happy years at Christ Church have a fitting memorial in the cemetery, Bronze ~ the Ageless Metal of Eternity.

A Change in Status

Cathedral Archives
Hi Stuart,

I have a question about the transition of Christ Church mission to Christ Church parish. I have heard that it happened during Vicar McKinney's years, which were 1968-1970. But I have no facts to verify this (and as you know, most of the old records here were destroyed.) Do you know?

Dear Nancee
Two sources state that Christ Church attained parish status in 1969. A small article in the Honolulu Advertiser, dated August 6, 1969, stated that Bishop Hanchett would be visiting the Big Island the following week to install three Episcopal clergy. The third paragraph reads: "The following day (Tuesday) the Ven. Irwin McKinney, archdeacon of Hawaii, will be instituted as the first Rector of Christ Church, Kona, marking that church's growth from mission to parish status."

Sandol Stoddard confirms this in an article she wrote for the Hawaiian Church Chronicle in August of 1989. Here is an excerpt: "In the years to follow, Christ Church gradually flourished, coming under the aegis of the Protestant Episcopal Church of America at the turn of the century, and in 1969 attaining parish status."
Stuart

Dear Nancee,

Regarding your question about what was the benefit of becoming a Parish, the answer is that it was of dubious benefit. Bishop Kennedy had a long standing principle of encouraging congregations to become self-supporting, and there was a lot of prestige in graduating up to Parish status. The requirements (short version) is to be self-supporting and be able to pay a full-time priest. The long version is in the Canons of the Diocese, which can be found on the Diocesan web-site under legal documents, Canon IV, 19, 20, 22, and 23. Additional benefits are they have more autonomy and less control by the bishop.

In 1969, Hawaii (and many other missionary dioceses) changed from being missionary dioceses supported by the National Church to dioceses which were supposed to quickly become self-supporting. When we were a missionary diocese, the national church gave us a LOT (actual numbers in the journals) of money to pay the priests. Afterward, the diocese was given 5 years to become self supporting. The pressure was on for the congregations that could to become self-supporting and transition to parishes.

Rev Carol

BLESSED ARE THOSE WHO MOURN

When I was growing up, the American flag was taken down every day before sunset. It was handled with the greatest care and dignity. In fact, in the old days, the flag was not allowed to touch the ground. If it did, then it was burned in ceremony. It was against the law to use a flag to make curtains, or a shirt. The stars and stripes were sacred.

Although there is no marker or plaque to announce it, the flagpole outside on the grass stands as a memorial to the Christ Church sons that died in the Vietnam War. There were two: Wayne Hedemann (May 1970,) and Joseph W. Gaa Jr. (Jan 1971.) They are buried in our cemetery.

Charlotte Miller Melrose remembers an earlier Gaa from her childhood; he was the church gardener at the time of Rev Miller. She says he was a lovely man, and her father enjoyed working with him. When the Gaa family had a party, they would always ask Rev Miller to come and bless it. Joseph would have been the yardman's son.

Wayne Hedemann was the son of Wattie Mae who is still with us every Sunday. I asked her for a newspaper clipping about him. She looked through her scrapbook and offered several; here is the one from the Hilo paper.

Letters Ease A Family's Grief
By Bill Benham   Hawai'i Tribune-Herald   June 9, 1970

Edmund and Wattie Hedemann, parents of Warrant Officer Wayne Hedemann, who on May 13 was the first Big Island flier to die in Cambodia, have received letters of condolence from throughout the United States after a tragically ironic juxtaposition of events caused word of their son's death to be carried by wire services and national news media.

A letter from the 25-year-old Kona helicopter gunner supporting President Nixon's decision to order troops into Cambodia, accompanied by a letter from Mrs. Hedemann asking support for Nixon's move, had been published in the Tribune-Herald the same day word was received of his death.

Despite their grief, the Hedemanns reaffirmed their support of the President's actions. Their story was carried by news services and syndicated columnists to people throughout the nation.

In addition to messages of condolence and appreciation of their patriotism from President Nixon and her public figures, Mrs. Hedemann displayed touching letters from other mothers who had lost sons in the war and even from children at an interview with a reporter in her Kailua real estate office.

"The only consolation I can offer is the profound respect of the nation he died to serve," read the letter from the President.

"With patriotism such as yours for an example, your son brought to the battlefield not only his life but something transcending it: the spirit of freedom that can never die as long us America has families such as yours." Mrs. Hedemann said she has received about 600 messages, including telegrams and donations, from virtually every State. Many of the letters congratulated the family for its stand in support of President Nixon and stated the necessity of supporting him at this critical period of the war.

But Mrs. Hedemann said she was especially touched by letters from servicemen who had served with her son and by heartwarming notes from children.

Two boys, seven and eight, whom he had met while home on leave, sent flowers they had picked and a donation of 62 cents to a scholarship fund being set up in the soldier's honor.

"It's still a beautiful world; strive to be happy," a 13-year-old Waimea girl wrote.

A friend in Vietnam said: "We all feel the loss of him and the aloha in his heart for us all."

Pilots in Hedemann's unit expressed support of the Cambodia action, and the pilot of the helicopter in which he died wrote: "Wayne, like all of us, felt proud of our mission and died doing what he believed in . . . He was one of the best."

Other warm letters came from Sen. Hiram Fong, Mayor Frank Fasi of Honolulu, and Gov. John A. Burns.

One note earned a special place in Mrs. Hedemann's heart. It came from a Kaua'i man who had been hired to find mokihana blossoms and make a lei for the family. But when he learned the Hedemanns' story, he asked that his employer give them the wages he had earned, along with the lei.

Follow-up: The Scholarship Fund

According to another old newspaper article, The Rotary Club of Kona Mauka announces the Wayne Hedemann Memorial Scholarship Award in the amount of $1,000 and renewable for a second year. Based on active participation in school and community activities and financial need. Any senior planning to attend any community college or 4-year college or university may apply.

Wattie is proud of this scholarship; it keeps her son's name alive but it also helps students. Wayne had been dyslectic at a time when teachers did not know much about it.

Different Voice, Different Pen: Acknowledging the Fallen

By Kyra Boyle

Kyra wrote this reflection for a high school English assignment when she was fourteen.

During the Prayers of the People we will observe a moment of silence while the bell is rung once for each military life lost in Iraq and Afghanistan in the past week, as well as for all who suffer in war.

I like the way the sound rings throughout the silence.

.o.0.O.0.o.0.O.0.o.

The sound of the felt-covered stick clanging against the rim of the copper bowl was the only sound in the room. An endless, almost otherworldly noise, it reverberated off of the walls and wove eerily between bodies and through small, ghostly clouds of breath being projected into the cold air. It wriggled its way through their ears and toyed with their heads, causing them to wonder, dimly, if there was somehow more meaning to what they were hearing than they could have ever guessed. It was a haunting sound, and yet, strangely musical.

When the man tapping the stick against the bowl stopped doing so, the noise did not also cease. Rather, it echoed into the silence, no less felt than heard and seeming to last eternities instead of seconds. Pulsing, as if it too could breathe, the sound faded quickly back into the air and the masses it wove between, still haunting, still somehow ethereal and musical. It was almost as if it were dissolving back into the air, never to be heard again.

That is, until the next time. For the spell-binding moment had passed, just like it did every time, and the masses dared to speak amongst themselves again, just like they always did. Children again dared to breathe, and they gasped and sucked in dramatically, and their parents chortled at their antics.

And no one noticed the way the sound still pulsed in the air, no longer heard, but still something that they felt without acknowledging it. Nobody felt it, and nobody cared that they didn't, and that was how it was.

Until next time.

The War Memorial

What are the names of those from Christ Church who died in World War Two and the Korean War? There does not seem to be a list anywhere. There is a war memorial at another cemetery, down at the bottom of the hill and across the street. On a sunny, vog free Saturday morning I go to see it. The war memorial is right up front, the closest to the road, and the tallest thing on the property. Five little American flags decorate the memorial. An engraving at the top announces "Erected by their fellow residents of Kona." There are three plaques.

The plaque on the north side is for the Vietnam War. I find the names Gaa and Hedemann right away. There are eleven more.

"The Sinking of the US Royal Frank" is the only part of the Second World War acknowledged on the memorial. It looks as though all the local boys were on the same army transport ship torpedoed in 1942.

The third plaque is the Korean War dead: twenty-two names. None is familiar to me, yet I imagine they were once the young boys in Father Linscott's Japanese Boy Scout Troop.

Doctor Theodore Yeh, 15ᵗʰ Vicar of Christ Church 1970-72

Only one of the priests still living accepted my invitation to contribute to this writing project; that was Father Linscott. For learning about our leaders we must turn to vestry notes, letters from bishops, newsletter articles, and stories told by people who remember them. The exception is Dr. Yeh; Reverend Carol hit a gold mine of information when she googled his name and found that he had written an autobiography. The forward was written in 1973, which suggests he wrote it immediately after he left Kealakekua in 1972. The title:

> Magnificent Miracles: A Spiritual Journey
> Now and Then
> Here and There
> For a Citizen of Two Kingdoms

Here, in his own words, Theodore Yeh tells us what he brought with him to Christ Church. Here, in his own words, are the times and ways God intervened in his life. Here in his own words, are the details and analysis of his great challenge at CCE, and why he eventually resigned.

What did he bring to CCE? He brought a rich cultural heritage, a wealth of education, and perhaps a bigger world view than any priest before him.

Theodore Yeh was born in 1918 in Honan China. He was 5ᵗʰ generation Christian on his mother's side. His father was an Episcopal priest. Yeh wrote about long term hunger and floods, one revolution after another, and the terror each one brought.

The most interesting detail of his childhood to me is that Yeh's mother had bound feet. Her dainty, deformed feet prevented her from living a normal life; she could only hobble. Perhaps in the old order, had she been wealthy, it would not have been such a problem. But in 1918 most people were poor; they scavenged for food, washed laundry in streams, carried water; daily chores were extremely difficult for the handicapped.

Theodore's father taught him how to read from their Bible. When Theo began school in the third grade, he says the teacher spanked him every day. He wanted to quit and become a farmer. It was not to be. His dad let him stay home for a while, but eventually he had to return to school.

Yeh remembers arrogant missionaries that visited his home during his childhood years. He confesses that he felt rebellious against church legalism and institutionalism, as did his father: "My father thought that Christianity in practice is sometimes a farce."

He also writes about gentle servants of Christ. Midway through Theodore's childhood, the bishop's wife trained his mother to make silk lace. She, in turn, taught other Chinese women, and their work was exported to Great Britain. As a handicapped woman in a hungry region, this was indeed a great gift.

Yeh earned a scholarship to high school, and then to St John's University in Shanghai. He studied to be a doctor, but this was not to be either. God called him to the ministry.

It is the Confucian way that Chinese mothers do the matchmaking, and Theodore's mother chose his bride for him. *Shih Hua* was the one; CCE knew her as Barbara. The couple was married in 1945 in a simple wedding performed by Theodore's father.

When St. John's parish needed a new rector Yeh was given the position. He describes it:

> St. John's was a large parish of nearly two thousand people; most of them were fishermen. However, I ministered to anyone who had problems, Christian or non-

Christian. Since the parish was made up of six churches in six villages connected by canals, my responsibilities were great. . . usually I had to walk from one village to another. . . On Sundays [the parishioners] would come from the sea, often carrying their children in two baskets connected by ropes to a pole over their shoulders. The children sat in the baskets, swinging to and fro.

Imagine that! How different that culture was from life in the Western world! But Yeh did not come here straight form St Johns. Just look at his resume:

BA and BD degrees, St. John's University in Shanghai.

Both teacher and minister in China, England, and California.

Bishop Kennedy sent him to establish the Diocese of Taiwan.

Masters and Doctorate in theology, Church Divinity School of the Pacific, Berkley California.

Author of the book Confucianism, Christianity, and China, 1969.

Yeh describes his first view of the Big Island; "My Pan American flight was nearing Hawai'i when we were informed that there had been a huge earthquake on the Big Island, and there was volcanic action; so the plane circled the area to let the passengers see the volcano."

Yeh also describes his first welcome:

When the plane touched ground, I saw the bishop and others waiting for me. Miss Frances Tyau came over to me as I stepped off the planc and gave me a lei and kissed me on the cheek. I felt very shy, because Chinese custom would never have permitted a minister to be kissed by a woman. Instead such a minister would have been defrocked.

What about his wife and children? At the time of Yeh's arrival, they were still in China. Travel was dangerous, and expensive. They had to deal with Communists, thieves, chicken pox, measles, bureaucracies, exit permits, and different languages. But strangers (Christians and/or angels) showed up everywhere, intervening for their safety.

On Yeh's resume it states that Barbara is a registered nurse. This is a modest statement. In Hawai'i she was a nurse but in China she was a doctor. From the autobiography I learn that she went to graduate school and specialized in obstetrics. After completion, she taught at the university in Shanghai, and served as a doctor at St. John's Midwifery Clinic.

In Hawai'i, Barbara enrolled in night school to learn English. She learned how to drive a car. She worked as an RN at Ka-pi'olani Hospital. A fourth son was born in Hawai'i; Dr. Mitchell delivered him. The boys followed in their parents' footsteps in terms of education and excellence. But they were grown by the time that their dad was called to Christ Church.

When he accepts the job at Christ Church in 1970, Theodore and Barbara believe that they are moving toward retirement, a quiet position in rural Hawai'i. It doesn't go quite as they expected.

On Feb 14, 1973 Robert Greenwell, senior warden, writes to the Bishop:

> We believe you have been aware for some time of the strained relationship between Dr. Theodore Yeh and a number of the present and former established parishioners of Christ Church. We regret to inform you that this condition has deteriorated even further and that there is now an irreconcilable breakdown of communication

between Dr. Yeh, the Vestry, and the above mentioned groups.

I have switched from Yeh's autobiography and have been reading through the official records of the CCE collected chronologically in a red plastic notebook. Until this letter I don't know that there is a strained relationship. There have been things that caught my interest preceding this declaration, but not a word about conflict. The incidents that caught my attention were four *no* votes by the vestry spread out over several months. They are:

> The vestry of Christ Church wished to go on record as opposing the apparent action of the House of Bishops at their meeting in South Bend, Indiana, for offering sanctuary of the church to A.W.O.L.'s.
>
> Sept 29, 1970 one member pointed out that "he was against monies to support Black Panthers and other minority groups, i.e. Mexicans, Indians and SDS." He reported that the consensus regarding the Church as a sanctuary is NO.
>
>
> Jan 11, 1971 Vestry minutes "Archdeacon Richard E. Winkler of Maui, Chairman of the Devotional Committee of the Diocese....suggesting Christ Church invite Gertrude Behanna, authoress of the book THE LATE LIX, an ex-alcoholic and ex-drug addict, to speak here from the pulpit. Her subject would be "God is not dead," aimed toward alcoholics and hippies. The date for Kona would be Feb 23. NO.
>
> June 15, 1971 "Dr. Yeh reported on the sequence of development of events on a Nursing Home in Kona. The feeling of the Vestry was that the church should NOT be involved.

Were all these "NOs" the source of the conflict? There was no discussion reported on any of these possible outreaches. It appears that the Vestry was unwilling to take risks on outsiders. This perhaps shows the strong division in the country as well. For the World War ll generation, loyalty and unquestioning obedience to our country were cherished values. On the other hand, the kids of the Vietnam era were encouraged to question all authority, to follow their consciences; indeed, we were schooled in antiwar books such as All Quiet on the Western Front, Red Badge of Courage, Catch 22, and Slaughterhouse Five. For evening TV entertainment we watched *Mash*, and *All in the Family*. With this as a background, the idea of offering sanctuary to AWOLs, Black Panthers, Mexicans and ex-alcoholics might well be a source of generational conflict.

Or perhaps the strained relationships had to do with the adoption of new liturgy. In the red book is a flier on Christian Maturity titled Grow in Grace April 21, 1970:

> Christian maturity demands of us that we continue to grow. We cannot cling to the past simply because to do so is comfortable. We must move toward deeper relationships with our Lord, and such movement is not always easy. This is not to say that change for change's sake is always good. There are values and understandings and disciplines from the past which should be preserved. But it must be faced that it is often expedient for us that the known, familiar, comforting Christ go away in order that we may find new strength as we grow in Him. Such growth is risky business, but only risk can lead us to Christian maturity.

These differences of opinion are briefly mentioned in the Yeh autobiography, but the real issue—according to him—is his relationship with the Jesus People.

It all started with a letter from Bishop Hanchett, "I mean to speak with you about…the hippies. Anything you can do to develop a ministry to these young people would be good. Of course, you will have to work carefully because some of the people of CC may not understand. I stand ready to help in whatever way I can."

In Chapter 17 of his autobiography, Yeh details the events that led to his resignation. He supports Ken Smith who is baptizing hippies on the beach and helping them turn their lives around. The Bishop has made plans to ordain Ken in order to carry on the work. Yeh offers the new believers odd jobs at his home so that they can buy food. Barbara, a nurse, offers medicine. Yeh gives them Bible studies and befriends them.. In gratitude, they come to visit CC.

> Suddenly the church began to fill with these young people at both services. My church was in an uproar! The older members asked: can they receive Holy Communion without confirmation? Are they, then, all members of the church without going through our Episcopal rites? Will they have the right to vote at the end of the year? Shaken by these doubts and questions, some members stopped their church attendance and contributions...
>
> The church will never be peaceful again, I thought. The adults and the Jesus people will never be able to mix with one another. The adults are not accustomed to the folk music, holding hands, Lord-praising, and addressing everyone as brothers and sisters. All of this was too much and too heavy. What was the solution? My duty was to serve both groups. However, the Jesus people would not join the church, both because of their inner anti-establishment, anti-intellectual, and anti-liturgical feelings and because of the resentment of the Old Guard against them.

In the CC red book I find a shocking letter in with the vestry notes. Ken Smith (the one who is working with the hippies,) writes an Old Testament style letter to CC. It is so full of Bible references that it is hard to read so I have removed them. I have also taken out one paragraph in the middle that heads off in a different direction.

Open Letter   July 29, 1972

> May I call your attention to the following quote from "The Walk #1 by R. Stevens titled "Contend for the Faith": . . . . "We're not going in to help teetering denominational churches back on the foundations: we will kick them down. We'll not say to some, "Oh dear brothers, you're losing the fire; we're here to help you." We're here to shake them! They are already set in a mold that is deadly. People are limited by the memory of the things that are past/let's go back to the old time religion? Forget it. . You don't know how sickening the old order denomination can be, unless you came out of it/ remember the pit from which you were digged and give glory to God. I would rather be a doorkeeper in one the churches in this walk than to be a pastor of the greatest old-order church you can find. I'd rather be an elder in this walk than the greatest Potentate of High Pontiff you can think about. This walk is not reactionary: we're not trying to put Humpty Dumpty back together again –we're stepping on the eggshells!

> In January of 1971 my brother in Christ, Brent Brody, and myself were sent to the island of Hawai'i to build a New Testament church with a balance of His Love, His Holiness and His Power with the fruit, gifts and ministries of the Holy Spirit in full evidence to the Glory of Jesus the Church.

> In your study book on "First Principles" I find instructions in 50 subjects of need and interest but not one on love; two on giving, according to the OT, but none on love. . .

Twice now members of your denomination have sought to proselyte among the sheep of this body without first seeking to instruct the elders and shepherds and in violation of the Holy Scriptures. There has been no scriptural exhortation. In fact the fruit has been brother divided against brother and that over minor doctrines. Members of your denomination minister the letter of the law in the spirit of pride, violence, and legalism with respect to no other work of the Holy Spirit. We could have used help with the 200 young Christians but instead received only pressure to JOIN your church. It is with much regret, that as shepherd of this flock, I MARK your denomination on the island of Hawai'i as DIVISIVE, CONTENTIOUS, PRIDEFUL, VIOLENT, LEGALISTIC and greatly lacking in love toward the true body of Christ. I pray that you might REPENT and return to the "Old Time religion."
– Ken Smith

Finding himself in an impossible situation, Yeh gives notice to the church. In his book he concludes this painful chapter in his ministry: "I must not be biased toward the church which supplied me with my bread and butter, as the vestry claimed, or the Jesus People who need the love, concern and acceptance of the adult community. My attempts to bring them together caused much tension, pain, and loneliness to myself, the church, and the Jesus People."

Dr. Yeh left in 1973. He died in 1977. He is buried in the Christ Church cemetery in the shade on the south side. There is a space for *Shih Hua* (Barbara) next to him. There is a photograph of them together inside the back cover of the autobiography. Underneath is a poem in Chinese characters. The translation says:

> Together with Him, He and I view, /Over the hill, beside the sea. /His everlasting mercy is always upon me./With Him is fraternity,/For one day I shall fly into eternity.

Different Voice, Different Pen: Dr. Yeh and his Cookie Story
By Maile Melrose

Dr. Theodore Yeh was a great story teller, but some pre-sermon stories delivered from the pulpit caused a little consternation in his congregation. His strong Chinese accent, his loud laughter, and his pride and delight in all things Chinese, were unexpected in a small Episcopalian church. This story, repeated many times by teenagers who enjoyed their parents' raised eyebrows and appalled looks, is typical.

When God decided to make-a human beings, he mixed up a big-ga batch of cookie dough. He patted the dough to make the shape of a man and a woman. (There may have been hand motions for this.) Then he put the cookies in his oven to bake. Oh, no! The first cookies stayed in the oven too long and when they came out, they were all burned! Too bad! These are the black people.

So, God made a second batch of cookies and he put them into his oven. This time he tried to watch more carefully, but when he took them out of the oven, they were not cooked enough. They were all pale and soft. Not so good. These are the white-a people.

Then God stirred up a third bowl of cookie dough. When he put these cookies in the oven, he was extra careful. Time not too long and not too short, oven not too hot and not too cold, everything just right. This time, when he took the cookies out, they were cooked perfectly golden yellow. Oh, God was so happy. These are the Chinese! Ha, ha,ha!

CHAPTER 6

Christ Church and graveyard, 1927. (Courtesy Kona Historical Society.)

THE REVERENDS DAVID AND ALICE BABIN, 1980-1986

Before he came to Christ Church, David Babin was Professor of Christian Ministries at Seabury-Western Theological Seminary, Evanston, Illinois. Alice had been his student. He was older; she was younger. He was short; she was much taller. He was married;

she was single. When they arrived at Christ Church in 1980, they were both ordained priests, and they were married to each other.

David Babin, priest and professor, was also the author of several works on practical theology: *Doing the Eucharist, The Celebration of Life,* and *The Supreme Festival of Life and Death.* Those who knew him say that he was brilliant.

In an old file I find a few typed pages titled "Draft: Notes toward a History" with a paragraph or so on Christ Church priests. There are a few things in the margin in the hand writing of Sandol Stoddard, so I believe that she is the one who wrote the following:

> Revs. David and Alice Babin called as a single Rector. First By-laws of Christ Church written. Long-Range Planning and Stewardship Committees appointed. Lay persons training programs begun. Choir and Altar Guild organized and trained. Pre-school begun. Newsletter begun. Bible studies and seminars, etc.
>
> November 1980: church declared unsafe for occupancy. Repairs/reconstruction under way the following 9 months, during which congregation meets out of doors, 8:30 a.m. for a single Holy Eucharist service Sundays. Church attendance and budget by now more than doubled; community building single service continued for practical as well as theological reasons when church again occupied. Plans begun for a new, larger worship facility. "Let's Make a Difference" program is adopted, with half of money to be raised/spent allocated to new facilities and half for outreach, locally, nationally and internationally.
>
> David's final illness. Hospice of Kona spearheaded by members of the congregation as a memorial. David's death, February 1985. Rev. Alice continues as rector until August, 1986, when she leaves Kona to be remarried in Massachusetts.

Next I turn to my interview with Cynnie Sallie for information about the Babin years. She speaks freely and with warmth:

> Although it was 1980 when they arrived, the new prayer book was not in use. In fact the 'trial books' were still in boxes. The Babins initiated a lot of dynamic shifts. The place filled up. It was a time of new blood, new ideas, new teachings, new ways of looking at Christ.
>
> They got committees active... Everything had over the years become older and older, and in some cases staler, and staler, including people. As far as I was concerned, it was just a real shot of new blood, new ideas, new thoughts, good preaching, good teaching. All of these things—it was very appealing to me. New ways of looking at things, new ways of looking at Christ. Just a whole lot of new stuff.
>
> David and Alice were each gifted. David, first of all, was an unbelievable preacher–the best preacher I have heard by far–a golden tongue, really good. Not only was he a good preacher but he was a teacher, so every opportunity he had, he talked. So whether it was in a quorum, or a sermon, or sermon feedback, or classes... David was extremely organized, one fabulous teacher, great preacher, whether he was an administrator or preacher/teacher.
>
> Alice was in the second wave of women priests ordained in 1977. She was more warm and fuzzy. She was a wonderful counselor. I would go to her for counseling for anything. She, too, was a good teacher, more teaching from the heart than from the brain. She was a good preacher. Interestingly enough, neither one of them let you off the hook really with their preaching, but Alice left you a little more uneasy about where you were in the Christian journey than David did; but they both had their gifts.
>
> Spirituality became a focus; programs like EFM started. Outreach became a priority and new programs like Hospice and the Peanut Butter Ministry were formed.

But even these were not without some controversy: when the Randalls offered towels and showers to the hungry who came for sandwiches, some of the congregation objected. Insiders and outsiders, old ways and new ways are in conflict once again.

Cynnie concludes:

> When David died, it didn't take long for the chauvinists to move in. As far as they were concerned, David was the one. ... . Alice continued, actually was elected, so it was not actually just a continuation.
>
> The congregation was OK with a woman priest as long as she worked in tandem with her husband, but when David died, that changed. Some were unwilling to have her in charge alone. She might have been an exceptional teacher, but she smoked, drank and cursed. Although a church member might do all these himself, it did not fit his picture for a woman in the position of a spiritual leader.

Sandol Stoddard came to Christ Church after a professional life as an author, and first advocate of hospice care in America. She had hoped to retire here in paradise. When David Babin became ill, however, she helped create a hospice program for Kona.

Sandol reflects on the Babins' contributions:

> David was one of the writers who worked hard on the "new" Episcopal prayer book of 1976. That of course represented a radically democratic change from the 1928 version that was filled with "thees and thous" and humble admirations of the churchly hierarchy. One of the main changes that he and his wife made at Christ Church was in sync with that – insisting that it open up and offer a sincere welcome to one and all.

Additionally, "they both insisted that baptism was a solemn, life-changing commitment, rather than a social event to be held at the convenience of the wealthy and their friends."

Jasmine Locatelli arrived at Christ Church during the Babin years. She agrees that David had a brilliant mind. She also says that David was a dwarf. This is something I have not heard, and I realize that I have never seen a photograph of him. Apparently David was born with a physical abnormality, and this made him particularly sensitive to the challenges of others.

Jasmine had a special needs child of her own. Nick was not comfortable in crowds, but he was ok at church. There was something about it that made him feel safe. She remembers that there were about 30 children in Sunday school. She remembers the energy and excitement of children running into church. "Being at Christ Church felt like being part of a global community. It was exciting."

Different Voice, Different Pen: the Children, by Jasmine Locatelli

When Alice and David Babin were priests at Christ Church, the congregation had one service. The attendance at church had grown so much that chairs were placed at the end of the pews in the central isle. A group of ushers welcomed everyone with seat finding and prayer books and they usually stood at the back due to a lack of chairs.

Amongst those who attended were families with children. One family had four elementary school age children. Another woman, with a beautiful voice in the choir, had six. The children ranged in age from newborn to middle school. The older boys were instructed as acolytes and sat next to the altar with the priests. The infants were numerous enough that a hired baby sitter spent her time in Wallace Hall with those in cribs. It was the Sunday School that was the heart and soul of the membership.

The children went to Wallace Hall at the beginning of the service while their families crunched together in the pews with the choir packed into the stalls. At the time of the Eucharist, one of the standing people ran over to tell them it was time for

Communion. What a time it was! A motley crew of boys and girls in various emotional states burst into an adult group of Episcopalians working at devotion. The teachers tried to maintain some dignified approach and succeeded only in preventing a complete stampede. You had your front runners; they were the ones who came every Sunday and clearly knew the ropes. They vied for front position and felt completely at home. The stragglers were those shy ones that clung to the teacher's hands and had that wide-eyed shell shocked look as they searched for a parental face. All sat on the steps leading to the altar. Some faced the altar while others turned towards the congregation looking for discreet hand waves from reassuring family members. After Communion they ran out to play and headed for Aloha Hour.

The very creative Sunday School teachers always had liturgically appropriate art activities for this very active crowd. My favorite is *The Hallelujah Butterflies*. Just before Lent the children made large brightly colored butterflies and they were a thing of beauty. Bold strokes of crayola crayons on precut forms. On the Sunday before Lent a great ceremony took place where the butterflies were buried on the church grounds to await the resurrection of the Hallelujahs on Easter. With great anticipation, Easter morning arrives. The butterflies are duly unearthed and each child retrieves her treasure. At the appropriate moment they enter the church holding aloft the most malodorous paper butterflies while everyone says "Hallelujah!"

What I remember most about this time are the indelible images that flash through my mind. Little snapshots of color and life. The smile on the children's faces, the smiles of the congregation. The giggles as we watch our children act like puppies on the steps waiting for bread and wine. The little girl who wore red rubber boots with her Sunday dress but forgot her underpants. The covert pushing and shoving, the siblings looking out for one another, the older children lifting the younger ones so they can have a sip from the chalice, the occasional tears from a slight. It was orderly chaos and a wonderful time.

Reg Rodman, rector of Christ Church 1987-1996

Once again without a priest, the Senior Warden describes the situation:

> Christ Church is composed of a complicated and sophisticated congregation; [it] is bursting its seams with growth and widely varying opinions on almost any subject."
>
> There are approximately 150 members; there are chairs in the aisle, the choir is full, there is an extra pew, some sit on the stairs.
>
> With each passing day we are, as a community and as individuals, learning more and more what it means to be Easter People, and to experience the joy of living together in harmony.

In July of 1987 the Search Committee interviews four candidates for the rector's position. They carry on a very thorough search. In September the vestry elects Reginald Rodman, who stands out for his charisma. When he preaches he makes the people laugh and cry.

According to Pat Taylor, Reg Rodman was hired for conflict resolution, which is ironic because of all the trouble that followed. Rodman made it clear from the start that his wife was not part of the team; on the contrary, Terri Rodman was an artist, and on her own. Some people thought she was too much on her own; some said she was just too pretty. But Pat was friends with her.

Meg Greenwell describes the Rodmans as "fun, fun people... wonderful people.. good hearted...scatterbrained...always off on a tangent, always entertaining." She remembers that Reg made a sign that said 'The Minister is Not the Star,' and it really made her think. Meg Greenwell chose Terri Rodman as godmother for her son.

Brenda Machado says that the Rodmans were very supportive when she planned her father's funeral. The family wanted to be creative, use real doves and give away plants, to sing the ginger song. It was out-of-the-ordinary, but he allowed it, encouraged them because they were part of the 'disestablished order.' She explains that there were two distinct groups at that time and Reg tried to humble the established ones, those in charge of the church.

Billy Paris said he knew Reg, and liked him. Said he loved to paddle and was very active in the canoe club. But, boy, he said, did he create fireworks over tearing the old church down.

As I move through church history the story gets tangled up here. In the interviews, tempers flare and temperatures rise when we reach this point in the chronology. I can't figure out how to write about it, or get past it. To ignore the conflict seems unfair to those who suffered. To tell it is to open a can of worms. I don't want to create a trial on paper, to examine the witnesses and the evidence, to weigh the testimonies and ask the reader to make a verdict. That is too much work, too much negativity, and to what purpose?

What exactly is Reg Rodman charged with anyway? It depends on who you ask. The conflict begins with the historic church. Rodman is told that it is his job to create a new modern church. He (and/or the vestry) decides the historic church will be torn down, to make way for the new. This creates immediate anger for the many members who love the historic church, who wish for it to be restored/ moved/ and kept as a wedding/ meditation chapel and for small intimate events. The congregation divides over the issue and apparently, Rodman tells each side what they want to hear. Accusations fly. There is a secret vote on the issue, but some say the ballots are tainted. Things fall apart. The issue is no longer about the historic church, but about personal slights, confidences broken, trust destroyed.

I find three things in the files that touch on this issue. A letter from the bishop, an article in the Star-Bulletin, and an architectural report.

The first one is the letter from Bishop Hart to Reverend Rodman, dated November 30, 1989. He summarizes the situation, clarifies both sides, and offers his advice on how to proceed with the conflict.

Dear Reg and Friends on the Vestry:

I have received your letter explaining your decision about moving the church and I appreciate your willingness to consult with me.

To tell the truth I have also received letters from several of you and from those associated with the Committee to Save Christ Church! My mail has been more than full for the last several weeks. If it is true that a live church is one in which people are excited even to the point of controversy and letters begin to fly around (not unlike in St. Paul's day), then truly Christ Church is alive!

The situation that has developed is a difficult one. I can feel the emotion and the frustration in all the letters. Everyone cares deeply about what is happening, and I have to believe when that kind of caring is around good things will result. God will not let this opportunity pass by.

I hear the Vestry's sincere attempt to move the church forward on a plan that has been around for several years. The present old church building is no longer adequate for the size of the congregation nor for its worship needs. If Christ Church is going to be a vital witness in the community - a community that is growing and changing - it needs a liturgical space where it can express its new life and strength. I do not hear anyone criticizing the old church or putting down the past. The old building has served faithfully and well in bringing you to this point. It has an honored place in your history. Good stewardship of your resources and good planning for the future move you to the decision you have made.

You are surprised and hurt by people who do not agree, who hold to the past, who speak out of the past. People who have not been an active part of the life of the congregation for a long time, people who have not been regular supporters of Christ Church through the hard years of maintaining an old building, suddenly claim an interest and a part in your decision. Do they have the right to make this claim or have they forfeited that right by their inattendance? What part do they have in the future?

And then I hear their voice—those who want to save the old building. They are a cry for recognition, a voice of conscience that says the church does not belong just to the Vestry or to those in the congregation now. The old church building is a symbol, a sacred place, a sacramental outward sign of something deeper in the life of the larger community. It's a place where joys and sorrows have been lifted up to God and where healing and strength have been found. So few places like that can be found anywhere. The thought of losing it is frightening, even with the assurance that another place will be built in which the same things will happen.

These people are surprised and hurt that plans for a new worship space can so overwhelm the sacred past. They claim a place in your decision-making on the grounds that they are among those who have been touched by the ministry of Christ Church, that they know the sacredness of the place. Perhaps they have not "earned" any rights by their support, but earning rights in the church on any subject is problematical at best and sometimes close to heretical.

Arguments on both sides have holes. I am more impressed by the truths on both sides. You both have got hold of good things you want to do. The issue is how to work together.

I think Christ Church needs to move ahead with its plans for a new worship space which will accommodate growing numbers and new liturgical experiences, which will reflect in new and helpful ways, who the church is as it moves into the 21st Century. You need to be clear about your mission, about who you think will be served in the years ahead, about what a growing Kailua-Kona area will mean to you. We will have to plan on a new church in that area in a few years. How will Christ Church relate to the community it serves?

I think, in the light if the strong feelings for preserving the old church, you will carry on your mission better by leaving it where it is. The Committee to Save Christ Church has made a generous offer in their willingness to restore it. You need good will in the community around you in order to carry out your ministry. They are right in reminding you that Christ Church is not an island unto itself. I hope in preserving the old building they will move beyond being an historical society only and will catch the excitement of being part of a church with a mission. The chance to catch them, however, will never come if they are cut off from the start.

I hear you say that the difficulties of building the new church on another part of your property are too great. I ask you to take another look at that and consider carefully the advantages of a new location somewhere on your property, and the possibility of preserving the old building. If zoning or rights of way are the problems you certainly should be able to count on the help of those on the Committee to Save Christ Church to join with you to solve the problems. You need to work together in a common effort that will build good will. Without that, the possibility of years of controversy and the rector using his time and energy to deal with endless small brush-fires of discontent becomes too real a probability.

I wish you well and keep you in my prayers, as you have been. I know the decisions you must make are not easy and you have not come to this point without much hard work and prayerful thought.
I am happy to have the chance to meet with you if that would be helpful.

Faithfully yours,
The Rt. Rev. Donald P. Hart
Bishop

The second source in the file is a Sunday edition of the Star-Bullet in Honolulu, Jan 7, 1990. There is a photograph of the chapel and a story under the headlines "Saving an Episcopalian church becomes a divisive Kona issue."

Reg is quoted, "it's important to keep this place. I think it's like a beacon, an old navigational aid....that's part of respecting the culture and the past." But Cynnie says that Reg complains, off the record, "This building has a lead roof...prayers can't get out or in."

The Historic Hawai'i Foundation is asked to evaluate the old church and to provide some insight into what restoration would entail. The verdict is made: the church is in good structural condition, but requires repairs. The vestry hires Spencer Mason Architects to make a detailed investigation.

The third resource is the *Existing Condition Report* written by Spencer Mason Architects, May 1990. There are 12 pages of history, inventory, code evaluation, and additional drawings and photographs. Dated photographs—1872, 1885, 1900, 1930, 1939, 1950, 1957, 1962 and 1974—from the Kona Historical Society are used. The paper says, "Due to the very few changes the structure has had, it is an extremely important resource to the scholarly research of Hawaiian history and architectural design. There are few, if any, structures that are this intact from this period."

The evaluation reports the original roof was shingles with square nails. A corrugated metal roof had been laid on top. It reports on the original gutters, the air vents, roof overhang, soffits, and long term water damage and termite activity. There are technical details on the exterior walls and steps, the bell tower, the floor, and the condition of the windows. The glazed paper on the inside of the sacristy window is deteriorated, delaminated and discolored.

The structure is "grandfathered" with respect to the building code (1985 at the time) but unsafe conditions have to be corrected. Handicapped access and handrails are recommended. At the conclusion, the architect urges that "the work must be done by skilled carpenters who are sensitive to the extreme value of the structure historically."

Betty Hodgins told me about the restoration and how much her husband Groggy loved working on it. He spent a year (minus Sundays) on it. Stained glass windows are commissioned. A committee spends a great deal of time on the design with artist Rita Cowel. They are to be memorial windows.

By 1996 the restoration of the historic building is done, but it seems it is too late to restore the confidence of the membership. People on both sides of the original conflict have left. One of them, a successful author, catalogues a list of offenses concerning the rector: A Litany of Sorrows recounts the stories of 26 members who felt hurt and betrayed by their pastor. Numerous behaviors unbecoming to a priest are recorded, some unethical, some immoral.

Reg Rodman, however, is not here to defend himself, so it seems we really can go no farther.

The Bishop removes Rodman, and once again, Christ Church is left without a shepherd.

October 5, 2007 Interview: Pat Taylor

Being in community is what Pat has valued most in her years at Christ Church. When I ask for specifics, she says that working for hospice was a high point. She explains,

> When Reverend David Babin was diagnosed with cancer, the congregation gathered their concern and their energy and began putting together a hospice. In addition, they updated the chemotherapy unit at Kona hospital. Then June organized the volunteers to paint the interior of the hospital wards. Other volunteers prepared dinners for all the painters afterwards. As we responded to this immediate need, the work really did bind us together. That time of focused, intense ministry really created community, togetherness, belongingness.

Pat remembers the day Reverend David died. She and her husband Bill were heading out of town, south toward Volcano. They saw June on the road. She waved them over and told them the news. Pat says that they turned around and went home to get the big pot of lentil soup she had made that morning. She can't quite remember the funeral, but she does remember having the soup to share.

Who is June?

"June Kerr. . . she was an active parishioner at Christ Church. We served on the vestry together. She had a gift for bringing people together to work as a group on community outreach. She single handedly did more to introduce Christ Church to the Kona Community as a caring, concerned entity then anyone else I can remember. She brought out the best in us."

What are some other examples of community for you?

"Participating in EFM gave that sense of family too. And the time spent with the *Let's Make a Difference Campaign*."

Currently [2007] Pat serves on a discernment committee for Heidi Edson, our seminarian. "Over the months of listening and sharing together, we really came to care about each other. As we discerned for Heidi, we eventually had to discern for ourselves. It was an ongoing spiritual experience."

In the years that you have been worshipping here, does one particular Sunday stand out? Pat says no, considers it, and then changes her mind.

"The Sunday after 9/11. The church was full. Garrett was in front leading the music. Jesse Colin Young got up from a back pew and walked forward. "I gotta sing," he said and took Garrett's guitar from him. Jesse sang the song he is famous for:

> Love is but a song we sing. Fear's the way we die.
> You can make the mountains ring, or make the angels cry.
> Though the bird is on the wind, you may not know why.
> Come on people now, Smile on your brother,
> Everybody get together try to love one another right now.

Pat has a faraway look in her eyes as she concludes, "He just had to sing. He couldn't hold back his feelings. Everyone was deeply moved."

When it is time to leave, I stop to admire a weaving on the wall. It has shades of beige, tan, wheat, with accents of teal blue. There are sticks woven in, very neat, very precise. "The colors capture all the landscape outside," Pat explains. "It is one of Terri Rodman's weavings." I knew that Terri was an artist; this is the first work of hers I have seen.

Follow up: Hospice

I went to the local office of Hospice, next to the USPO in Kealakekua. I talked to the receptionist first, and then the director. Neither had been there for a long time, neither knew the history of this particular hospice. The director looked for some old brochures, and found a one page "Company History." One paragraph speaks to my inquiry:

> Hospice of Kona was organized in 1985 after the Rector of Christ Church Episcopal Church died of cancer. A member of his congregation, Sandol Stoddard, who authored The Hospice Movement, brought Dr. William Lamers from California to instruct on Hospice Care. A committee of dedicated volunteers from Christ Church organized, and Hospice of Kona was begun.

Interview: Betty Hodgins

Betty Hodgins' living room is all white like her hair. It is elegant, neat and trim, also just like her. On the way to the lanai, we pass by a blue-green Hawaiian quilt on an ornately carved bed. She made the quilt when she first arrived in Kona in 1970. She didn't really want to make it, but her mother-in-law insisted.

Betty's husband, Groggy, (Gordon) restored the wooden bedstead. They found it painted red, dismantled and in disrepair in an antique shop in Honolulu. Betty explains that her husband loved to make old things new.

The Hodgins were from Oahu. Groggy's father had been a doctor at the Queen's Hospital. The family had vacationed on the Big Island annually. When Groggy, and his brother, Bill, were ready to retire from Dole Pineapple, they brought their wives to Kona. As a foursome they found their way to Christ Church. Although they had been devoted to their church on Oahu, they were not comfortable with the leadership at Christ Church. When it changed, however, they joined the congregation.

During the Rodman years, Betty's daughter, Sally, and her babies attended Christ Church. The children sat on the front steps while the Reverend spoke to them. He was a wonderful speaker and obviously very smart.

Betty worked in the office for Rodman for four years. Being in the office she saw the problems behind the scenes. Rodman was always late. Things were piled up on the floor. He was not good with the business side of things. When it was overheard that the historic church would be torn down by New Years, things fell apart.

Betty is more comfortable talking about her late husband than about herself. She explains his part in restoring the historic church. He was chairman of the restoration as well as the inspector. He discovered that the floor was bad, and the belfry. He also was in charge of replacing the waxed paper windows with real stained glass.

"He had the time of his life," Betty laughs as she remembers it. "He worked every day but Sundays for about a year."

I want to know the story about the stained glass windows. She remembers that there were a great many meetings about them. She remembers that they were memorials.

"Were there two artists?" I ask. "The windows up front seem to be designed by a different artist than the side windows... The colors and the overall style look different."

Betty says no, only one. (But she calls me later to say maybe I am right. She tells me to look in the Red Book for the details.)

Now the sisters-in-law, both widows, attend the early service together. They sit on the right about half way back. Wilda Hodgins is quite hard of hearing, but like Betty, she is always warm and welcoming. And she is elegant too.

At the end of our time together, Reverend Carol asks Betty to share one memory, or one story of something special that happened over the years at Christ Church. Betty thinks for awhile and then laughs again. "Everything changed for the better as soon as you arrived!"

Follow-up

During the reconstruction and repairs, workers found a blue "W" painted on the crossbeams of the foundation. The same blue "W" was painted underneath one of the old handmade pews. They are believed to be the mark of our first vicar, Charles Williamson.

The Windows of Christ Church: Epiphany

The first pew is very seldom used, but this morning, a young couple is seated there. I am directly behind their infant daughter; she has initiated a game of peek-a-boo with me. I am transported back in time to when I was a little girl in my grandfather's church. I remember that I was afraid to sit behind the elderly women who wore fur stoles. In those days, the tiny feet and heads of the creatures were left on. I thought they had been sacrificed like the animals in the Old Testament, and I was quite horrified. I avoided the dead foxes, and tried to position myself behind babies instead. Then I quietly played with them during the service.

Now, in Epiphany season 2008, Josephine, in a pink sweater, bats her eyes at me, and I am defenseless. Pretty soon Rev Carol is distracted too. Josephine is a star attraction with her contagious smiles and dove-like cooing.

The sermon is about baptism. Carol gives an historic overview of this sacrament throughout Christianity. There was a time when all baptisms were done at the Saturday night Easter vigil. She talks a little about infant baptism, the reasons for it and the tradition. She brings it up-to-date in our own tiny church. She tells us that baby Josephine had been baptized while visiting her grandparents on the mainland. Since we feel that this baby is technically ours, we will offer prayers for her too. Her parents stand up; they turn to face the congregation. Now we know why they are in the front row.

The first row is the one closest to the Epiphany window. The author of the stained glass window guide explains it:

> The season focuses attention on the manifestation of Jesus as the Christ. Here water, with all its theological significance, is pouring from a gourd out of a white cloud on the solitary figure of Jesus. The cloud is a symbol of the presence of God and the gourd a vessel which signifies life. The ti leaves are representative of purification, blessing and healing, reflective of the Gospel accounts of Jesus' ministry read during the season of Epiphany.

We read three prayers from the red Book of Common Prayer. Josephine throws one hand in the air, palm wide open with fingers spread out; it looks like a Pentecostal move, the outward show of an inward, enthusiastic, *Alleluia!*

INTERVIEW: CYNNIE SALLEY

Wise, calm, committed, involved, Cynnie Salley is one of the pillars at St Jude's Episcopal Church in Oceanview. She started out at Christ Church, where she became involved for the sake of her children. She was in charge of picnics and potlucks, participated in the Women's Guild. That is, until the larger church decided that women could serve on Vestry and as delegates to convention. Then Cynnie's ministry focus changed, her contributions broadened, and her spirituality deepened.

She was one of many who left in frustration, during the time of Reverend Rodman. Now she is on friendly terms with Christ Church again; she participates in *Disciples Of Christ in Community* and *Education For Ministry* and attends special events.

Cynnie was born in Honolulu. She remembers her first visit to her family ranch in South Kona in 1943. She moved to Kona as a newlywed in 1960, and then to the ranch in 1976. We are at the ranch today, a beautiful sprawling mauka ranch. We sit on a lanai surrounded by large, lovely antiques.

Cynnie began attending Christ Church during the time of Reverend Alter. She explains, "The kids were going to the 7th Day Adventist School and I figured if the kids ever needed God, they needed to know what he looked like. So I started going to church."

Her memory is clear and strong, the details precise. She is careful to separate the facts from her personal opinions. Although the priests are not the focus of our attention in this history, each priest helps to define the era and gives us a structure to hang our observations on. Cynnie sums up each priest's era.

> Alter was a wonderful, sweet man: I think everyone liked him. He was the one who came to give me a confirmation class. He said 'Well, what do you want to know?' I really didn't know enough to know what I wanted to know, and so he said, 'Make me a martini.' So that was Mr. Alter – I tried to make him a martini – and I pulled out the Vermouth and it was all full of ants and he said 'That's ok – just strain it.'
>
> Alter was made Rector Emeritus when he retired. He and his wife, Marjorie, built a house in Puuloa and lived there until they died. They continued to attend Christ Church. Cynnie remembers "every once and a while he

would substitute for Bob Brown. Then he got the mumps and it was down hill after that.

Bob Brown was "young, had little kids the same age as ours, and it was kind of a different perspective. Here was someone right out of seminary, played the banjo and it became fun – church was fun. His wife was fun – she had a fabulous personality – bleached blonde who wore mini skirts. This was in the early to mid-sixties. Mini skirts weren't really in and she also wore bikinis; those weren't really in either. But I think a lot of it was to keep the ladies from dropping in. They lived in the rectory.

Bob started the *Aloha hour* between the services. He gave folk masses. "We set up a Halloween Spook House, and part of that Spook House was falling down the trap door. The church did lots of fun things and families were happy." The Browns also shook things up in the faith department:

> A lot of the people did not like Bob Brown mainly because there was so much spirituality involved, and so much theology involved, and so much learning involved, that it was just this really big shift in the dynamic of the congregation, a big shift in the spirituality, a big shift in looking at our theology and looking at Christ and just a big, big shift. ... All of a sudden it became meaningful, for me anyway. All of a sudden this church-going experience was becoming really meaningful.... The "ought tos" became the "want tos." What it was all about just kind of clicked. It is a little scary; I mean it was a little scary because there is so much responsibility that goes with it. You are a Christian by your baptism but you have a choice as to do it well, or do it poorly.

But really, the Browns wanted a downtown ministry; they wanted to minister to the homeless. "I think he felt this place was a little too provincial. He hadn't gone to seminary to be in a little rural church, in a little island in the middle of the Pacific." So they only stayed 2 years.

Reverend McKinney was next.

> He gave a little mini sermon to the children before he went into church and he would invariably talk down to them and, you know, kids somehow were intuitive – so he wasn't really popular with the children. He was dear and sweet and grandfatherly and all of that kind of thing. So the older people were really happy with him, but most of the younger people left. . . I wrote to the vestry at that point and begged them to get somebody young – bring somebody younger. The mean age of that congregation was pretty close to 70. We had a really old congregation.

Dr. Yeh came. Here Cynnie shifts in her chair, raises her eyebrows, and makes a face. "He was different and controversial from the start. The Jesus People were coming in flocks. Ken Smith was a self-proclaimed evangelist and had started these entrepreneur things – he had an ice cream parlor in Kealakekua where (he said) through Jesus he was saving drug-addicted hippies."

Cynnie has more stories, and a good amount of anger about how Yeh dismissed the Vestry, how she was treated, about potential law suits. The parish was seriously divided over Ken Smith and the Jesus people. Yeh had to leave.

Cynnie adds a positive P.S. on the Yeh family: "Yeh had a bunch of sons – three or four sons. One of them is a doctor I think, one might be a lawyer. His wife Barbara was very, very nice and she gave Chinese cooking classes. She was a sweetheart."

After two years, the bishop sends Reverend David Paisley.

> What can I say about Dr. Paisley? I was the general warden when he came and I remember helping him unpack his trailer. I don't know if he had been a printer, but he had all these heavy, heavy printing supplies that

all went under the house at that point. David Paisley was just strange, but certainly non-controversial.

Under Paisley the church dwindled to 9 tithing members. His wife hated living in Kona and threatened to take their son and to leave, with or without him. She hated it here – absolutely hated it. So he left.

After another *two year* break David and Alice Babins came—both ordained. (See Cynnie's description in the section on the Babins.) These were magical years for her as her faith deepened. But David died. Alice stayed a while, but she left too.

Then Reg Rodman came. There was a honeymoon period, but things fell apart. Cynnie left Christ Church.

Let's end on a good note… share something positive. Cynnie considers a moment and then shares:

> The guild was the Women's Club of Kona in its day. I used to go – everyone went. You did not even have to be a member of Christ Church to go. They had their basket of sewing stuff – so every meeting someone was in charge of the basket. This wonderful basket would come out – all kinds of booties, receiving blankets; they made all kinds of neat stuff.
>
> I stopped going when women could go on the vestry.

HISTORY DETECTIVE: NOT THE OLDEST TREES

Jenny Huisam knows who planted the cypress trees that line the walkway from the street to the church. Jenny says that her husband, Bart, took cuttings from the older "Chinese Cypresses", and planted them to replace the old ones. So, they are not the oldest trees on the property, although they may be the keiki of the oldest.

Jenny writes that her husband loved Christ Church:

> When in Hawai'i, he never missed a service. While I played tennis at Higasihara Park he would go down to the church and always found something to do. For instance, he placed the Red piece of cloth above the entrance of the church. . . I believe the opening is heart shaped. We bought the material; it had to be RED. Of course it is all faded now, but at the time it looked nice. He brought a ladder into the church and climbed into the opening, then I went up the ladder and the two of us fastened the material. He nailed it in place.

I looked for the heart shaped cut-out; the cloth is old and almost colorless now. I asked two Altar Guild members, Peaches and Jasmine, about replacing it. Neither had ever noticed it before. But they did remember Bart, and fondly.

Bart rests in the Christ Church cemetery. His headstone honors the memory of his brothers; "ter nagadactenis de broers in Holland," Jan, Aat, Frans, Joop, and Wim.

Jenny comes by from time to time to visit the site.

The Kingdom

For people in the church, the Kingdom of God marks a time when "God will be All in All." What does that mean? To me it means that in the realm of God, the rules are different. Here and now, the world runs on competition, and sometimes greed and injustice. The rich and the strong, the mighty and the fearless, tend to rule or manipulate things the way they want it. But in the realm of God, things are turned upside down; love reigns, peace prevails, goodness overcomes evil. Those not considered powerful—children, widows, the sick, and strangers—will be first rather than left out all together. God will be "All in All" means that love will be inside and around and underneath everything.

To work for the 'Kingdom of God' means to work for peace, goodness and love, and to help those who have no power. This, I believe, is the mission of the greater universal church, although it often gets lost in dogma.

It is my understanding that the vestry of a church is an elected group of elders who strive to keep the church on this path. It is an honor, a blessing, and sometimes a headache, to serve on the vestry. I asked Ed Geer to talk about his time as an elected member. He did not feel he was qualified to answer my questions because he thought I should ask someone serious and well educated, and he is neither. But I know Ed as a great story teller with a beautiful heart, and I pressured him to say yes. In the following pages he will first explain how he came to Christ Church. Then he will answer two questions: *How has your work on the vestry contributed to the Kingdom Of God?* And, *how has Christ Church contributed to your own faith journey?*

DIFFERENT VOICE, DIFFERENT PEN: ED GEER

My experience here at Christ Church starts 33 years ago and ironically began with a stolen car, a handful of money, and an 18 year old kid. Now I was wondering if such a tale might not be inappropriate in a book about church, but then I thought, well, this is a group of people that meets week after week reading stories, verses and chapters from a book that features a brother killing his only brother.

A father ready to slay his beloved son.

A mother and son conspiring against his older brother, and father.

Another father tricking his new son-in-law into marrying the wrong daughter.

Jealous brothers doing away with their youngest sibling.

As well as other such tales of deceit, lies, and murder ....And that's only in the first chapter. So I thought, why should my story be considered inappropriate?

Well let's just say that the car was used more so to escape a "Bad situation" (which I won't elaborate on,) more so, than for mere thievery. When it was all over, the car was left at the police station with the keys in it. The young man, of course, was me, and the money... well the money was taken out of anger, or aggravation for being put in such a situation. That money ...about 30-40 dollars... was placed in the collection plate at Christ Church. It was the first service that my sister Gwen and I attended here.

My next recollection would have to be a Sunday morning when my girlfriend and I were having a serious disagreement. I remember coming to church with a very heavy heart, still embittered by our disagreement. At that time Christ Church was in-between rectors, and had various ministers filling in. When this particular gentleman opened his mouth to welcome everyone, it was obvious from his accent that he was Australian. At the time I was a waiter in a fine dining restaurant. And, as all waiters at that time knew, the worst people to wait on were Australians. Not because they were not nice people, but because at that time they were not known to tip. At all! I'm thinking "Oh great, an Aussie minister... those guys never tip." So I hunkered down in my pew and prepared for the worst.

Well this man proceeded to blow me away with his sermon. For some reason his talk that morning seemed to parallel my exact situation. I was convinced that somehow he had knowledge of what was ailing me and his sermon was a direct answer to all of my frustration. I can't recall the exact message that he gave, but the lesson had something to do with how God would make the mountains level and raise up the valleys. As he gave this unbelievably profound sermon, he seemed to almost glow. Something like what Moses or Jesus may have looked like after conversing face to face with God. Now I can't say that anyone else could see this, but I surely did. And at the end of the service, as each parishioner shook his hand, he stopped me for a moment, looked straight into my eyes and said, "God has a special plan for you"

[Ed Geer is no longer a waiter, but has his own successful DJ business. Now that you have been introduced to him, here are his answers to my questions, 33 years after his stolen car adventure.]

How has my work on the vestry contributed to the Kingdom of God? What a difficult question that is. My life has been somewhat peaks and valleys, and at times darn right turbulent. My belief is that if you try to follow what I call "the vibration of God," life seems to go a lot better. I am grateful to God for allowing me to both have this understanding and to just have a smoother life.

The reason I bring this up is because when I was first asked to be on the vestry my initial reaction was "Well, this is not really a good time for me . . . I'm kind of busy right now. Maybe later." But because I had this sense of gratefulness, and because when I'm in that "God Flow" I think about God a lot, I felt "Well, I guess if you want me here God, I pretty much will follow your lead." So I had my first stint on the vestry.

Those days in the church were different. I think I was different too in some ways. I think I was still searching for "The Flow." I knew that I found something good with the people I was meeting and taking classes like DOC & EFM. I loved talking about God and how we felt about God and maybe "The Flow".

The main thing we were focused on as a vestry back at that time was the community center that was going to be built. The whole feeling of the vestry meetings was different from the ones today. If an agenda came up there wasn't much discussion on whether it was a good idea or not. It just seemed like we were informed of what direction we were going and what committee people should be on. We, as a church, would all pitch in. Much as we still do. (Well, at least those who go in for that type of stuff.) We had some successful events and projects, and some not so successful ones. So many times our meetings consisted of the nuts and bolts, and bean counting that it takes to run any organization. As my time on the first tour on the vestry ended, I was somewhat relieved and elated to be going off.

Well, time has a funny way of just marching along and wouldn't you know that enough time had passed so that I could be up for another round as a vestry member. Again sensing how blessed my life has been, and again not having any intention of turning God down if that is where He (She, or Whatever) wants me to go, I once again agreed to sit on the vestry. This time though, everything was different. Our rector had relocated and we were left with the prospect of finding another one. I had been on the outside for at least two other searches.... Back in the late 70s and 80s all of these things were done behind closed doors...

Now I was actually in on the process and eventually I would have a vote on who would be our next rector at Christ Church, which would also mean what direction we would be going. Our vestry meetings would be lead by our senior Warden Doug Edson. Doug is as unassuming of a person as you will ever meet. When Doug led a vestry meeting there were no personal agendas that we had to follow. We all had a say in whatever the business was for that month.

The biggest business that we had to attend to was finding a new rector. With some directives from the Bishop's office we would elect among our congregation a search committee, interview candidates and then select our new minister to lead us for the next 10 years or more. The beauty of this was we actually had to trust in God to guide us. We had to have faith that we would make the right decision. We had to all work together as a vestry and as a congregation, not only to get through a year without a minister—and having financial difficulties—but also to make this incredibly tough decision. Through this process, with all of the different people from different backgrounds, all working together for a common good... I believe that we had some semblance of the Kingdom Of God in our midst.

How has Christ Church contributed to my own journey of faith? I would have to say that even though the church has constantly changed over the years, it has offered me a sense of community and solace. When I may feel out-of-sync spiritually, I could recharge and regroup and try to get back into "The Flow." Whether I would come to church on a weekly basis, or not show up for years at a time, Christ Church has always been there for me. On more than one occasion I found myself late in the night, or in the wee hours of the morning, on the church doorstep praying, and sometimes weeping over the hardship of a broken marriage.

Being in that place where you feel that you are truly in the "God Flow," a place that you feel more in harmony with God's will. ...that place may be the Kingdom of Heaven here on earth as much as we can sense it.

Commentary: Married to the Ministry

In the library I find an old book on religion and society written by a New England minister. In a chapter about pastor's wives, he writes, "More is expected of her by the public than of other persons, and generally her words and actions are considered with less charity than are those of others."

The author lists the requirements for a missionary's wife, as if young pastors carried a checklist with them when they courted. The job description included:

- a thorough knowledge of the Bible and experiential piety independent of his;
- the caretaking of husband and children" [essentially all of the caretaking of the children as he would be unavailable to do so];
- care for members of the congregation;
- the endurance to withstand the special trials of itinerancy.

A missionary wife is always starting over: making a new home, making new friends, proving herself all over again. I suppose one should also add the proverbial *Wife of Noble Character* ideals to the list of requirements for a missionary's wife. Why not? Why not add that she gets up in the dark, is like the merchant ships, considers a field and buys it, then plants it, makes scarlet winter clothes and coverings for the bed, which she spins and weaves herself out of wool and flax. Her lamp does not go out at night, and she does not eat the bread of idleness. Of course, she speaks only with wisdom, and she laughs at the days to come. Of course! She is expected to be all things to all people at all times, and to do it, be it, model it with dignity and grace!

How lovely it would be if we could have all of the missionary wives from Christ Church sit down together for tea and conversation. How they felt about their years in Kealakekua would be one rich subject. How they actually arrived here (a hospital ship, a freighter…) might seem a bit heroic. How they felt they were regarded by the membership would be something else altogether.

Were they regarded as submissive wives? Were they too timid or too forward? Too pretty or too plain? A helpmate to her husband, or too uninvolved? How she wore her hair, her dress, her make-up, what she made for the potluck, what she gave as shower gifts: all these would have been open to evaluation.

Our first minister's wife was Mrs. Davis. She arrived with her husband and the Anglican Bishop Willis in 1872. We know that she was a nurse from St George's Hospital in London. She is briefly referred to both in the journals of the first Greenwells, and the published letters of Isabella Bird. The comments are not complimentary; HNG writes "Mrs. Davis' foolish tongue makes enemies wherever she goes." At some unknown time, Mrs. Davis returned to England alone. Indeed she is not with her husband in our cemetery.

Only after a great deal of hunting did we find that there even was a Mrs. DuMoulin, but we know nothing about her except that she gives birth to a son, here.

Mrs. DD Wallace was clearly beloved. Her memoriam published in the Hawaiian Church Chronicle is full of thanksgiving for her life. She came from Ireland, and served Christ Church for 25 years. We have photographs of her, and a good deal of praise from an adoring congregation. Even Bishop Restarick, in his history book, credits her: "No account of Christ Church would be complete without special mention of the wife of the priest, who has endeared herself to the community in a remarkable way."

We know she was a nurse and that she ran the local Red Cross, but we don't even know her first name.

We know much more about the personalities of Gertrude Miller, Jeanie Linscott and Marjorie Alter. A loving daughter, a widowed spouse, and a grandson share their memories of these women in the interviews.

Mrs. Downey is always described as the Girl Scout leader. Her influence on the girls in her care can never be measured, yet those girls, grown now, speak with obvious affection.

The first thing I always hear about Mrs. Yeh is that she gave Chinese cooking lessons at church. In her husband's autobiography I learn that her first name means *God-Given Flower*. Their marriage, in China, was an arranged one. There are photographs of her with her four stair-step sons: Tommy, Timothy, Tobias and Theodore Junior.

Some wives were criticized for being too pretty, or too sexy. Mrs. Brown wore a bikini around the rectory, supposedly so no one would come to the door.

Terri Rodman kept herself separate, devoted herself to her work as an artist. One person told me she cared for her mother-in-law who had Alzheimer's.

The very first thing I always hear about Alice Babbins (at least a dozen times) is a description of her with a cigarette hanging out of her mouth. The second thing is about her obvious pleasure in swearing. *Then* I hear about her gifts in ministry, her gifted counseling, her spirit-filled sermons. In the minds of some, these two pictures are completely incompatible. (I know other women who attended graduate school in the 70s who also adopted cussing as a kind of badge of honor. Becoming "liberated" meant being freed from the restraints women had traditionally been held to.) Alice was both clergy wife *and* reverend, so she is in a category of her own. I invited her to participate in our storytelling, but she declined.

I imagine that each would agree that *more was expected of her by the public than of other persons, and generally her words and actions are considered with less charity then those of others.*

I wonder what Christ Church gave these women. Were they lonely here? Did they suffer from the heat or the vog? Did their grown children and sisters visit them? Did they swim in the ocean? Grow flowers? Write music? Did their busy husbands give them enough attention? Did they grow closer to God while they served here?

Anne Morrow Lindbergh, a writer of my grandmother's generation, wrote much about the desire for focus and renewal in her busy and demanding life. She saw the church as a great centering force, especially for women. Here, through the ages, they could have,

> that quiet hour, free of interruption, to draw themselves together. . . Here were the advantages of the room of her own, the time alone, the quiet, the peace, all rolled into one and sanctioned by the approval of both family and community. . . Here, finally and more deeply, woman was whole, not split into a thousand functions. She was able to give herself completely in that hour in worship, in prayer, in communion, and be completely accepted.

Between the requirements deemed best by the New England minister, the work ethic of Proverbs, the changing role of women in society, and the personal spirituality Anne Morrow Lindbergh writes of, our clergy wives have had a challenging job. I don't suppose we have ever thanked them enough.

Chapter 7

Christ Church from East side, 1938. (Courtesy Kona Historical Society.)

Interview: Thelma Tyler

Reverend Carol takes Eucharist one Sunday a month to an Evening Prayer service at the Regency. This is where several of the elderly church members now live, some with assisted care, others still quite independent. We have scheduled an interview with Thelma Tyler. She invites us to come early and join her for lunch, so we look for her in the dining room. Thelma and I have not met before, but she graciously says that she already knows me from my book reviews.

I can never imagine the way most elderly women looked when they were young, but Thelma is different. I can imagine her as a little girl. Today, at 88, she is very pretty in pink. She offers us iced tea and menus, suggests the taco salad, the special of the day. Dorothy, another Episcopalian, joins us. As each new person enters the dining room, Thelma and Dorothy take note and tell us something simple about them... "She's 94...She eats a lot...She just got married to that gentleman she is with...She just moved to a different floor." I can imagine that Thelma and Dorothy have spent much of their lives in the role of hostess.

On the table is a note announcing a hula show at 2:00. Thelma waves the invitation away, "I've seen enough hula," she proclaims.

After our taco salads, she offers us ice cream. She wants us to say yes, so we eat chocolate ice cream together. We learn that her husband had an ice cream plant in Kainaliu, where Kona Medical is now.

But let us start at the beginning: Thelma was born here in 1919. Her father, William Weeks, was half Hawaiian. "His family was well known for their wood work. They did beautiful Koa dining room chairs, whatever you wanted – custom made."

But her father didn't like doing that, "He was crazy about automobiles. So he got his first automobile; then he opened a garage and he had that. My brother, who was the oldest, was very, very sick all the time with asthma, and so he never married. He ran the service station."

"The Kainaliu Store, where the Nasturtium Café is . . . that was your family store?"

"That's where the garage was. The garage and service station."

Thelma's mother was an Ackerman, one of 11 children born on the Kealakekua dairy farm. Betsy Ackerman Weeks was active in the Christ Church Guild. Rev Carol has brought a framed black and white photo of the guild dated 1931. The event is the 63rd anniversary of Granny Greenwell's arrival in Kona. She sits in the middle, all in black, surrounded by many Victorian looking women.

Thelma would have been 12 at that time. Thelma looks at the old faded photo with bright, eager attention. She says that her mother had this photo on a little nightstand in her bedroom. She can identify almost everyone. She points to each one, tells us who she is, what her husband did, and where they lived. The names are ones I have seen in the cemetery. She is most complimentary about Mrs. Cushingham....

"Oh, she was wonderful. She was the best parishioner we had. She always met the planes, she and her husband; he was manager of this national bank and they would always go down and pick up whoever was coming and have them for dinner at her house . . . She was so devoted...the best parishioner...loved to entertain... so loyal....never missed church."

Thelma's earliest memories of church are of running and playing on the grounds. "The only playmates we had were our cousins, Alice, Marty, Jacque and Ching. . . It seemed like we climbed guava trees." She remembers being dropped off early for Sunday School. Her mother came back when it was time for church.

Thelma and her sister, Bertha, walked to school each day. "We went to school where the library is. . . The little school. . . There were about eight or ten students. Miss Baybrook was a teacher but we had another one, Holly – we hired her from the mainland – Miss Hall; she was the first one."

"What was the social life for teenagers? What did you do? Were there movies?"

"We went to church. I don't think we had movies until 1926... We went up to Kealakekua to the first movie house."

Thelma went to Hilo and lived with a second cousin for two years of high school. Then she boarded at Punahou for the remaining two. After high school she attended one year of business school.

Thelma explains how she met her husband: "I worked at the pineapple company for a summer job. I was a guide and that is really the way I met him. And then we went to a tea dance and he came to the tea dance – he met my sister first, and he was dancing with her, and then he said *'I met a girl; saw a girl at the pineapple company.'* 'Oh' she said, 'that's my sister.'

Curtis Tyler was in the naval reserve:

> He was on a cruise, and he was at the University of California, and he was attending college... Anyway, he came here and he was here 3 days and he went back and he wrote to me. He couldn't call because it was so expensive – $45.00 for 3 minutes. We were married in Honolulu and he was called to active duty July of 1941, so he had to report to Pearl Harbor and we lived in Makalava. That was the officers' house.

Thelma's dad gave them two acres of land to build their home on. In Kona, Curtis worked for American Factors, and for a second job, started a little ice cream plant.

They were very involved with the church; she was very busy with the altar guild, Easter especially.

All of her memories seem to be happy ones. She looks over a list of all Christ Church vicars/priests. Yes, she remembers Reverend and Mrs. Wallace... "They were very nice people."

Yes, she knew Reverend Miller. "I was quite young then. He led the children in a Christmas play."

Father Linscott? "Oh yes! He was a wonderful man!"

Pickens? "A nice person."

Thomas? "He was only here a short time. He was frightened away by the earthquake."

Downey? "He was another nice man."

Alter... "Very well liked... Very relaxed... always had a drink."

She does not remember Brown or McKinney. But she remembers Dr Yeh "...his whole family...he had four sons... they were very bright people."

Paisley... "His wife was not happy here."

David Babbins... "He died. Curtis (her son) helped care for him. Took turns in care giving."

Today is her second son's birthday. Charlie, she explains, was a special needs child. They always took him to church when he was young, "but he stuck out like a sore thumb." They left Hawai'i for a number of years to educate him at the *Devereux* School, first in Philadelphia, then Santa Barbara. He is now 52. "Unfortunately," Thelma admits regretfully, "he has lost so much of what he had learned."

Thunder and lightening surprise us all. It is only 1:30, an unusual time for such a display. Intermittent flashes of light startle us, and the booms silence us. We talk around the interruptions. Soon we hear drumming in the distance. It must be time for the hula. Thelma tells us again with emphasis, "I'm not going! I've seen enough hulas!"

Different Voice, Different Pen: My Labyrinth Tale
By Diane Aoki

Years ago, when I went to a conference at the University of San Diego, there was talk of a labyrinth there that seemed to be drawing attention. I had no idea what it was about, so I did not bother to go. Having the labyrinth at Christ Church next to the Community Center had the same impact on me, minimal. I was impressed that Jane Mowry had generously funded the labyrinth in memory of her husband, Glenn, who was known as a kind and generous man.

Oh, it was neat. Pretty. Pleasant to look at. Great to see the kids hopping around on it every Sunday. I even read the brochure. Okay, that's interesting. But I was not drawn to walk it, to use it "as a tool in contemplative prayer and meditation," as the brochure says.

When I came to pull weeds the day before the blessing, I saw the plaque for the first time. "Hele me ke Akua I loko o Kalani, Walk with our Father in Heaven," it reads. That's nice, a little local touch, recognition that we are in Hawai'i. Could that be the mental bridge that would get me to walk the labyrinth for the first time? It's been here for a year and I still haven't walked it. No one around but Brenda, another weed-puller. Okay, I'll do it. I did. I had not realized that there was an in and out pattern, taking you towards the center, then out towards the edges, before taking you to the center and out again. It was fun. Still, no flashes of inspiration or insight.

Now, after attending the blessing on February 12, I understand the value and wisdom of having a labyrinth in our own back yard. Perhaps the combination of the program: the prayers led by Rev. Carol Arney, the reading by Jane Mowry, the music by Garrett Webb and Stephen Cline, the hula by Nancee Cline, the recognition of Terry Angeleo and his family as the builders, the prayerful yet celebratory atmosphere, and most especially the exciting and articulate guest speaker, Eve Hogan, contributed to me finally "getting it."

In her presentation, Eve gave guidelines for walking the labyrinth. What I came away with may not be exactly what she said, but is my interpretation of her talk. She suggested that when you begin your labyrinth walk, you look at yourself from above, practice seeing yourself, becoming aware of your thoughts and the issues you are facing in your life. You become conscious of whatever comes to the surface as you walk to the center. When you reach the center, you become centered. This could mean a realization of God as your center. You pause, breathe it in. As you walk out, you walk out with an awareness of God as your center, and perhaps make plans, resolutions, or have a clearer sense of direction than you had when you started your walk.

What impressed me most about her talk was the idea that the labyrinth is a metaphor for your journey in life. You don't need a physical labyrinth to have a labyrinth walk. The mental and spiritual process can be experienced in your everyday life. I connected that idea immediately to my life. I recently decided to take our dog for walks as often as my schedule allows. This was a life-changing decision for me, and I did have somewhat of a labyrinth walk experience on my walks with Koa. The only thing that I knew I didn't have was a center to go to, a turn-around point at which I was aware of my center. After speaking to Eve, I decided to incorporate a significant turn-around point into my walk.

Though I now feel I do have a "labyrinth walk" when I walk my dog through my neighborhood, I now know the potential that the Christ Church labyrinth has to be a blessing to our community. The idea of the labyrinth has the advantage of seeming to be "New Age," but it is really an 800-year-old practice, so there is somehow a sense of newness that has deep roots. Though it is historically Christian, it is appealing universally and has the potential to attract people from all faiths and backgrounds. For me, it serves as a reminder of the labyrinth walk of life. However, the labyrinth can be more than a reminder, but an actual way to practice the spiritual process of increasing self-awareness, and bringing this to the Lord, who is at the center of all things, and then walking with Him through life's pathways.

INTERVIEW: BRENDA MACHADO LEE

Brenda brought her high school scrap book for our interview. The very first page shows a beautiful, tall, high school sophomore in a bathing suit, high heels and a crown. Miss Billfish Queen. Miss Aloha Hawai'i. Konawaena Queen. On other pages are church youth group mementos; a letter from the bishop, a program from camp, the liturgy from a celebration. The scotch tape is yellowed; some of the papers are crumbling. As *Miss Aloha Hawai'i* she won a scholarship for college. It was Reverend Alter that drove her to UH Hilo to begin her college life. She earned her BA and a teaching credential; she taught at Ho'okena and Konawaena until she started her own family.

When did she first start attending CCE? It was shortly after her grandfather, John Machado, was buried at CCE. It was decided that the five Machado children needed to be baptized. Father Linscott brought them into the church. Soon the kids attended the elementary school in Wallace Hall. Brenda describes the school as two stories with a trapdoor between them. The kids loved the trapdoor. They ran and played all over the grounds. There was a little thrift shop on the church property operated by Maud Greenwell. Brenda remembers that her mother, Hester, took her children's outgrown clothing to it.

I find Hester's name throughout the old Vestry minutes. Brenda describes her mother as a hard worker, always busy with running the family store, a plantation store converted to a tourist shop. Hester taught the kindergarten Bible class and contributed to church work that she thought was important. She had no time for such things as parties though, so sent Brenda and Caroline to represent the family. Brenda has a dreamy look on her face as she reminisces. "All the parties: Halloween! Easter! Christmas! Dressing up as a flower! As an elephant!"

We have old photographs to show her....groups of children in the 50s. So many children! In the first photo is a church procession, in another a group of little girls in their brownie uniforms, another shows children holding bouquets of flowers. Many of them are Japanese Americans, or a lovely Kona blend. Brenda knows them all...and names them one by one.

The church became an extended family for Brenda. Eventually, after her parents divorced, it was Reverend Alter who became a father figure for her. When the Reverend replaced the altar Bible, he gave the old one to her. She is clearly moved by this memory.

She says that her father built the baptismal font

So many pastors served at CCE. She remembers them vividly, or not at all. In some cases, she remembered the wives.

Rev Linscott baptized her. When she was a little older, she babysat his children.

Rev Pickens was tall.

Rev Downey's wife was her Brownie and Girl Scout leader.

Rev McKinney officiated at her wedding.

Rev Rodman buried her father. Mrs. Rodman was an artist.

What do you remember about the Rodman years? She answers that Rev Rodman went through a time of conflict with the established order. He befriended the Machado family, who was part of the "disestablished order." He ran into lots of problems...did not get the financial support he needed. He tried to humble those with power.

When it came time to plan a funeral for her father in 1994, Rodman encouraged her to be as creative as she wanted. So her family did things not in the traditional Episcopal way. For instance, they burned Buddhist incense, and released doves. They did these things with his blessing.

Brenda often spends time in the graveyard now. She sees it as a way to honor the dead, to show her respect, and to make herself available to their wisdom from afar. She speaks of her ancestors, Hawaiian, Chinese and Portuguese. She wants them all to be remembered. Brenda knows her Hawaiian genealogy the best and the beautiful long names roll off her tongue. She talks about her ancestor who was the first Hawaiian to go to China to set up the sandalwood trade. Now, generations later, she works for Hawaiian sovereignty.

Brenda is soft and warm. All of her stories about her life in Christ Church are happy ones. She laughs frequently and I capture a glimpse of Miss *Aloha* every time she does.

When I first attended Christ Church there was a very large Hawaiian man who sat near the back on the left side of the chapel. I always sat near him because when he sang, his deep, loud, beautiful voice made the whole pew vibrate. He is Brenda's brother

Barry and he is now buried in the cemetery, near his mother, Hester, and his grandfather.

Different Voice, Different Pen: First Impression
By Linda Melson

It was Easter Sunday of 2000. Bill and I were here looking for a home to buy. We were retiring the following June and had decided to move permanently to Hawai'i. We had been here to dive many times, and I'm quite ashamed to say that we had never gone to Christ Church while here on vacation. (I truly admire all the tourists we have visit.) We drove up the parking area (then unpaved) to park and go in to the church. We looked over and saw a beautiful Hawaiian lady helping another beautiful Hawaiian lady out of the car and into the church. The older woman was wearing a snowy white muumuu. Her hair was done up, and my first impression of the church was one of joy because it felt like it must really be part of the "real" Hawai'i. Later, I met them. Brenda Lee is still a member of our church, but her mother, Hester, passed away shortly after we met them. When we got inside, the people were warm and welcoming. We stayed for coffee hour and I met a lovely lady who had a Yorkshire terrier on her lap. She introduced herself as Jean Greenwell and laughingly told me that half the graves in the graveyard outside were from her family. It was a memorable beginning of our life at Christ Church.

INTERVIEW: STEPHANIE ACKERMAN

Stephanie Ackerman is the person in charge of the cemetery.

"How did you get this job?" I ask her when she gets settled on my lanai.

"It got dumped on my lap."

"Did you have special qualifications? Interest? Experience?"

"No."

She explains that David Merkel had been in charge in the past. When he died of AIDS, the position was left empty. Vestry member Pete L'Orange said, "Get Stephanie to do it. She's young and knows everyone."

That was around ten years ago. It is true that she knows everybody, but she knew nothing about the cemetery. So she went to her aunt, Helen Weeks, for all the cemetery records. Helen however, still angry from a run-in with the Babins, refused to turn over the documents. So Stephanie searched through the church office and found some remaining records in five different drawers. But a lot was lost with her aunt! Stephanie had to pretty much teach herself through trial and error with random documents, old maps and scattered letters. She has since learned how to use a computer and to create spread sheets.

Tommy Greenwell is the official gravedigger and he has helped her with the hands-on site work. He has shown her how to use a probe to locate a buried vault; how to *use chop sticks* to measure; how to use an *empty beer can* as a level. He taught her how to decorate a new grave with ti leaves and ferns. Stephanie laughs as she admits that the first grave she decorated solo looked like a hula girl.

The problems are many and surprising. Tommy and Stephanie always open a grave the day before a burial because they never know what they will find in it. Like somebody in it already. There are problems when there are four wives. There are problems with disputing families. There are problems with the markers being lost, or dented, or with names spelled wrong. The weather is rough on cemeteries: roots push graves up, storms blow trees and rock walls over, earthquakes crumble everything, and floods wash soil away. Ants and critters and time make their own steady contributions.

Stephanie has many funny stories. As you might imagine, the subject matter inherent in the work is so touchy, so sad, sometimes so tragic, that to carry on, one must at times joke around. We talk about good literature with this very theme. I give her titles to look for; she promises me some official documents from CCE to read. As she walks to the door I ask her if she gets paid for this work that she does. She answers in the negative. I ask her if she has her eye on a successor. She answers that with a big sigh.

Interview: Stephanie #2

Since I have spent so much time wandering through the cemetery lately, it occurred to me that I ought to have my own plot. I talked to my husband about it. Ashes at sea are fine with him, he says, a lifetime surfer. But for my sake he would be willing to have his ashes buried with me on the pretty rolling green grass of Christ Church.

On Lent, Reverend Carol makes the sign of the cross on my forehead with ashes, and reminds me that I shall return to dust. After the service I give her an envelope with $300 and ask for a space to call my own. She sets up an appointment for me with Stephanie Ackerman.

It is a gray Saturday when I meet Stephanie. She is setting up the coffee for the Sunday *Aloha Hour.* Stephanie wears many hats at CCE. She interrupts her tasks to get her official cemetery stuff from her car. She has a cardboard tube, mat board, four clothespins, and a notebook. We walk down to the front row of graves, and sit in the shade of an old cypress. She takes off her glasses and sets them on top of the gravestone of J.W. Atkins, who died in 1913. She removes the map from the cardboard tube and spreads it out over the mat board, clips it on with clothespins.

She asks me what I want. Like: what do I want for breakfast? Or, would I prefer coffee or tea? But this seems a much bigger question, and I don't know what my choices are. What about all the separate space next to the church where only old Rev Davis and young Esther Waha are buried? What about down by the road? Is it all open, or do we need to "buy and die" in neat orderly rows?

The answer is "buy and die" in neat, orderly rows, and that narrows the field greatly. So then, what should I consider? An ocean view? Shade for mourners? Who would be my neighbor? Is it picturesque? The rock wall is homey and charming, but the chain link fence with tricycles is not.

I'm choosing where to spend eternity? Well, not exactly, only where my ashes will be buried, and where a marker bearing my name will rest. I have no doubt that I will be forgotten, but it is kind of sweet to imagine that over this whole globe, one tiny speck of it will announce that I once was. Someday, children might stumble across it hunting for Easter eggs.

We look at the map, all the plots and the walls and the buildings and the trees a long time ago. There was once a jacaranda on the side by the rock wall opening. I wish it were still here! There is an available ½ plot within the range its shade *would have* reached. Even better, the plot is within range of the lovely purple carpet of blossoms the tree would have dropped each spring. Jacarandas in Hawai'i, in spring, are absolutely breathtaking. This is the plot I want, the one in the shade of a beautiful ghost tree.

I tell Stephanie that my surfer husband will like that there is a tiny bit of ocean view if you stand on your tip toes. I confess that he would be happy to have his ashes scattered at sea, but that he is just as happy to do this for me. She is quick to explain that he can have them half and half. In fact, she explains that our dear Jane Mowry, the one-time French countess, is going to have her ashes divided into three separate places.

How long has cremation been acceptable here in the Episcopal Church in Hawai'i? Stephanie's guess is since the 1940s, but the records do not indicate what type of burial is given, only the dates. But that is not quite true: according to the notebook, Wattie Mae's son and husband had military funerals with their remaining ashes. And the notebook says that Anderson Russell, who was struck by lightening, had his ashes scattered over the sea at Honaunau. Stephanie points out the grave of Kathleen Marquardt, once a beautiful musician, and tells me that her remains are in a ginger jar.

Stephanie believes the Kimuras were the first to offer cremation service locally and suggests I stop by the fabric store and ask. I will also email the archivist at the cathedral in Honolulu.

As we roll up the map we talk about the damage to the J.W. Atkins gravesite, the one we are working on. The gravestone fell down in the last earthquake, and it is crumbling so much that it cannot be put back up without a lot of repair first. We have been sitting on a little cement wall around it. According to the cemetery rules and regulations, little walls are no longer allowed. Neither are big ones like the post and chain thing around the Lambert grave.

"That grave used up 6 *plots*!" Stephanie exclaims.

I tell her a little about the sea journal of Lambert's parents, who brought the gravestones by sail boat from England after their son's drowning in 1874. That took several *years*, and then they carted the stones up the cliffs by oxen. It was a tremendous testament to their love and loss. Stephanie still seems to think it is extreme.

I ask her about herself: does she have a gravesite picked out? She laughs and says that the Ackermans, a very old family here, have used up all of their space in the cemetery; she will have her ashes thrown into the sea in front of their ancestral beach house.

Follow-up: Christ Church Cemetery Rules and Regulations

Nowhere does it say who wrote this document, but it is 6 pages double spaced and is dated October 2001. Stephanie already told me that it was Betsy Strance (then a lawyer, now a judge) who cleaned up the laws and updated the language. It is actually quite easy to read.

The first rule is that Christ Church Cemetery is a private cemetery for use by its own members and their families only. The rules define who "immediate" family includes: parents, siblings, spouse, life partner, and children.

The second rule limits the use of the plot: it can be used for burial only.

An additional detail: when a member buys a plot, he or she is not really buying a piece of land, but making a reservation to use that piece of land.

A member may buy a full plot for a full burial, or a ½ plot which is enough space for two urns. The costs for grave digging, installing a plaque with concrete, or a headstone, etc., are additional and not part of the "reservation."

The Church requires that each grave have an appropriate plaque, preferably bronze. There are restrictions on how big one can be, and restrictions on any fence or wall that might interfere with mowing the lawn.

Only cut flowers or potted plants are allowed.

My favorite rule is number 7 (c) on the last page. It is so very Christ–like. "Special cases may arise in which the literal enforcement of a rule may impose unnecessary hardship. The Vestry, therefore, reserves the right, for itself and the Cemetery Committee, to make exceptions, suspensions, or modifications, without notice." Sounds like grace.

Follow-up: Cremation

Dear Nancee,

I know that the Roman Catholic Church did not allow cremation in the past (and maybe even the present without special permission), but I'm not sure whether it was ever an issue in the Episcopal Church in Hawai'i. Although the church registers in the archives record burials, they do not specify whether they are full-body or cremated remains.

If the issue was debated in our diocese, there may be some record of it in the diocesan publications, including the Anglican and Hawaiian Church Chronicles, Journals of Convention, or

Standing Committee minutes. But as you know nothing in the archives is indexed - a situation we are trying to rectify, though very few have come forward to volunteer for this project. It will take some time to plough through the records to see whether the issue was ever debated.

If there was a theological reason why cremation was not permitted by the Episcopal Church in Hawai'i, perhaps the Bishop might know. I will copy him on this email.

Aloha,
Stuart Ching

(The bishop writes back.)

I suspect that there was nothing formally that precluded cremation; it would just not have been practiced at the time here in the Islands. By the late 1870s, cremation was being accepted by bishops of the Church of England. Frankly, as long as there was enough land on church owned property, it appears that burial was the norm. The Church's acceptance of the practice was driven by a lack of space, urbanization and industrialization.

I suspect that in the years of the Kingdom, it rarely came up in the Church here in Hawai`i because the population was low, life largely rural and land was available for "church" burials.

By the beginning of the twentieth century, it was a moot point in Anglicanism worldwide.

Bob The Right Reverend Robert L. Fitzpatrick Bishop

Dear Bishop Bob and Archivist Stuart,

Thank you both for your responses. I have been writing a history of Christ Church and spend regular time in the cemetery here to think and wonder and make connections. I bought my own plot on Lent and had to think through some of my own details (full burial or urn?). In light of my research and story collecting, deciding was much more interesting.

I'll share with you the one old reference I have found on cremation. On a chapter about Bishop Willis' opinions, Restarick writes that Willis opposed cremation. In response to an article in the Anglican Church Chronicle, May 1900, Willis wrote, "We sincerely trust that no clergyman of the Anglican Church will be found to carry out the program which would turn the Christian Burial Service into a farce." He considers it a return to paganism.

Restarick's book, published in 1924, states that by this time "this method of disposing of the dead is now so common in Honolulu that it causes no comment..."

Quite a change in less than 24 years!
blessings,
Nancee Cline

Dear Nancee,
Bishop Willis would have come from a High Church very 19th century point of view and Restarick from far more Broad Church 20th century modernist one. This points to major theological shifts in the diocese driven by external political and social ones. Very interesting and helpful.
Bob

Interview: Mona Ewing Gurrobat

Mona is the church treasurer. When Carol and I met her for this interview, she was on her lunch break at her monogram store. We were surrounded by baseball uniforms and a rainbow of work smocks with embroidery. She gave us boxes of overstocked items to use for the next church rummage sale.

Mona Ewing was born in 1954 and grew up at CCE. We ask her to tell us what she remembers about being a child at church.

* standing by the side of the road with her sister waiting for a ride to church on Sunday mornings.
* lots of sleepovers at the rectory.
* Christmas pageants.

* Dying Easter eggs, and then finding them in the Easter egg hunt
* Girl Scouts after school in Wallace Hall... earning a merit badge using the pine trees that lined the walkway... Signs on the trail...rocks stacked up, or twigs laid in a certain direction.

She remembers
* Mr. Cushingham was the bell ringer, and Mrs. Cushingham wore a fur coat for Christmas Eve.
* Grace Ackerman was her Sunday School teacher, and she told stories with flannel boards.
* Confirmation class met in the choir stall. . . Lots of memorization.

She names all the other students. The Bishop came to confirm them.
* In junior high singing the Eucharist...she found that so moving, and the old Prayer Book... that too really touched her. She remembers the old words now, but not the new ones.
* She is proud to report that she had perfect attendance at Sunday School.

Reverend McKinney took Mona to lunch at the Kona Inn. He wanted to know how he could make the church exciting for teenagers. He helped her get involved with the youth group in Oahu. She remembers "flower power," and rock and roll at summer camp. She remembers writing poetry there. And that the youth minister, Frank Chun, gave her a little cross. It is *still* in her wallet, she confides rather shyly.

Mona gets excited about one summer adventure. She volunteered to participate in a church sponsored shelter for runaway girls. Mona was only 14 or 15 at the time, but she went to Honolulu to live with the runaways, as one of them. She explains that there was a two story house next to the fountain at the cathedral, which became her home. First she was trained, and then she and 2 other volunteers were dropped off downtown at 10:00 at night. The police picked them up for curfew. Mona said they could not stop giggling because it was so embarrassing. The police decided that they must be high. At the police station, the girls' parents were contacted. The parents said to release them into custody of the church. So their social ministry started off in a very authentic way. Mona remembers several girls in the shelter, one was pregnant, and another was blind. The blind girl ran away because her parents said she couldn't go to college. The shelter helped her to enroll, and Mona counted steps with her to the bus stop, counted stops on the bus, helped her find and memorize her way to UH. Mona stayed the whole summer; she is totally caught up in the memory.

Mona went to the mainland for college. Once she had children, she came back to CCE to baptize them. She has a story about her daughter, and an incident at church. Bree was an acolyte and really enjoyed serving in this way. One Sunday morning, however, she found that she had been replaced. No one told her why. Bree was very hurt. Mona's eyes fill with tears as she remembers her daughter's sense of rejection. Whatever happened, whatever simple, unintentional misunderstanding took place, it left a scar. Bree never went back to church. Even now.

Mona stopped attending church because of the Babins. When Mona returned, Reg Rodman was there. She says they did things at church she didn't appreciate. She didn't like church any more. But she did go to Reg for counseling; he let her talk out her problems, listened as she eventually came up with her own answers. She admits that he helped her a lot.

She has another story, of an issue that came up while she was on the vestry. The Rodmans wanted to buy a modern dishwasher. Mona believed that since everybody else in the parish washed dishes with their hands, they should too. The church did not have much money, and she did not think it right that the parish treat them as socially superior. The social disparity bothered her.

Mona was married a second time, and this time at church. Rev Carol, the new priest, performed the ceremony. Mona's children stood as her witnesses. Mona remembers "blubbering like a baby." Carol remembers the butterflies that decorated the service leaflet.

Mona does not attend church regularly, but Rev Carol points out that Mona is always present for the Good Friday service. Mona agrees, it is "really, really strong for me. I can miss Easter, but not Good Friday. It is really, really special to me....the gift... the promise of Easter is meaningful *because* Friday is so stark... everything has been taken away."

FOLLOWUP: KING KAMEHAMEHA BUTTERFLY (FROM THE INTERNET)

The pulelehua, or Kamehameha butterfly, is one of only two butterflies that are native to Hawai'i. With its bright red wings, bold black borders, and 2 1/2 inch wingspan, pulelehua are often seen fluttering near koa trees, where adults feed on the sweet sap oozing from broken branches.

The Kamehameha butterfly lays its eggs on the mamaki plant, a native shrub that was sometimes used by Hawaiians to make a coarse tapa (the leaves are also used to make an herbal tea). Young caterpillars protect themselves by cutting a flap of leaf, pulling it over themselves, and securing it with silk to make a shelter. As they grow older, the caterpillars sit motionless on the branches, waiting for nightfall. Once the sun has set and the forest birds have gone to sleep, it is safe for the caterpillars to venture onto the leaves to eat. Even their chrysalis is well-camouflaged, looking like a withered leaf. In a little over two weeks, the chrysalis splits open, and out pops a beautiful pulelehua!

INTERVIEW: EDWARD AHUNA SEPTEMBER 16, 2007

Edward Ahuna explains his ancestry to me first thing. His mother and great grandmother are both named after Queen Emma. This is clearly very important to Edward. His great grandfather was Joseph Karooluri Nawahi, cabinet minister under Queen Liliuokalani, long time legislator in Hilo, and advocate for the independence of Hawai'i Nei.

Edward Ahuna has two books to share. One is <u>Hawai'i's Story by Hawai'i's Queen</u>, and there is a chapter about his great grandfather in it. The Queen writes about Joseph Karooluri Nawahi after his passing; "No private individual in our land had ever received such a demonstration of love and respect as was shown to the lamented member of the house."

The second is a beautiful old book with a tapa cover. Inside are photographs of the elaborate funeral of Joseph Karooluri Nawahi.

Edward also has Scotch and English blood in his veins. This part of his family has a coat of arms. His "Anglo Saxon roots go back as far as the Knights of the Round Table." He says that he is proud of his ancestry. Both sides.

Edward has attended Christ Church for about 17 years. He sees it as "a beacon of the English influence in the Pacific." He speaks of American history and Hawai'i and the history of kings with facts and figures, names and dates. He understands the currents of religion and politics and money behind the scenes. He is intense and sincere. He stops the flow of conversation to ask me about *my* family heritage.

No one has ever asked this question in an interview, but I'm happy to share it. My brown eyes come from my mother's family, from Holland, a long time ago. My name and my hair color come from my father's side; DNA research points to Northern Europe as the source for the red/strawberry blond gene mutation. As I was reading about Captain Cook and his early life I found (to my surprise) that his mother and I share the same maiden name. She was Grace Pace and I am Nancee Pace.

So Edward is related to Hawaiian royalty and I am related to Captain Cook.

Follow-up: Genealogy

If we go back far enough—if we could do the DNA research—we would find that we are all family. There was not a Polynesian Eve, and a haole Eve, an African Eve and a Middle Eastern Eve.

There was one mother from which all others came forth. The most recent DNA research deals with the Y chromosome from 'Adam', and it can be traced back to the beginning.

According to geneticist Spencer Wells, Africa is the birthplace of humanity, and the DNA proves it. As families followed migrating herds, they moved northward up the continent and eventually divided. Some went west and developed Western Civilization; some went east and developed Eastern Civilization. There were many migrations and many divisions. Remote and isolated places, such as Tibet and Siberia, have gene pools that have been stable for many generations, but most populations have been on the move. Because of different climates, mutations, natural selection, and genetic drift, great diversity resulted. The journey of mankind can be charted on a map, literally, following the changes in the Y chromosome.

When European explorers sailed west, they eventually met those early ancestors who went east. *First Contact* is the name of this event; the Vikings met the Beothuk, the indigenous people in New Foundland, a little over 2000 years ago.

Wells offers an amazing story of this genetic odyssey. His book and documentary, both titled <u>The Journey of Man</u>, have contributed to the success of a worldwide National Geographic DNA project. You can send in a sample of your own DNA to contribute to the study.

One of the stunning things Wells explains is how quickly our family tree fills out:

> We acquire new ancestors in each generation as we go back in time, and they start to pile up pretty quickly. Each of my parents had two parents, and each of them had two parents, and so on. The geneticist Kenneth Kidd, of Yale University, has pointed out that if we double the number of ancestors in each generation (around twenty five years), when we go back in time about 500 years each of us must have had over a million living ancestors. If we go back to the time of the Norman invasion of England,

around a thousand years, our calculation tells us that we must have had over one trillion ancestors — far more than the total number of people that have existed in the whole of human history.

How can this be? The math is right, but it assumes that each person in the genealogy is unrelated to each other. On the contrary, we share many direct ancestors. (For instance, siblings share the same parents, so for 6 children there are two parents, and four grandparents, not twelve parents and twenty four grandparents.)

Different Voice, Different Pen: Lao Tzu

At the same time that the Old Testament prophets were calling the Hebrew people to justice in the Holy Land, Lao Tzu was compiling *A Book of Virtue* to guide the people of the east. The ancient wise one who wrote Tao 31 knew the truth of DNA thousands of years before the geneticists could prove it. Here are a few lines:

> . . . every being is born of the
>   womb of Tao (the source of goodness).
> That means that his enemies are his enemies
>   second, his own brothers and sisters first.
> Thus he resorts to weapons only in the direst
>   necessity, and then uses them with
>   utmost restraint.
> He takes no pleasure in victory, because
>   to rejoice in victory is to delight in killing.
>
> . . . Observe victories as you observe a
>   death in the family: with sorrow and mourning.
> Every victory is a funeral for kin.

Race Relations

On the first day of classes at Hawaii Community College, my students read a speech that Martin Luther King gave to junior high kids in Philadelphia. It is a wonderful speech and my students find it inspirational. Before we start, I ask them what they know about Martin Luther King. Most remember that he was a black leader and that he had dreams. This week [August 2010] one student answered the question in a way that really got my attention. She said with complete confidence, "Martin Luther King freed the slaves and ended racism forever."

Since I lived through the Civil Rights Movement, I have stories that help bring the movement and the message alive for my students. I tell them that the work of MLK affected every one of them; 'Black is Beautiful' translated to 'Brown is Beautiful' too. All the minorities symbolically lined up behind MLK, and the women's movement as well. The fact that our class is a rich ethnic mixture of Hawaiian, Japanese, Korean, Chinese, Portuguese, Filipino, Spanish, Tongan, and haole is part of the Dream come true. Hardly anyone recognizes it as the miracle it is.

Martin Luther King visited Hawaii and spoke at Punahou School in 1959. I don't know for sure, but I doubt there were any black students attending then. It was not too many years, however, until Barack Obama did.

Two young black/Korean boys at church are being groomed to attend Punahou some day. I asked their mother, Dr. Joy McElroy, to speak to the subject of race at church. She thought about it for a couple of weeks, and she talked to her mother about race and church in the past. Joy's mother's story starts with the Catholic Church in a little town in Missouri.

Different Voice, Different Pen by Dr. Joy McElroy

The do-gooders of the Roman Catholic Church invited the colored children to learn about Jesus at a makeshift Sunday school.

Majestic nuns in billowing robes and starched habits gathered their flock for a special-and-separate class. They had colorful little prayer books and serious looking statues to look at. It was almost a party-like atmosphere at the town cinema. An audience of white children gathered on a second floor balcony to give 'extra attention' to the potential recruits. The extra attention, however, meant spit bombs and threads of saliva dangling from the second story seats.

The spit bombs would have been tolerable, but when the colored kids learned that the cupcakes (with sprinkles in the shape of a cross) were only for the children upstairs, their taste for high mass was ruined.

Weeks later, the Episcopalians hosted a recruiting session for the little colored children too, a battle for little souls. "The Episcopalians never launched spit balls on us," my mom said. "They had a separate-but-equal class, only this time, everybody got cupcakes."

By the time I was a young adult [Joy continues], my Episcopal priest gave me gifts. Not Fire and Brimstone, or Heaven and Hell, but an approval to think, to question, and to reflect about God and our special relationship with him. We learned everybody has been given the gift to doubt, to stray, to be too smart for our own good, and the greatest gift of all, permission to come back to belief, come back to God, to church, the audacity of a personal God. No intercession. No go between. The door is always s open.

Its no surprise the uber-cool Episcopalians ordain women: loud mouthed women for Christ's sake! And they don't gawk when gay couples walk in and sit down together to worship. "Love who you love" they seem to imply. Episcopalians toll the bell every Sunday for the soldiers killed in Iraq and Afghanistan. They try not to politicize; after all, these dead are not only patriots, but somebody's children.

At Christ Church they wear muumuus and jeans, linens and slippers, Nihau shells and diamonds. They drive pick-up trucks and Mercedes, bicycles and BMWs. They have money; boot-strap wealthy; and landed gentry, but give what they want when they're ready . . . not when they're told. Episcopalians are the common sense essence of the American dream. They are a mirror for our community to see itself, not a window to look through onto something else.

Christ Church is a cross section of the true and the new Hawai'i. Different and varied, but all interrelated and tolerant. Every day, everywhere, in the good, the bad and the ugly. With provincial stained glass windows of voyagers, a koa baptismal font, and a PowerPoint screen of the doxology in Native Hawaiian. It's brown and white, lucky and unlucky, broken and fixed. It's Christmas trees and champagne brunch, hula and high mass. We take the best of all of it. It's the church that was home for Harriet Tubman, Jane Austin, Charles Darwin, C.S. Lewis, Van Morrison, so many presidents and Supreme Court justices.

It is the church that gave strength to the indomitable Queen Emma, and the church that gives the sprinkled cupcakes to everyone.

FOLLOW UP

I talked to Joy later, after she wrote her answer. I asked her again about race and church, here and now. She thought awhile but didn't answer, so I asked her again. Finally she shrugged and said, "It's all good."

HISTORICAL CONTEXT: EVENSONG SEPTEMBER 30, 2007

Garrett Webb, music director, leads an ecumenical choir for this one Sunday night a month. Garrett looks like Abe Lincoln in an Aloha shirt. He is lanky and relaxed, 6' 10" tall, and he is crazy about music.

For this special service, he chooses Renaissance and Baroque music. He has invited a harpsichordist and a flutist. Garrett plays recorder and guitar. My mainland friends can't believe this kind of music is offered in Hawai'i.

Many years ago it was explained to me that the Episcopal Church kept classical music alive in the world. When popular music and recording technologies completely changed the music world, the church kept organs and choirs and glorious old music. Even before there were Episcopalians, it was the greater church that gave the masses access to beautiful music. All music was "live" music then, and only the wealthy could afford instruments and musicians in their homes. But the church offered it to all, for free. A gift for believers and non believers alike. For rich or poor. For young and old. A true gift. Imagine the desperate poor crowded around the church doors, listening in awe to what must have seemed heavenly music. Imagine how it fed their souls even when (especially when) their bellies were empty.

Evensong is always a lovely event; the sunset purpling the sky over the ocean as we sing and pray and listen together. Tonight Evensong begins with Sonata Metodiche 6 by Georg Phillipp Telemann. This piece was written near the same time that Kamehameha the Great was born. It seems unlikely that they could ever—even in their wildest dreams—imagine the existence of each other.

Interview: Robert Mist

What history I have gathered thus far has been rather neat and tidy. It is usually linear. People talk about a specific date, a particular person, and extraordinary event. It is true that the stories don't all match or agree, and facts are open to interpretation, but Robert Mist's memories know no bounds. For Robert, boundaries don't really seem to exist. He knows the land from generations back, knows who owned what, who used it, what it was used for. He knows genealogy, and not just his own. He knows Ali'i, as well as the prominent Japanese, Chinese, Portuguese and haole family trees. He speaks about the distant past as if he had been there. The boundaries between now and then blur. The boundary between the living and the dead (the ancestors, the kumus, and the saints) blur too. The myths and legends and heroes seem to swirl around him.

He is a storehouse of knowledge. In other cultures, other times, he might have been the keeper of memories, the one whose sacred duty was to keep the stories alive. As Christians around the world remember and admire and make reference to Moses and David, Ruth and Naomi, Robert remembers Cook and Vancouver, Queen Emma and the Kings. He says adamantly that we are still connected to them, our stories flow out of theirs.

It is a sunny, summer Sunday morning. During the announcements, Reverend Carol reminds us to sign up for the *Aloha Hour*, to take our turn providing snacks to go with the coffee served after each service. This happens 52 times a year, so if everyone takes a turn it won't be a burden on anyone. Robert Mist raises his hand.

"*What about the ulu trees?*"

"What about them?"

"*They have enough breadfruit to feed everyone, all year.*"

Carol pauses, unsure how to respond.

"Well, we would need someone to teach us how to fix it and everything."

To Robert, the problem is solved. To Rev Carol, it is too much trouble. Robert is silenced in disbelief. Here is a gift from God! Food from our own land! Effortless abundance dismissed!

Reverend Carol goes on to remind us of the empty basket by the church entrance. It is to keep us ever mindful of the hungry of our community and the need to bring in food donations. Near the coffee pots at the *Aloha Hour* is the large box with the collective donation of canned foods. Robert eagerly suggests that the breadfruit be offered to the food bank. Carol answers,

"They want non-perishables."

"*Like what?*"

"Like this." Carol reaches over and picks out a plastic bottle of corn syrup with imitation maple flavoring. "This is the kind of thing they want."

Robert says (or maybe just thinks it, and tells me later) *"But many, many Hawaiians are diabetic.. . . I thought we wanted to help them, not hurt them."*

Two days later Robert shows up at the church office with 4 sheep. He has taken seriously Carol's request to feed the hungry, and he has gone hunting. Carol is not there, and the secretary does not know what to do. She calls around, but everyone is too busy to deal with this. Robert takes the meat to another church.

These three small encounters illustrate a major disconnect. Robert sees the bigger picture. He sees the land, the island, rich with fresh, healthy, delightful food. Providing food is the purpose of the land! In this little bit of Eden, we are to be careful, grateful, and ethical stewards of it. We are called by God to love it and care for it and to share its bounty.

"Why are there hungry people when there is an abundance of fruit, nuts and meat?

"Why does CCE have two acres if not to feed the people?

"Why have most of the fruit trees been cut down and the ornamentals left standing?"

None of this makes any sense to Robert.

Rev Carol is the daughter of a real estate man. In her tradition land is bought and sold at ever changing prices, a source of currency. For her, the fruit trees are messy (as is fresh meat.) Carol is practical; she sees check lists and bottom lines. Robert Mist sees himself as a guardian of the land, and he sees Eden being abused.

Part of this communication "disconnect" is personal history, family values, and life style differences, but part is the way information is processed. One seems to be right-brain dominant and the other left-brain dominant. What does this mean and why does it matter?

People use both sides of their brains, but like right-handedness and left-handedness, we tend to have one clearly dominant. Individuals who are right-brain dominant are intuitive and subjective. They process information in a holistic way, and prefer elusive, uncertain information. Those who are left-brain dominant process information in a linear way; they are intellectual and objective, prefer established, provable facts. Reverend Carol and Robert Mist are perfect examples of each one. They really speak different languages.

A Few Old Photographs

A little boy named Lyle spent an afternoon at my home and taught me something very interesting. Tired of playing with him and needing to fix dinner, I suggested that he might like to watch some old cartoons we had on video. They were old, I explained, so were in black and white. He said yes, he had seen movies of when the world was still in black and white. He had no concept of the history of film making; he believed that the film told the truth – the world really was once only black and white.

The earliest photographs I can find of Christ Church are printed as a montage and labeled 1872. These must be from Reverend Davis' glass plate photographs. They were once black and white, but now they are brown and orange with age. The building is clearly our church, but there are no trees at all. There is a parsonage as well, with a lanai.

Another old photo is dated 1881; it is a Xerox stapled to a copy of The Voyage of the Wanderer, the story of the Lambert grave. Is this a photograph that the grieving parents made? There is no explanation, but 1881 is the year they arrived. There are still no trees, but the photo shows a rail fence enclosing the upper part of the cemetery.

Finally, by 1885, the abundant wildlife has reasserted itself; the church and the parsonage are surrounded, shaded, and softened by trees.

I don't know if the dates are written by the hand of the photographer, or by someone far later making an educated guess.

The photos are in random places, old envelopes, inside a book, in a file folder.

Another photo shows a Tin Lizzy (?) on a dirt road, looking like a toy next to towering trees and a steeple rising out of a lush landscape. There is no date, but the automobile helps provide a time frame. The internet offers no mention of early cars in Hawai'i, but there is a reference in a Davis journal: August 27 '05 "Mac came to church in his automobile and it startled the Wallace horses who broke their harness making the family late to church." (And if that weren't enough excitement for the morning, "Then Mac's dog came into church, and when he took it out one way, it came in the vestry.")

An advertisement in TIME magazine features a color photograph of Christ Church and an invitation to **"Come see the great cathedrals of Hawai'i."** The date is May 1972. (To get the historical context we need only look at TIME's red cover: a portrait of North Viet Nam's General Giap.) A young woman in a long dress and straw hat stands in the Christ Church cemetery where sunlight pours out of the sky with rainbow-like colors. The model is Noel Black Ackerman. The ad is charming:

> Perhaps you've seen the cathedrals of Chartres or Cordoba or Milan. They're monumental, but then that's what Europe is there for.
>
> Perhaps you didn't know you can see some remarkable churches in Hawai'i as well. To be very frank with you, in terms of architectural splendor, ours offer no contest. But if it's soul you're after, come to Hawai'i.
>
> On the Big Island of Hawai'i, and on Maui and Kauai, you'll find interesting old churches by the dozen. The best Christian examples date from the early nineteenth century when the missionaries set out to recreate their native New England structures here in "Owhyhee." Despite grave shortages of skilled labor and appropriate materials, moral fiber won the day.
>
> The men of the cloth left Hawai'i a mixed bag of blessing. For example, the muumuu, which you will certainly

see and may even wear on your visit here. It was originally designed to conceal the charms of our Island girls for the spiritual betterment of our Island boys. In point of fact, it does no such thing: humanity has yet to create a more provocative garment. Again, you'll see.

While you're here, you ought to get Hawai'i's complete religious picture. So visit some of our beautiful Buddhist temples. Our Shinto shrines. Our tabernacles. You'll be warmly welcomed in any of them....

Hawai'i ITS MORE THAN A PRETTY PLACE.

Reverend Norman Alter used a photograph of the inside of the chapel for a number of invitations and for the Hawai'i Church Chronicle in 1963. It shows the Altar back against the wall, with the painted panels above it. The three tall narrow windows above it use the same space but are not stained glass. (Perhaps they are the transparencies that the Altar Guild purchased.) Jesus is in the middle window with a dove over his head. The candles and the linens all look the same as now. The text with the photograph has the chapel itself speaking in first person. . .

"I Am Christ Church, Kealakekua. . . I am a quaint church, noted for my spire that tells others I am in this area. I also have a very beautiful Church graveyard surrounding me, where beloved members of the Church have been buried through the years . . ."

The last photo is also an inside one. There is no date, however Reverend Carol is in it, and she looks quite young and pretty. She is sitting by the Altar with a small cross in her hand. It is clearly during a service; there are white orchids, and the candles are lit. A brown sheep has entered the chapel and walked up the aisle to the communion rail. Carol has stopped whatever she was doing to enjoy the unexpected visitor from a very old parable.

History Detective: Sand Dash Finish

The East wall is being repaired, repainted and refinished.

Between the two services, Doug Edson gets a plastic bag full of sand from his car and carries it to the historic church. Standing at the east wall, he compares the sand on the wall to the sand in the baggy.

"We tried to figure out where the first builders would have gone to get it," he explains.

"We thought the sand in front of the Ackerman and Greenwell beach houses would be a logical possibility."

But it is not a perfect match.

When I see Doug between the services the next Sunday I ask him, "What was decided about the sand?"

"Ho'okena. . . Ho'okena sand was the perfect match. A perfect salt and pepper."

"But that was a long way to transport when there was sand nearby."

"Well, with the storms and tides and all, we can't really know what was where 140 years ago. But the sand at Ho'okena today is the match."

Follow-up

Tom Quinlan, the historic restoration expert, repainted the church in spring 2007. The sand is put on top of grey paint. According to his records, the sand is 80% coral sand, 3mm sieve, 15% black lava sand, 5% shell and beach deposits.

In the journals of HNG we find a reference to this very practice, March 10, 1884, "JW Smith began painting and sanding the houses at Kalukalu today."

How many of you have ever actually touched the outside of the church?

Interview: Norman Wessel / Profile Reverend and Marjorie Alter

"Eddie Would Go" states the bumper sticker on the big white truck in the church parking lot. Everybody knows who Eddie is, and laughs when they read it.

The real Eddie of the bumper sticker fame is Eddie Aikau, Hawaiian big wave surfer, lifeguard, and hero. During a reenactment of the voyage between Hawai'i and Polynesia, the ship got in trouble. Eddie Aikau went for help, alone, on his surf board, and was never seen again. His bravery and sacrifice are celebrated in a biography titled "**Eddie Would Go**," thus the bumper sticker.

He is a folk hero on the Big Island, but anyone who knows the family who drives the white truck knows another Eddie: Edward Allen Weaiu Wessell to be exact, the intrepid four year old great grandson of Reverend Norman Alter. Eddie attends his great grandfather's church, and he lives in his great grandparents' home. Although they have been gone for some time, the house is still full of the Alters' dusty books. The lovely rolling property with low rock walls for climbing is Eddie's territory. He tromps over and around and through it with an attitude of abundant confidence and absolute manifest destiny.

Today we celebrate Eddie's birthday. We arrive at the ancestral Alter home and are greeted by pirates. We are given grog, tattooed, and invited to play pirate games. Rev Carol arrives late with a really cool gift for a boy.

One of the best ways to know someone is to look at their bookshelves. I ask permission to browse the Alter shelves, and soon lose myself in old titles. "The Girl's Own Indoor Book of Practical Help to Girls on all Matters Relating to their Material Comfort and Moral Well-Being," 1888. "Polly Anna" 1914. Old editions of Edgar Allen Poe, Louisa May Alcott, the Oxford Book of English Verse, Isabella Bird, Stephenson in Hawai'i, William Ellis.

Another party pirate asks what I am doing. When I explain he is incredulous; "You are learning about dead people?"

"Knowing what a couple read shows a lot about them.... especially if they had a whole collection of something."

He is clearly baffled, so I explain.

"Like here, for instance: a whole row of bird identification books....different editions, different artists, from different climate zones, different countries. Bird watchers share certain characteristics: they have an amazing ability to pay attention to detail; they are good at waiting; they can be very still and very quiet for long periods of time; they enjoy being outside in nature; they keep a *life list* of each variation of bird they identify, as well as if it is male or female, adult or juvenile. Dedicated birdwatchers will travel great distances and spend a lot of money for the possibility of spotting a new rare bird. Most of us don't fit this combination of personality traits, so seeing a whole row of bird identification books here, offers me a window into the life of the person who collected them."

The pirate considers me as if I might be a lunatic.

"Well, what if I don't have any books in my house at all?" He asks this as if he has tricked me now, for sure.

"That tells me a great deal about you as well."

He can't believe this either!

"Like What Could You Possibly Know?" he roars.

"You probably didn't enjoy your high school studies too much... you decided to go straight to work rather than attend college. ... You are probably someone who enjoys working with your hands."

Now he is really confused, not sure whether I am crazy or a genius.

I struggle to pick up a gigantic old yellow dictionary, 1944, and heave it toward him.

"How much do you think this weighs?"

"At least 12 pounds," he estimates.

"Whoever owned this was a lover of words," I venture.

After the piñata, the presents, the birthday cake, my husband and I walk down the gentle rolling front lawn, so beautifully designed by the Alters decades ago, past the old tree with the bench built around it, past the giant jacaranda almost ready to bud, and on to our own home just up the street. We are neighbors actually. I have talked to Eddie's Dad, Norman, and arranged to come back and interview him about his grandparents at a later, quieter time.

Imagine my surprise in the shower when my tattoo does not wash off.

※

It is a later, quieter time, and we are sitting on the Alter's lanai with the ocean view, having pupus and drinks and calling up old memories. Eddie, uncommonly shy, sits in his mother's lap and feeds pupus to the cat.

Norman, named after his grandfather, the much loved Reverend Norman R. Alter, has very little to say about him. Yes, he knew him, but the Reverend didn't really spend time with children.

"People said he made a mean martini, he always kept a frozen one in the freezer, and he told a good joke." But this was not part of a child's world. I keep pushing Norm to share some little memory of his grandfather and finally he says, "He hummed to himself."

Norm has a lot more to say about his grandmother, Marjorie, the reverend's wife. She was the lover of words. She was a strict, precise, demanding high school English teacher at Konaweyna High School. She and the Reverend used to argue over word usage and meaning. She found mistakes and made corrections in almost all the books on the shelves I looked at.

Norm remembers picnics at the beach at Napoopoo and Honaunau with his grandmother who loved to swim, and his mother, the bird watcher. The grandmother's attention to detail in language manifested as a love of ornithology in her daughter. What about your grandfather? Your dad? "The men didn't ever come," Norm explains. "Picnics were for women and children." When he was older, Norm played golf with his grandmother.

"Did your grandfather play too?"

No.

"Did you ever play chess together?"

No.

Norm really has nothing to say about his grandfather although they both lived here, several decades, on this island. The words he will not say are becoming louder and louder. Norm does want to talk, but only about his grandmother. He shares story after story of her.

After Marjorie Alter retired from teaching English, she taught herself French. Norm says that she could read it, but not speak it. She read French mysteries, at least a hundred of them.

She learned all the constellations month by month.

She took correspondence courses.

She collected literary bloopers.

She typed books in Braille for David Fraser, a blind, deaf, and crippled young man at Christ Church.

She did all these things besides being an officer or volunteer for the Woman's Guild, the Democratic Party, the Outdoor Circle, the Historical Society, the Public Library, and the Bridge Club. Norm said she used to sit down by the phone with a list of club members, and call them all. She would not say hello; she would not identify herself; she would not say goodbye; she would leave her precise message and promptly hang up.

She loved blue; all the glass in her house was blue, and all the flowers in her yard were blue. They were only allowed to be blue.

When Reverend Alter retired, they built this house. They stayed at Christ Church. When he died, his wife refused to allow Christ Church to have a funeral for him. Why? He was so beloved! Norm shrugs. He explains that his grandfather had made arrangements for his ashes to be sent to a Buddhist Church in Kauai, to a place that kept ashes in little pigeon hole boxes.

At some point, Marjorie Alter, widow, was offended by one of the priests at Christ Church. She didn't think things were done right any more, so she refused to attend services. She was a woman of principles. Things were black and white. (Except when they were blue.)

When Grandson Norm and his second wife, Jeanette, were married, they moved into the Alter home and cared for Marjorie. Jeanette, with plenty of spunk of her own, takes over the story telling. She describes how she would give her grandmother-in-law whatever she wanted. For instance, everyone else worried about this 97 year old woman eating a healthy diet. But not Jeanette.

"What would you like for dinner?"

"Chocolate."

"Chocolate éclairs or chocolate ice cream?"

Jeanette saw no reason at all not to give her what she wanted.

In another instance Jeannette describes tiny, old Mrs. Alter sitting at her desk balancing her checkbook while wearing white cotton gloves. When a house guest asked her what she was doing she answered,

"Balancing my check book."

"But why are you wearing gloves?"

"Because my hands are cold."

Norm wanted to tell the following story at his grandmother's memorial service, though his mother would not let him. I'll let him tell it here.

Marjorie Alter was once invited to speak at the statewide Guild Meeting. She was asked to give a talk about humility. She accepted the invitation. She stood up in front of a large crowd, and spoke about the realities of being a missionary wife, how she had come to Hawai'i with her husband during the war on a freighter. She recounted the good times, and she recounted the hardships. Then she went back to her seat and sat down.

One of the Guild members raised her hand and asked, "Well, what about the humility?"

The Reverend's wife answered very clearly and concisely; she announced that she did not believe in humility.

Norm loves this story because it sums up his grandmother. She was the wife of a priest but she knew her own mind. She told the truth. She was a no-nonsense woman who knew what she wanted, worked hard, stayed independent and busy.

Little Eddie, who has really been far too quiet, throws up in the bathroom. Clearly it is time to leave.

A last question for Norm:

"How are you like your grandparents?" It is a big question, but he carries their DNA. It seems an important question to tie all of this together. I collect my papers and prepare to leave, as he thoughtfully considers this.

"How am I like my grandmother?" He asks aloud.

He finally decides on one word, "Intellectual." Norm is a lawyer, and already retired at a young age. He is happy to spend the whole day alone with a math book.

"How am I like my grandfather?"....... he stops to smile, and looks surprisingly like the Cheshire cat..... . "I like to drink."

CHAPTER 8

Altar, 1962. Photo by Adrian Harvey Saxe. (Courtesy Kona Historical Society.)

THE WEAVING METAPHOR

On the very first page of this writing project I wrote "Here, in this tiny piece of paradise, is a cloud of witnesses freed from time and space. I shall be a gatherer of their stories, a weaver of memories. I shall sort them out and tease out the tangles." Looking back, I am amazed at how over-confident I was, and how very naive.

Even though the research didn't go the way I expected it to, the weaving metaphor still works for me. I used to be a weaver with very ambivalent feelings about my big Swedish floor loom; I loved working with colors and textures and design, but I dreaded the math involved, and the process of dressing the loom. Try to imagine having one piece of silk thread eight yards long. Now imagine one thousand silk threads. The weaver must thread each one twice without breaking it or crossing any other thread. She has to keep them all straight and keep the tension even as well. It always seemed impossible to me, and in fact it was; I always had broken threads, crossed threads, lose threads, tight threads. It was just too complicated... There were too many variables. I used to cry over the warping, but then I would sing once I actually got to weave. Writing a history book was very much the same.

I used to find comfort in an old legend about ancient Jewish weavers. They believed that since only God was perfect, it was presumptuous for them to weave a perfect piece of cloth. As an act of humility they always made a mistake on purpose.

I didn't have to make mistakes on purpose in my weavings or in this history. So many stories have not been told, so many loved ones unacknowledged . . . old names in the cemetery, and new names. . . Entire families left out. But how many early members left letters or journals behind? And if they did, who is here now to hand them to me? The records I have had access to have been scarce, incomplete, scattered, and random.

Some people will be sorry that they are not in this book. Perhaps others will be sorry that they are.

We do have historians in our past. First was Reverend Miller. We have his handwritten letters of inquiry and the notes he compiled for Christ Church's 75th anniversary. He was our first history detective. Sixty years later, Sandol Stoddard went all the way to England to verify the details in letters sent to the Anglican Church and the Mission Societies. Thanks to the foresight and dedication of the Greenwell family—Amy, Jean, Sherwood, Maile, Megan—the Kona Historical Society exists, and a great deal of the past has been saved.

But many valuable historical documents were simply thrown into the trash.

To be honest, there was both too much history, and not enough. There are years of vestry reports full of facts and figures (too dull to pass on.) And there are great big blanks; several priests are not even mentioned in this history. I would love to know what was preached the Sunday after Queen Emma died, the Sunday after annexation, and the Sunday after Pearl Harbor. But there were no sermons left behind. What about Prohibition in Hawaii? What about the Great Depression? What about the Civil Rights movement? There are dozens of questions I never could answer, and the fact that I may have spent hours and hours looking, does not show up here for you to see.

If I had had any idea of how hard it was to be a weaver, I would never have taken it up. The same is true with this history.... If I had any idea how much work this was going to be, I would never, never have attempted it.

And yet it has, at times, been a work of joy.

Commentary: What is a Church?

If life is a beach, if every day is a winding road, if all the world is a stage, then what is a church? Not the church as a world wide body of believers, but an actual structure dedicated to communal worship and fellowship?

In the midst of a crowd at an interfaith prayer vigil, I thought about the room we were in. A church is a room with doors and windows, but not just ordinary doors and windows. Double doors allow multitudes to enter, and windows of glowing color allow for new ways of seeing.

The night of the prayer vigil—September 11—I saw the church become a container to hold grief. It was like a beautiful jeweled bowl, large enough to fill with fragile people, strong enough to hold their pain. Not solve it, but hold it.

I realized that the same was true for joy. Friends and family congregate inside sacred space to share in their most heart-felt celebrations, to bring lovers for weddings and babies for blessings.

A church (temple, mosque) then, is a container created to hold the full range of our most profound emotions.

A church seemed like the only safe, or sane, place to be on September 11, 2001.

A Backward Glance

"The Lord made the earth and it was good." It was, and is, rich and fertile, beautiful and abundant. The earth has a life of its own, and integrity. For our ancestors in Hawai'i, daily life was shaped by the land. Whether it was in taro fields, or sugar plantations, coffee or orange groves, dairies or cattle ranches, people lived by the rhythms of the land, the harvest, the weather. Living off the land took constant vigilance, dedication, strength, ingenuity and physical endurance. As I walk through Christ Church cemetery and read the names and dates of the early ranchers and farmers, their wives and their workers, I am grateful for the hard work of their lives. Their work was honorable in ways not necessarily affirmed by our fast-paced world where immediate gratification now reigns.

The values that once defined life here are rapidly disappearing. Small farmers are easily forgotten by history, and too often unthanked. As Hawai'i embraces change for the sake of progress or tourism, much of significance is being lost. Who will defend the old time values?

Author Wendell Berry does. He writes a lot about the beauty of the past, when life was simpler and folks were more dependent on each other. He is a farmer and he loves the land with great tenderness. In his novel <u>That Distant Past</u>, Berry talks about the mystery of time, and the connections between the generations and the land itself. We cannot escape the past, nor should we want to. He explains:

> When I stand in the road that passes through [town,] I am standing on the strata of my history that go down through the known past into the unknown; the blacktop rests on state gravel, which rests on county gravel, which rests on dry creek rock and cinders laid down by the town when it was still mostly beyond the reach of the county; and under the creek rock and cinders is the dirt track of the town's beginnings, the buffalo trace that was the way we came.

Berry believes that even the unknown past has a great influence on us.

As Christians we are people that honor the past...we tell and retell stories and sing about people and places and events from 2,000, even 3,000 years ago. These stories help us know who we are, and remind us that we are connected. Looking at history—distant or recent—we begin to see patterns. We discover that the problem we are struggling over now is not new; on the contrary it is as old as humanity.

The main issue that has come up over and over again throughout my interviews is the tension between honoring tradition and embracing change. Changes in the prayer book, in the music, and in the upgrading of the historic church have all created division. Giving up old British ways/manners/preferences to make room for new ethnic groups has challenged every generation. Welcoming hippies was one thing, but giving them a vote was something else altogether. The behavior of priests' wives has created debate; when one wore a bikini, and another swore like a sailor, strong opinions were expressed. Presently there is disagreement on the use of the community center for worship. Some love the quiet, meditative atmosphere of the old church, and some love the modern, extroverted style in the new building. Some like getting up at dawn to attend services, while others welcome sleeping in on the official 'day of rest.' Like congregations all over the world, we accept some change and resist others. We forgive and go on, or we don't. People have left the church over issues of change, but other things too: money issues, decisions made at Lambeth, and a multitude of hurt feelings.

On the other hand, the congregation gracefully welcomed a Chinese rector in the 1970s, two women priests, a divorced rector in the 1990s, and openly gay members into the church family. We have members who hold a very conservative view of Christianity, members who call themselves liberal and/or progressive, and those who take positions on both sides. Our life together invites the dynamic tension and the willingness to compromise, which are foundational to Anglican ideals. We are a work in progress, never arriving, but sustained by hope, and love, and grace.

Then and Now: Dancing for Evensong

One night every November, we celebrate the lives of Queen Emma and Kamehameha IV. We gather in the historic church at sunset to acknowledge once again, the great gifts these two gave Hawai'i in general, and our tiny church in particular. There will be music and hula at the luau following the prayer service. Brenda and Mona and Sparky and Roth and Reverend Carol will dance. It will be lively and joyful and fun. But in the prayer service, the music will be more subdued. It will still be joyful, but more of a quiet, inward joy. Garrett has been practicing special music for the night, and he has asked for dancers. Diane Aoki, Julie Lyle and I will dance hula. But dance in church will not be like dance in the luau: liturgical dance serves a different purpose. Symbolic movement invites the audience to go deeper into their faith.

Garret has chosen the song *Kaleleonalani, Flight of the Heavenly Ones*. This is a welcome song: Queen Emma has been away and now she is returning. Imagine the Hawaiian flag waving in the breeze. Imagine the waiting crowd throwing lehua blossoms out onto the waves. See them float out to meet the Queen.

It is a lovely song. Garret and Kathy sing while Cindy plays a gentle melody line on piano. But what, I ask myself, does it have to do with our faith? Why dance this in church? I read the words over and over until I find my way into the heart of the story. For the songwriter, the point is that Queen Emma has been gone, and is now coming back to her beloved people. Where has she been? If we know her history, we know three sad times that she went away. When the Queen's only child dies, she retreats in mourning. She returns to her position as protector of her people. A year later, the king dies; Emma goes away again, both literally and symbolically. She retreats to another island to be alone with her grief. But she comes back again. Later Emma campaigns for the royal office and although she is sure of her place as *protector of the people*, she loses the election. Again she goes away to heal her wounds. But she does not retreat into permanent resentment or bitterness. She returns once again to become a role model of grace and dignity.

History tells us that Emma is not diminished by her heartbreak or her failure. This beloved Queen survives her pain, *and we can too*. We can survive our own brokenness, our own despair; we can survive injustice, and our own failure. This I believe is the greater meaning of the song; it is universal and it is deeply personal. We honor Emma for starting our church, for building a hospital, for educating girls, but more than all that, we honor her for her faith, her inner beauty. Queen Emma became a saint because she pointed the way to holy living.

My favorite line in the song is "there is no thing without beauty." We hold first one hand in the air and turn it quickly, then the other. Think of this gesture as similar to shaking your head no. For me, this is the heart from which the story radiates. In her role as wife to King Kamehameha, the Queen is addressed as Emma or Emmalani. Her family calls her Kalanikaumaka, "the chiefess to whom everyone looks." When her son dies, Emma takes on a new name: Kaleleokalani, "the flight of the heavenly one." When her husband dies, she makes the name plural: "The flight of the heavenly ones." Picture two birds slowly, gracefully ascending to heaven. A lovely image, a lovely name. *There is no thing without beauty*; indeed suffering can be transformed into beautiful things. This is why we dance this song in church; this is the heart of Christianity.

Acknowledgments

Sincere appreciation to all those who agreed to be interviewed, and those who wrote down their stories.

Thanks to my scholarly consultants: Maile Melrose of the Kona Historical Society, author Sandol Stoddard, Stuart Ching from the Cathedral Archives of Honolulu, and Cliff Thornton, President of the Captain Cook Society, London, England.

Thanks to Reverend Carol Arney, for all her early work in planning interviews, trips to the archives, and a multitude of behind the scenes details.

Hugs for my son, Brady Cline, for designing the book cover, and to Nat Oshiro-Aoki for her lovely watercolor art.

Lastly, I want to express my gratitude to my three readers: Charlotte Melrose, Stephen Cline, and Pam Grisham. None of them saw the manuscript until the very end, and each responded to it with surprise and enthusiasm.

This book was funded in part by a publication grant from the *Hawaii Council for the Humanities.*

Photo Credits

⚜

Cover photo: Christ Church, 1962. Photograph by Adrian Harvey Saxe. (Courtesy Kona Historical Society.)

Chapter 1: Queen Emma. This appears to be Emma dressed in widow's weeds, in London, where she visited Queen Victoria, 1865. (Courtesy Bishop Museum Archives.)

Chapter 2: Christ Church 1881. (unattributed, Xerox stapled to The Wanderer.)

Chapter 3: Charles Lambert and HN Greenwell graves, @ 1892. Photograph by Rev. SH Davis. (Courtesy Kona Historical Society.)

Chapter 4: "The Little Grass Shack" at Christ Church, William Gaa, civil defense and grounds keeper, and M. Talbot, USO director. 1945. (Courtesy Charlotte Miller Melrose.)

Chapter 5: Christmas Choir @1940. (Courtesy Kona Historical Society.)

Chapter 6: Christ Church and graveyard, 1927. (Courtesy Kona Historical Society.)

Chapter 7: Christ Church from East side, 1938. (Courtesy Kona Historical Society.)

Chapter 8: Altar, 1962. Photo by Adrian Harvey Saxe. (Courtesy Kona Historical Society.)

BIBLIOGRAPHY

Berry, Wendell. That Distant Land. Berkeley: Counterpoint, 2004.

Bird, Isabella. Six Months in the Sandwich Islands. Honolulu: Mutual, 1998. (first printing 1875)

Cavaletti, Sofia. The Religious Potential of the Child. New York: Paulist Press, 1983.

Chauvin, Michael. Hokuloa, The British 1874 Transit of Venus Expedition to Hawaii. Honolulu: Bishop Museum Press, 2004. [George Forbes Papers, Incoming Correspondence, 1874, no. 14, University Library, St Andrews, Scotland.]

Cline, Mychilo. Power, Madness, and Immortality. University Village Press, 2005.

Da Jesus Book. Orlando: Wycliff Bible Translators, 2000.

Daws, Gavan. Shoal of Time. Honolulu: University of Hawaii Press, 1974.

Dibble, Sheldon. A History of the Sandwich Islands. Honolulu: Thomas G. Thrum, 1909.

Heckman, Marsha. Lei Aloha. Honolulu: Island Heritage, 2002.

Horwitz, Tony. Blue Latitudes. New York: Picador, 2002.

Hyde, Lewis. The Gift, Imagination and the Erotic Life of Property. NewYork: Vintage-Random House, 1979 (1983).

Jarves, James Jackson. History of the Hawaiian Islands. Boston: Tappan and Dennet, 1843.

Kanahele George S. Emma Hawaii's Remarkable Queen. The Queen Emma Foundation, 1999.

Kona Historical Society. A Guide to Old Kona. 1998.

Lambert, C & S. The Voyage of the Wanderer. London: Macmillan, 1883.

Liliuokalani. Hawaii's Story. Honolulu: Mutual, 1990.

Lindbergh, Anne Morrow. Gift From the Sea. New York: Pantheon Books, 1955.

McLaren, Brian. A Generous Orthodoxy. Grand Rapids: Zondervan, 2004.

Mulholland, John. Hawaii's Religions. Tokyo: Charles E. Tuttle Company, 1970.

Oaks, Robert. Hawaii, A History of the Big Island. San Francisco: Arcadia, 2003.

Nakano, Jiro, Kona Echo, A Biography of Dr. Harvey Saburo Hayashi. Kona: Kona Historical Society, 1990.

Portrus, Stanley. A Century of Social Thinking in Hawaii. Palo Alto: Pacific, 1962.

Restarick, Henry. Hawaii 1778-1920 from the Viewpoint of a Bishop. Honolulu: Paradise of the Pacific, 1924.

Rappolt, Miriam. Queen Emma, A Woman of Vision. Press Pacifica, 1990.

Stoddard, Sandol. The Eloquence of Silence, A Testimony to the Life and Character of Charles George Williamson, Priest and Builder of Christ Church, Kealakekua, Hawaii. 2007.

Tayman, John. The Colony. New York: Scribner, 2006.

Walker, Brian Browne. The Tao Te Ching of Lao Tzu. New York, St. Martin's Griffin, 1995.

Wells, Spencer. The Journey of Man, A Genetic Odyssey. Princeton NJ: Princeton University Press, 2002.

Yeh, Theodore T.Y. Magnificent Miracles. Hilo: Transcultural Press of the East and West, 1976.

Papers

Arney, Carol. The Episcopate of the Rt. Rev. Harry S. Kennedy, Bishop of the Missionary District of Honolulu. University of the South, 1995.

Staley, Thomas Nettleship. Five Years' Church Work in the Kingdom of Hawaii. London, Oxford and Cambridge: Rivington 1868.

Melrose, Maile. KINUE, The Life of Henry Nicholas Greenwell and Elizabeth Caroline Hall.

Clark, Blake. "Blood Donors of December 7, 1941." Hawaiian Anthology. Ed. Gerrit P. Judd. New York: Macmillan, 1967.

Abraham K. Akaka, *The Hawaiian Statehood Service*, LP record, recording, 1959. [Quoted in Hawaii's Religions, p18.]

LIFE Magazine. January 26, 1959.

TIME Magazine. May 1973.

On-line Sources

Lagaris, Christina. www.kosmix.com/topic/kamehameha *butterfly*.

Espenak, Fred. http://eclipse.gsfc.nasa.gov/transit/catalog/Venus Catalog.

missionbf.tripod.com/USO.html.

Music

Cogswell, Harrison, and Noble. My Little Grass Shack in Kealakekua Hawai`i. 1933. (Lyrics)

Liliuokalani. The Queen's Prayer. Translation by Jean Greenwell.

Kotani, Ozzie. To Honor a Queen. (CD Liner notes)

Young, Jesse Colin. Get Together. 1967. (Lyrics)

Made in the USA
Charleston, SC
25 January 2012